IT WAS TWENTY YEARS AGO TODAY

DEREK TAYLOR

A Fireside Book
Published by Simon & Schuster, Inc.
New York

A FIRESIDE BOOK
Published by Simon & Schuster, Inc.
Simon & Schuster Building
Rockefeller Center
1230 Avenue of the Americas
New York, NY 10020
Published in Great Britain by Bantam Press
FIRESIDE and colophon are registered trademarks of Simon & Schuster, inc.
Design – Jonathan Raimes, Tim Peplow
Picture Research – Sheila Corr
Manufactured in the United States of America
10 9 8 7 6 5 4 3 2 1

Library of Congress Cataloging -in-Publication Data

Taylor, Derek, 1932—
  It was twenty years ago today—

  "A Fireside book."
  1. Rock music—History and criticism. 2. Popular culture—History—20th century.
I. Title.
ML3534.T37   1987   784.5'4'009   87–386
ISBN 0–671–64201–4 (pbk.)

To Joan

'It is only through the development of an inner peace in the individual and the outer manifestation of that reflection that we can ever hope to attain the kind of peace in this world for which we yearn. We must strive, if we can, to make living into an art itself, although it will always remain a tremendous struggle.'

His Royal Highness, the Prince of Wales

CONTENTS

LIST OF COLOUR PLATES

Though he was sitting up in his pram before Hitler came to power, before Roosevelt's first term, and before the then Prince of Wales realised that Mrs Simpson was Mrs Right, **Derek Taylor** is still young enough to know that Van Halen is *not* the name of the doctor who outwitted Count Dracula. He was born in Liverpool, raised in West Kirby, and after grammar school was indentured as an apprentice newspaper reporter on the local *Hoylake and West Kirby Advertiser*, before becoming a sergeant in the Army during, but not in, the Korean War. He left newspapers while on the *Daily Express* (after passing through the *Liverpool Daily Post* and *Echo*, the *News Chronicle*, the *Sunday Dispatch* and the *Sunday Express*) to join the gang around the Beatles in 1964, becoming personal assistant to their manager, Brian Epstein, and the band's press officer.

For three years including the period of this book Derek Taylor and his wife, Joan, and children (now three sons and three daughters) lived in Hollywood where he was publicity agent for most of the pop stars of the golden era of 'folk-rock': the Byrds, the Beach Boys, Paul Revere and the Raiders, Captain Beefheart, Paul Butterfield, Sir Douglas, Van Dyke Parks, Judy Collins, the Mamas and the Papas, and Chad Stuart and Jeremy Clyde. He was a founder and the publicity director of the Monterey International Pop Festival.

In 1968 he returned to Britain with his family to become press officer for the Beatles' new Apple Corps, staying until it passed into dismay and book-keeping, when he joined Warner Elektra and Atlantic Records as director of special projects. In 1975 he was made managing director of Warner Brothers Records in Britain, and in 1977 he returned with his family to California where he became Vice-President of Warner Brothers in America. He gave it all up a year later to walk in the barley-fields of old Suffolk, trying to avoid writing for a living. Despite this, he has written a number of books, including two volumes of autobiography. In 1985 he began working with Granada Television as a freelance consultant for John Sheppard's documentary film, 'It Was Twenty Years Ago Today'.

Aside from all this, Derek Taylor has contributed to *Punch* and produced light music on albums by Harry Nilsson, George Melly and Peter Skellern. He is happily married and has no pension plan. He neither smokes nor drinks, and wishes to point out that, while the book has to deal fairly and squarely with the enthusiastic ingestion of illegal drugs of an explorative nature during the period covered in the mid-sixties, there is no intention to encourage anyone at all to follow suit. As Proust might have said: '*All* drugs is dodgy.'

ACKNOWLEDGEMENTS

The author wishes to thank the dozens of people who have made this book possible, whether by living through the events and arriving in the Now to celebrate them, or by writing and talking about them to provide much of the substance of this book. There is a particular, unseen, indebtedness to Charles Perry, who wrote the history of the Haight-Ashbury, and to Jeff Nuttall, who wrote *Bomb Culture*. In personal and professional terms, the author owes special thanks to the director and co-producer, John Sheppard, the lofty cosmonaut of inner space whose idea it was to approach Granada Television to engage in a two-hour documentary about the year 1967, using *Sgt Pepper* as springboard and the author as consultant. Without the programme there would not have been a book – all gratitude to them. Without co-producer Simon Albury and researcher Colin Bell, without their energies and their interviews, there would have been neither programme nor book. Much thanks, too, to Mike Scott and Rod Caird; also to Jules Burns, David Fraser, Pip Pia, Celia Dougherty, Jane Wright and to Andrew Robinson.

Ursula Mackenzie, editorial and rights director of Bantam Press, has been a safe harbour and beacon against the batterings of deadlines, rewrites, special pleadings, time compressions and self-doubts. Here an enduring place of honour is offered by the author to Miss Mackenzie's team of professionals. Lynn Curtis, editor, Sheila Corr, picture researcher, and John Raimes, designer, have brought substantial additional layers to this book to deepen and broaden its appeal. We should also acknowledge that the Royal Mail was seldom late, British Rail seldom on time, and each got through eventually. Thanks to them, and to Caroline Crowley, photocopyist, for safeguarding the manuscript. Ray Coleman provided timely help with a bound copy of *Disc and Music Echo* for 1967.

Reg Davis-Poynter, once my publisher, now my friend and agent, has changed my life. I never had an agent before. How did I manage?

The city of San Francisco, Neil Aspinall of Apple, George and Paul formerly of the Beatles have all been at the heart of the affair, and Ringo was friendly and supportive. Finally, and as ever, the author thanks his wife, Joan, for everything; for all of thirty years of intelligence, encouragement and love, and for holding hands on that daring and dangerous dive into the black hole of what's-it-all-about nearly twenty years ago today.

Derek Taylor with his
pregnant wife, Joan, at the
Monterey International
Pop Festival in June 1967

INTRODUCTION

Only after completing this book and sweeping a generous eye over the middle distance now behind me am I able to say that I began by knowing far less than you will know after you're halfway through. I had *so* much to learn. 'I wouldn't have joined if I'd known the war was going to last so long,' said the GI in 1942 after being told that General MacArthur had promised to return to the Philippines. I would have been content enough, at one stage, to rest among the silken pillows of my certainty that the year 1967 was simply fabulous, bathed in ever-loving sunshine, cooled by light breezes, full of colour and delight, dominated by Sgt Pepper and the Monterey Pop Festival with a running story of street theatre out there in San Francisco produced by elves and pixies to divert the flower children.

Once into this thing, however, and holding on to dreams only with great difficulty, I found that I couldn't get out. There was so much to the story that I had to relive and relearn it. I had been in Los Angeles with my wife, Joan, and children from 1965 to 1968, three undeniably wonderful years for popular music and social change. Things did get better. No doubt about that. I had visited San Francisco several times, and the 'counter-culture' – those who became characterised as hippies or 'costumed people' or 'freaks' – was as good as its name: it was running directly counter to any culture I'd known. Even the Los Angeles pop stars found the Bay Area farther out than anyone could have dared to dream when they looked at the old fifties styles and shuddered that the sixties might be more of the same. But what I was to relearn during the preparation and writing of this book was that the connection between the young in years and the young in heart was more real, more sincere, less cynical and much more threatening to rigid forms than I had ever supposed. The years since, crowded with detractors and marked by some betrayals, had dimmed my memory of the vivid unity of the middle sixties, culminating in the Summer of Love of 1967. For all that, it did rain a lot that year and a few thousand of the unfamous and some of the very well known were busted for trying to raise their consciousness with illegal substances – but it was a wonderful watershed in the social history of Western youth, and I see with a greater clarity than ever that something good did happen and that it still casts a rosy glow over many lives.

I took LSD with my wife Joan at Brian Epstein's housewarming party in Sussex on Sunday, 28 May 1967. It was put in our tea, without our demur, by John Lennon and George Harrison. I took a double dose of the chemical because I drank two cups of tea by mistake. After that things changed. Salt-cellars became Chartres Cathedral *and* the Seven Pillars of Norman Wisdom at least, and barbed wire sprouted leaves in the windows of John's Rolls-Royce to the accompaniment of 'A Whiter Shade of Pale'. I had already been prepared to examine life through a prism of cannabised cigarettes. That had been good, but this new lark was ridiculous. How could a poor man stand such times and *live*? Well, I did, and so did Joan and our three sons and three daughters, through good times and through better and worse, and when the time came for Granada Television to consider making a documentary film of the year 1967, using *Sgt Pepper's Lonely Hearts Club Band* (the album and all that therein lay) as a springboard I seemed like some sort of suitable catalyst to take on a most pleasant role as – the credit says – Consultant. Why not? That's what I said. It took me back to America in mid-1986, to both coasts, and I raked my memory for old and happy associations, all either in good repair or comfortably renewable, and the production team and I put together an interview-list of about fifty people, forty of whom made it to camera.

There is no doubt that for many of us 1967 was a year to treasure beyond measure. We saw the Beatles as leaders. That was a view held from the edge of California to the World's End in Chelsea, and if they didn't see themselves like that – and their claim that they didn't is underlined in interviews given by both George and Paul – then that isn't to say we didn't want to follow them anyhow. They had it all – youth, optimism, unassuming wealth and a collective disposition to share everything with everyone.

On first sighting, in 1963, I knew my life should be inextricably entwined with the Beatles. I was in the fourteenth year of a comfortable career as a newspaperman headed for Fleet Street from my native Merseyside via the *Daily Express* in Manchester. The Beatles' sense of overwhelming cheerful confidence was too glad to be allowed to escape – they were a dream worth the harnessing. I became their press officer and personal assistant to their manager, Brian Epstein. Working for them in the heat of the mania turned out to be quite another sort of dream and, while retaining a friendship with them, Joan and I ducked under the wire and escaped to California where the Byrds were waiting for us, ready to release 'Mr Tambourine Man'. I picked up on that, we all worked together to make it a hit, and somehow I became quite a hot little item in Hollywood, impersonating a press agent for about two years, with the Beach Boys, the Mamas and the Papas, Chad Stuart and Jeremy Clyde, Captain Beefheart and Mae West among my clients.

On 31 December 1966, as part of a New (Cosmic) Year Resolution, I decided to 'drop out' – having 'turned on' but not quite 'tuned in'. Then somebody had the idea of a 'pop festival', and I dropped back in a little to be a co-founder of the festival in Monterey. And that, and the essence of 1967, has brought me to this typewriter tonight, in the thick of an English winter almost twenty years later.

This book moves between London, Amsterdam, Hollywood and northern California, and now and again we glimpse the eastern American cities of New York and Washington. But mainly it is about a lot of visionary people who had, for whatever reason, decided to have a good long look at something other than the competition. It was time, as the poet said, for the islands to stop glaring at each other and turn towards the ocean to see what might come of it. I hope you will enjoy the show....

January 1987
Suffolk, England   DEREK TAYLOR

ONE

A SPLENDID TIME WAS GUARANTEED FOR ALL

In Arcadian dreams of other times there was a belief that everything would turn out all right. It was often unspoken, more danced than dramatized. It was simply understood.

So it was when the sixties hit their stride. Poets Allen Ginsberg and Gary Snyder in America, Adrian Mitchell in Britain, Bob Dylan, young men who became the Byrds, the hip record-producer Jim Dickson, the young Texan dreamer Chet Helms, the shopkeeper Brian Epstein, the *New York Post* reporter Al Aronowitz, the novelist Ken Kesey and pre-eminently the Beatles – all these and many more were drawn towards each other's tribe in strange ways, as if on threads. Each didn't quite know what the others were up to, but hey! maybe something would come of it. It wasn't pop, it wasn't poetry, it wasn't politics. It was ... Something Else. Across the decreasing divide between America and Britain good things were happening. The tribes were gathering.

Remember, transatlantic travel, available to the rich or comfortably off for maybe a century, was not commonplace until the middle or late 1960s. None of the Beatles had visited America until George went to see his sister in 1963 and brought back stories that made the mind leap of the size and scale of the place, the fast food and the drive-in movies. When they did 'invade' America in 1964 as conquering moptops, the Beatles astounded not only the world but also themselves. You have to consider the image of the United States of America represented in the consciousness of every British man, woman and child in the forties and fifties by Hollywood movie characters seen on a huge screen, or else in person by handsome, affluent, masculine young GIs, overpaid, oversexed and over here since 1942. Dressed in fascinating shades of brown and beige and cream, with their Marvel comics, Glenn Miller glasses, Lucky Strikes and unlimited access to nylons, as well as their having virtually won the war for us, they were a whole lot larger than life. So, too, were Frank Sinatra, Danny Kaye, Louis Armstrong – all the collective power of the world-famous recording stars from the era of the big bands through to Guy Mitchell, Frankie Laine, Doris Day, Johnnie Ray ... and then there was *Rock around the Clock*, Elvis Presley, Chuck Berry, Little Richard, Eddie Cochran, Buddy Holly, the Everly Brothers and all the rest: columns and columns of heroes marching through the charts. And James Dean and Marlon Brando, Marilyn Monroe and Natalie Wood, the fireside presence of '77 Sunset Strip', the Western soaps – 'Gunsmoke', 'Wells Fargo', 'Cheyenne', 'Laramie' – and the science fiction and horror films from *The Blob* to *I Was a Teenage Werewolf*. It was a mighty popular culture; a timid boy could cringe before such a towering Colossus, get lost in its shadow, but a *brave* boy could aspire!

In America itself, however, there must in 1964 have been a basic longing to find something outside themselves and their experience, or Americans could never have taken to the Beatles in the way they did. For let's not forget the extent of Beatlemania; it spread – and quickly – from the screams at Kennedy Airport into every State of the Union and into almost every state of mind. The press, and those seen-it-all Sinatra/Broadway veterans who at first underestimated the Beatles' ability to stay and grow, they, too, came to understand that this music and these young men had the chance and the talent to seize the moment and engage the imagination of a country too long obsessed with itself. The Beatles tapped into a new post-Kennedy American need: to be charmed all over again as the doomed tragic President had bewitched them for so brief and seemingly magical a moment.

There had always been an awareness of quirky England, gently fading in influence in almost every other respect but still kicking up just enough creative sand to obscure its geopolitical weakness. The British had always been – well, *interesting*. There had been Ronald Colman, David Niven, Leslie Howard, Cary Grant, Alec Guinness, Errol Flynn (Tasmanian but from British repertory theatre and very anglicised), Claude Rains, Basil Rathbone, Charles Laughton, Laurence Olivier, Vivien Leigh, James Mason, Peter Sellers – actors aplenty with that certain quality of – what? – elegance? fearlessness? So the door was always ajar, but musicians for the most part had been dull or unwelcome guests at the American party. What could they bring back home that couldn't be cooked better in the big host country? Well, their own unique enchanted harmonies and merry essence were what the Beatles brought, and it was owing to the insistence of the children of the house that they were allowed to stay and quite soon excite the interest and engage the imagination of the elders, millions and millions of them.

Now America wanted to find out just what it was that could produce such cute guys. The answer was Liverpool, the centre of consciousness of the human universe.

David Crosby of the Byrds (*second from left*) at Abbey Road studios for a *Sgt Pepper* session. A favourite guest, he sang harmony on one of the tracks.

In Liverpool there was a drifting together of people of like mind which had in it something of pubs, something of poetry and folk-song, something of art school. It was pure Melting-Pot, as it would be everywhere. In that kingdom of the brave only the unwilling were unwelcome. The Beatles were a catalyst and levellers, bringing everyone together on one 'we're all one and life flows within you and without you' trip, captivating and capturing all hearts save the stony. The Beatles' detractors were and are a mean minority maddened by impotence – immovable, rocklike in their hostility. It was well that it were so. Had they had no pricks to kick against, they would not have been the Beatles, notable freedom fighters.

The Byrds' manager and encourager, Jim Dickson, living in Los Angeles, had seen and heard all of the developments in behaviour and music in the post-war pop culture. He was fascinated by the 1964 Beatles and their appearance on a scene that until then had only appealed to him through folk-music. Looking back, he acknowledges:

❝ The fellows who ended up in the Byrds were looking to be the Beatles. And we, as we worked on the process, we found our own way to go with a combination of folk-music and rock and roll.... The key group in folk-music was Peter, Paul and Mary, and they had done "Puff the Magic Dragon" and lost their audience as far as we were concerned. But when the Beatles occurred and their music was about as simple as music could be, except electrified, it seemed to McGuinn and the rest of us that something was happening here – that we could make a synthesis, use that strength and not have the insipid folk-music around.'

McGuinn himself remembers:

❝ We each heard them, saw them in *Hard Day's Night*, and I personally went out and got a Rickenbacker twelve-string like George had and David got a Gretch and our drummer got Ludwig drums and we just patterned ourselves after the Beatles immediately, and when they heard our first album I think it influenced them. We became friends, and then they would send tapes to us and we'd send ours to them; and we transmitted messages across the Atlantic via records, which is really a lot of fun. Then Dylan got to know them well, and we did actually have a nice kind of interaction where we all did influence each other for a while there.'

I had sent copies of the Byrds' first album to the Beatles, and when I went with them to England in 1965 they met the Beatles, who took a great shine to them and always contacted them immediately they hit Los Angeles on tour, attending Byrds recording sessions, exchanging riffs and tricks and innovations. It was David Crosby who first brought Ravi Shankar's music to the attention of George Harrison. In that year, too, a San Francisco group turned up at the rehearsal room in the suite of offices in Los Angeles on which the Byrds' management and I were paying the rent from our modest percentage of the very agreeable royalties from 'Mr Tambourine Man'. The Bay Area group wore little buttons that said 'Jefferson Airplane Loves You' (1965 was early for buttons). The link again was David Crosby, a ubiquitous enthusiast. In the way that people of like mind will relate to each other, Airplane and their context, hip San Francisco, instantly became part of the England–California axis.

Throughout the winter and spring of 1967 there was an understanding between the very wide awake that a fusion in the counter-cultures of London and San Francisco was taking place. Of course London and Los Angeles had been coming closer together as the accepted centres of the recording action and, though New York could never be counted out of the equation, there was a strong drift to the Coast. Young men and women were going West. The Lovin' Spoonful and the Mamas and the Papas had already made the trip to establish their own niche, and many would follow. It wasn't only vibes, man, though they were crucial. It was also the weather, the media and the myth. The Sunshine State ... the Golden Gate....

Aaron Copland said that, if you want to know about the sixties, play the music of the Beatles – to which you could add the Byrds, and Jefferson Airplane, and all those thousands of other less famous bands. Play *their* music, too, and souls will respond, as in other times soldiers did to martial rhythms. They were stirring times, and with most radio stations not yet alerted to the new music the message was passed by jungle drums or some such means. Osmosis? *Zeitgeist?* Have a dictionary by you at all times.

By their time of triumph, 1967, the Beatles had become accepted as the world's greatest communicators. They were perfectly cast and dead on time for Marshall McLuhan's 'Global Village', with electronic means of communication representing his notion – not, in my opinion, as specious as his detractors seek to prove – of an externalised nervous system.

In December 1966, at the entrance to EMI studios and the gateway to 1967, Ringo Starr was among the Beatles buttonholed or doorstepped by Independent Television News in a feature aimed at establishing the End of Beatlemania. Talking about the upcoming sessions, Ringo said there would be no point in appearing on tour during their present phase because the music was progressing so far: 'We can't do a tour like before because it would be soft us going on stage, the four of us, and trying to do the records we've made with orchestras and bands. We'd have to have a whole line of men behind us if we were to perform.'

In the same interview John said: 'We'll carry on writing music for ever, whatever else we're doing, because you can't just stop. You find yourself doing it whether you want to or not.'

Later he would say that during these sessions he was happier than he'd ever been in a studio. The Beatles were making the early tracks for *Sgt Pepper's Lonely Hearts Club Band*, a title which their road manager Neil Aspinall noted in his diary on 31 January: 'They wrote a song called Sgt Pepper's Lonely Hearts Club Band.' The team also included Neil's partner, Mal Evans, and it was this Scouse sextet who spent all those winter months at Abbey Road studios, stimulating their imagination with marijuana while Brian Epstein, also fully psychedelic, stayed close at hand.

Socially Brian was much involved, and their Beatle business was still under his control, but since they had retired from live performances in August 1966 he was much less active than at any time in the five astonishing years they had been together. From Boys in Black Leather to Lords of the Earth, they had known strange times, eaten strange fruits and remained wonderfully intact. When Paul McCartney and Mal Evans came to stay with Joan and me and the children in Los Angeles, Paul told me of a 'trip' he had taken with John Lennon in 1966. 'We had this fantastic thing. We had taken this stuff, incredible really, just looked into each other's eyes.... Like just staring and then saying, "I *know*, man," and then laughing ... and it was great, you know.' The LSD that was turning them into Timothy Leary's apparent avatars – mutants, messengers that come before the ultimate divinity – had done wonders for Brian Epstein, too. He had become marvellously relaxed, footloose, colourful and – for a man who had always liked a good time but had suppressed some instincts – free. He wrote to me skittishly in February:

Brian Epstein towards the end of his life

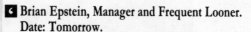

❛ Brian Epstein, Manager and Frequent Looner.
Date: Tomorrow.
Dear Derek,
It was sweet of you to send me the note about the Saville [Theatre, which he leased for a while] and very much appreciated. Very busy (but I must have a few days' rest to prepare myself to receive the Four Tops) but in Great Form (very happy about my Stigwood deal).

'Beatle single out here in February 17. Super smash without question one of their best. Title: Penny Lane and Strawberry Fields. John tells me the latter is between Menlove Avenue and Beaconsfield Road. Do you think it'll help our image in Liverpool? I used to get the tram (Number 46) from Penny Lane to Epstein's, Walton Road, when I overslept and was too late to accompany Daddy to work in his Triumph at 9.00 a.m. Anywhat it'll probably kill fifteen birds with one stone? The titles are being announced here next week.'

George Martin was the producer and arranger of *Sgt Pepper* and the preceding seven and four subsequent original Beatles albums, which comprise their basic canon. In addition he produced and arranged all their singles. He was an EMI staff producer with an impeccably broad repertoire, and a background in serious music as an oboist. Though a generation older than the Beatles, and therefore much more experienced in music and in life (he was a wartime officer in the Fleet Air Arm), he had an understanding, sympathy and respect that perfectly matched their special needs and strengths. His ability was somehow the right shape. He was not unfamiliar with genius having recorded Peter Sellers, Peter Ustinov and Spike Milligan among many others. He gave the Beatles all he had. They taught him all they knew. The combination was unbeatable.

The first two songs recorded for *Sgt Pepper* had been 'Strawberry Fields Forever' and 'When I'm Sixty-Four', and next came 'Penny Lane'. Then came the need for a single, and 'Penny Lane' and 'Strawberry Fields Forever' fled the album to become the greatest two-sided single ever released. The public couldn't buy sufficient copies in any one of the eleven

Filming the promotional 'clips' for 'Penny Lane'/'Strawberry Fields Forever'. It looks *very* cold, doesn't it?

George Martin in his prime

weeks it was in the charts to get it any higher than number two in Britain, but that is just ironic and perhaps irrelevant anyway. It became number one in America and sent strong signals of successful conquest of inner space to the 'hippies' of Haight-Ashbury and beyond. Writing recently in his *History of Haight-Ashbury*, Charles Perry states:

> ❛ The hit side of the single was "Penny Lane", a dreamy disconnected evocation of suburban English life, but the other side, "Strawberry Fields", was unquestionably about LSD. It charted the sort of acid trip in which a breath of escapism swells into a whirlwind of madness with each chorus of the song descending to a more ominous note.'

George Martin remembers the trips but, himself determinedly drug-free, he speaks from innocence. He just wanted to get the music right and make the best Beatles album he could. He has said since that the success may have been the result of dope (them) and no dope (him). In his autobiography *All You Need Is Ears*, he wrote: 'The time had come for experiment. The Beatles knew it and I knew it ... we had had an enormous string of hits and we had the confidence, even arrogance, to know that we could try anything we wanted.'

Noting that 'Eleanor Rigby' and 'Tomorrow Never Knows' from *Revolver* had hinted that something was going on that would signal a complete change of style, he admits that he didn't know how significant it was, or how it happened.

Interviewed in 1986, he said:

> ❛ *Sgt Pepper* is known as the psychedelic album, but what is psychedelic? The imagery was marvellous, but the media was too quick to find drug references all over the place. Of course I knew they were smoking. They tried to hide it from me; they'd go out into the canteen one at a time, Neil and Mal would have the joints already rolled out there. They'd come back and it would be obvious, but it seemed to help and they had an enormous enthusiasm for recording in those days. They worked very hard.'

The Beatles' expanded visions in *Sgt Pepper* were in pop terms beyond all precedent. When the music reached America it stunned people already inured to the Beatles' supremacy. Thus Jim Dickson, mentor of the Byrds:

> ❛ It was totally awesome. *Sgt Pepper* was so far beyond anything that we could imagine producing or doing that it overwhelmed us. It

23

was like Miles Davis with *Sketches from Spain*. He just left everybody in jazz with no place to go, and *Sgt Pepper* pretty much did that for us – left us with no place to go. What was new in it? Well, all that George Martin production, a backdrop of British music-hall and the tremendous construction, the continuity of songs, the braveness of the music. You could be frightened to death and hear that album and feel OK. It was magnificent. Overwhelming power.'

Beatles friend and Dickson protégé McGuinn is more low-key:

ᶜ I was already involved in the psychedelic thing when *Sgt Pepper* came out so it wasn't the big wonderful surprise for me I think it was for the rest of the audience, but it really had a strong impact on the world and it did change a lot of things. But, listening to the album recently, it didn't have the continuity I at first thought it had.'

Today the poet Allen Ginsberg sees it as a modern opera: 'One of the few opera triumphs of the recording century.' Ginsberg, a realistic, painstaking and ever-benevolent intellectual much humanised by his feel for the street, for the misfit, for the underdog, for Dylan's victim-figures in 'Chimes of Freedom', sees immense warmth and sympathy in the album. 'They were giving an example around the world that guys can be friends,' says Ginsberg today. 'They had, and conveyed, a realisation that the world and human consciousness had to change.'

Ed Sanders of the Fugs, hard, humorous and pragmatic, sees the album's arrival as dramatic.

ᶜ "A Day in the Life", that final terrific tune, was a short-story song. *Sgt Pepper* didn't stand for *my* year but it was an interesting thing. It brought into popular music a broader spectrum of concern – birth, death, sex, money, politics and religion – and it was kind of interesting four good singers talking about love, life and death in a way that nobody else was doing.'

It was astonishing that the Beatles' conquest should be so complete, and yet it is interesting that when top of the heap, aware of the power they had to start up, by their example, bands like the Byrds and Jefferson Airplane, the individual Beatles would travel to places where these bands operated and from where they drew their strength and whose local cultures they manifested. The Byrds were southern California cool, cerebral rather than sentimental, never strong on love-songs. Airplane were quintessential San Francisco 'acid' rock, from folk by way of 'mod' attitudes and clothes into a metaphor for the San Francisco identity of freedom and love and expanded mind, in God's nicest Californian city – not for nothing named for St Francis. Los Angeles may have had the money, but San Francisco had the spirit. Nothing of Los Angeles except David Crosby and his ethos could seduce Airplane into Hollywood. In that spring of 1967, in the middle of recording *Sgt Pepper*, McCartney, one of nature's searchers, ambled quietly into San Francisco with Mal Evans to check out the scene.

Airplane's Paul Kantner remembers: 'They came to [Jack] Casady's apartment one afternoon when they'd toured the Haight and, you know, traded licks and stuff like that.' He had a laconic view of the arrival of *Sgt Pepper* on the American scene.

❛ I said all ri-ight, another one on the bus! Because we were all sort of doing if not the same things then a lot of what was going on on the West Coast was sort of manic experimentation. Our first record took ten days in a studio. Our second took two weeks, and our third record took seven months, and we were probably one of the first bands responsible for the long studio hours that people use all the time now. So then we said all ri-ight.

'We were with the Byrds in Seattle, and kids would come back to your hotel, and this night David Crosby had a copy of *Sgt Pepper* before it came out and so he played it on his little tape machine in the hallway of the hotel, and all these fans were up in the hallway all night. There might have been a hundred of them! They had to call the police, but the police didn't throw them out because they weren't violent or anything; they were just listening to the songs, and it confirmed our suspicions of how mad everybody was. Something enveloped the whole world at that time and it just exploded into a renaissance.'

25

Now, let's not be naïve. None of the foregoing wisdom was in the mind of George Martin as he matched the demands of the Beatles' expanded consciousness with the ancient technology of Abbey Road studios. George Harrison remembers:

George Harrison

❛ Most of the songs we did we had to do as if we were recording live, like mono. We spent hours getting drum, bass and guitar sounds, then balancing them and then doing the take. That was in effect a backing track and then we later added overdubs. Nowadays you can overdub individually with each person having his own channel to record on. Then we'd have to think of all the instrumental overdubs, say, a guitar coming in on the second verse and a piano in the middle and then a tambourine. And we'd routine all of that, get the sound and the balance and the mix and do it as one performance. And if one person got it wrong we'd have to back up and do the entire overdub of all the parts again.

'We had old microphones and pretty antiquated machines, but we'd find new meanings in old equipment, and I think that it was largely because of the times and the state of mind everyone was in that it was exciting to try and come up with new ideas.'

The George Martin–Geoffrey Emerick combination of producer and engineer, so familiar to students of Beatles-album credits, was never more tested than by *Sgt Pepper*. In his book, Martin says that technically *Pepper* was 'a bit of a nightmare'. If he had had even eight-track recording facilities, it could have been so much better, but as he had only four tracks he had to stretch their use to the limit, dubbing from one machine to another not just once but twice. He used mathematics to ensure he didn't lose too much generational sound quality – for those with quick mathematical brains, it might be clear that by 'dubbing down' twice he could lose up to nine generations of quality. I don't understand it, but that is what I'm told. You have my word that Martin worked it out, and that he and Emerick succeeded is clear when you listen to the album. There *have* to be more than four tracks to achieve some of those sounds. The Beatles, more creative than ever, were demanding more than ever, and Martin served them well. Record albums were real hard labour then and maybe the better for it.

Neil Aspinall, first and senior road manager of the Beatles, schoolfriend, and still working with the surviving ex-Beatles and Big Brother, their holding company Apple, retains detailed memories of the *Sgt Pepper* days as of all other minutiae of their lives as musicians, artists, stars, colleagues and fellow-travellers through this vale of tears and laughter.

Uninterviewed until now, and even now only in brief and guarded bursts, Neil Aspinall is loath to claim any credit for anything ever, but it is uncommon knowledge that he put to Paul the suggestion that the Sgt Pepper song should be reprised, in part, as the penultimate song on the album, to the dismay of his close friend and fellow road manager Mal Evans, who always liked complete songs. As suggested by Neil the reprise would only be a part-song leading into what became 'A Day in the Life'. Neil remembers John (told of the suggestion by Paul) saying to him later with a wicked smile: 'Nobody likes a smart-ass.' 'That was when I knew that John liked it and knew that it would happen.' That was in February, as the world waited and 'Strawberry Fields Forever' and 'Penny Lane' were prepared for release. Neil doesn't see the removing of those songs for a single as a loss to 'the concept' of the album.

‹ No. It wasn't a concept. They were just songs. EMI wanted a single and they were just songs that were there. They were writing all the time. They were workaholics. They didn't say: "Let's do the Pepper album." It's just a bunch of great songs. They took a lot longer than before because they weren't on the road, they took three months and instead of working from two in the afternoon till three in the morning it was from 6 p.m. to 1 a.m. with weekends off.'

There was time at last for the Beatles to stand and stare.
George was grateful. He recalls it with pleasure.

Erich Gruenberg, leader of the 'Day in the Life' orchestra on the *Sgt Pepper* album

‹ Although we only toured for two years, it seemed like a lifetime. And 1967 was a year when we thought we'd withdraw a little bit. We just seemed to stay home a lot out in Surrey, in the dope-smokers' belt, and I remember wandering between my house, John's house and Ringo's house and sitting in gardens looking at trees for years and years. That year did take about fifty years to complete.

'The studio was one place to work where we had a bit of privacy whereas all the touring and stuff was non-stop, and being on display. A lot of time in 1967 in the studios was spent actually just trying to get sounds. We'd spend hours and hours trying to invent sounds. Nowadays it's pretty easy because there's so many sounds available just by hitting a button – in fact it's too easy, but it's because of some of those records in the sixties that they've invented machinery where you just switch on and instantly get an effect which we spent years trying to discover.'

The leader of the orchestra of forty-two musicians who played on the album, Erich Gruenberg, one of Europe's foremost violinists, remembers the recording session very well:

‹ The large studio at EMI has probably been used for all the most famous classical musicians and surely the most famous pop artists, but usually you came there to work and found it was a studio atmosphere which is cool and has as its purpose recording only.

'This time it seemed as if something else had taken over, and of course then we saw it was the Beatles – and not just the musicians themselves but their large entourage and friends. Well, we started our recording with them, and I remember that some things were clearly arranged and there were other things that were left on a slightly experimental basis, but they were always very clear about their intentions and what they actually wanted. On the song "A Day in the Life", for instance, they wanted certain effects from the string-players which were very difficult to convey in writing, but they explained what they wanted. It was an intensification of sound or a rise in pitch – if you remember there's a sort of spiralling chord that starts on a semitone "swirrel" and then rises up. The particular effect was created by everyone doing his own thing in a sense because it's the mixture of all these different ingredients that gives this special effect. The pitch rises, which means you slide up on a violin, and you slide and you slide, and if the slide is slow enough it takes a certain amount of time, and as it's quite a spiralling chord which lasts quite some time you retrace your steps – you go "waaaaaaaa", you go up and down. Now, if you heard about forty people doing basically the same thing but everyone does something slightly different, the mixture of sounds creates quite a unique effect.'

Paul's recollection of the 'Day in the Life' session and the progress towards it underscores the unity of the mood of those times.

◀ We were being influenced by avant-garde composers. For "Day in the Life", I suggested that what we should do was write all but fifteen bars properly so that the orchestra could read it, but where the fifteen bars began we would give the musicians a simple direction: "Start on your lowest note and eventually, at the end of the fifteen bars, be at your highest note." How they got there was up to them, but it all resulted in a crazy crescendo. It was interesting because the trumpet-players, always famous for their fondness for lubricating substances, didn't care, so they'd be there at the note ahead of everyone. The strings all watched each other like little sheep: "Are you going up?" Yes. "So am I." And they'd go up. "A little more?" Yes. And they'd go up a little more, all very delicate and cosy, all going up together. You listen to those trumpets. They're just freaking out.'

George Martin remembers using the largest number of musicians ever heard on a Beatles recording for this track, and that 'A Day in the Life' was recorded in an atmosphere of festival and fancy dress, producing an incredible sound. 'We recorded the sound four times and I added those four separate recordings to each other at slightly different intervals. If you listen closely, you can hear the difference. They are not quite together.' The final 'bunched' chords came from all four Beatles and George Martin in the studio, playing three pianos. All of them hit the chords simultaneously, as hard as possible, with the engineer pushing the

28

volume-input faders way down on the moment of impact. Then, as the noise gradually diminished, the faders were pushed slowly up to the top. It took forty-five seconds and it was done three or four times, piling on a huge sound; one piano after another, all doing the same thing.

From the *Daily Mail*, 17 January 1967. The newspaper was propped up on John Lennon's piano, so it's said, and the line just popped out: 'Four thousand holes in Blackburn Lancashire'. Nothing at all to do with the needle-marks of dark rumour.

No wonder people's minds were blown all across the seven seas; but, for all the psychedelia and special signals and secret messages and insights that came from the myriad 'listenings' and trips to which the record was the astonishing soundtrack and conduit, back there in Abbey Road it was a whole other world, incorporating the power of real inspiration, specialist knowledge, the best technology there was (for all that it seems clumsy today) and very hard work.

The big orchestral session was a riot of festive props, false noses and other notions provided by the Beatles for the musicians. Gruenberg, a former leader of the London Symphony Orchestra and the Royal Philharmonic, was wearing, in George Martin's recollection, a giant gorilla's paw on his bow-hand. Mr Gruenberg remembers it as

❛ Quite an occasion. The Beatles were very charming and musical, expressing their personalities like all truly successful people by being quite themselves. They had a good spirit, and in the studio there was a sense of occasion and momentum. Together we got the musical effect they wanted, and it was a particularly happy day. They sent me a copy of the record which I still have.'

Many of the songs for *Sgt Pepper* were written on the run, during sessions at Paul's house very close to the studios, or out at Weybridge and Esher. John sat at his piano painted by The Fool, taking his ideas from the day-to-day items around him: the famous circus poster of Mr Kite, the *Daily Mail* column of small news items which talked of four thousand holes being found in the road in Blackburn, Lancashire. Ringo's great and famous vocal on 'With a Little Help from My Friends' was put together by John and Paul, on guitar and piano respectively, at Paul's house. 'A Day in the Life', famously, is a combination of two songs, one by John and one by Paul. 'Good Morning' was later dismissed by its composer, John, but stands, with George Martin's sound effects, as a very smart little item on the completed album. Neil Aspinall's recollection of them working throughout that winter without any anxiety that they might run out of material is revealing. The group was obviously hot to trot. There was nothing they couldn't do or get in that last great year of unity, harmony and collective happiness.

Paul's leadership stance on the album went unchallenged. Each of the other three had plenty to do, instrumentally or vocally. Ringo's 'voice' as drummer is notably good, and his vocal on 'With a Little Help from My

The boys next door

Friends' has a presence and charm quite as fetching and musical as anything else on the album. George Martin has said there had to be some corner of each album that was forever Ringo. In *Sgt Pepper* he was wonderfully provided for with 'A Little Help', the last song to be written and recorded. In keeping with album's stance of being by someone other than the Beatles, their correct instinct was to have 'Sgt Pepper' announce the appearance of a friendly little chap, Billy Shears, whom everyone had known for years. It was a made-up name, apt, apposite and absolutely right for Ringo. It was also a very Liverpool name. The city had a lot of Billys in popular lore, in soccer, in humour or whatever, and Billy was a cosy name to suit a cosy man. The song, often sung and recorded by others, has never been rendered with greater openness, charm and wit than by Ringo.

Sgt Pepper was a first-rate stage for each individual to strut his stuff. Be it merely modesty and diligence, overt musical-hall rhythm, Indian-based nouveau rock or lyrical fantasy, *Pepper* would accommodate it. They could all sit comfortably side by side in this concert/concept. The programming was adroit and unmatched even by the *Abbey Road* album, which had some marvellous segues.

There was a wonderful absence of disputes in the making of *Pepper*. Paul was left comfortably to organise, John to explode into lyrical bliss with his tangerine trees and marmalade skies, George to respond to what he describes as the 'All You Need Is Love Consciousness' after the LSD period, and Ringo to change rock drumming for ever. It's been said there isn't a 'love-song' on the album, but that there is love in every groove is undeniable. Its unity is a reminder that group effort need not be dissected and credit apportioned exactly. As if that were possible anyway! That everyone was into their own thing for the common good rings out from the first tuning sounds at the album's opening to the final crashing chord and its fade away at the end of the record.

Everyone brought into the assembly of the album was on the good trip to artistic bliss. Peter Blake from the world of fine art clearly remembers the ambience of high creativity:

‹ What was exciting was that we were involved right through because they were still recording. We would go to Abbey Road for meetings. I remember one evening George was recording his track "Within You Without You". There was a carpet laid out, there was an Indian musician, and the whole atmosphere was different to other times. I liked their music, and they were interested in my art. They were at the height of their power and strength, so we knew we could pretty well do anything we wanted. You could come up with some pretty extraordinary ideas, and they would get done. Working with other bands – it wouldn't be fair to name them – you wouldn't get that power.'

Paul says now:

‹ Until this album we'd never thought of taking the freedom to do something like *Sgt Pepper*. Marijuana started to find its way into everything we did. It coloured our perception, and we started to realise there weren't as many barriers as we'd thought, we could break through with things like album covers, or invent another persona for the band. Let's pretend we're not the Beatles. That was a pretty big dare, you know, and it changed everything.

'For the cover we came up with a list of our heroes, like Oscar Wilde, Marlon Brando, Dylan Thomas, Aldous Huxley, Lenny Bruce. Everyone had their choice. It was really to say who we liked – it was about time we let out the fact that we liked Aldous Huxley. That wasn't the sort of thing we'd talked about before. No one had ever asked us in an interview!'

George remembers:

‹ We all wrote down the people we liked. I had a few Indian Yogis and also Gandhi, Lenny Bruce, Bob Dylan and Carl Jung. They were people who meant something to us.

Peter Blake

'I recall us talking as if we were Sgt Pepper's band, but really it was still us doing it. Still, it *was* a good idea. With the Billy Shears character [in "With a Little Help from My Friends"] and with the artwork combined with the Sgt Pepper song in the introduction and reprise, there was a feeling that we were stepping out from the old Beatles which is shown by the waxwork dummies on the front.

Brian Epstein had offered Robert Frazer to EMI as co-ordinator of the jacket artwork, and Robert had proposed that Peter Blake should design the front cover – an inspired choice.

The centre spread was supposed to be done by The Fool, the charming acid-drenched unit who did so much to pretty up London in 1967. Neil Aspinall remembers:

They hadn't somehow checked on the album size and their design was just out of scale. So they said, "Oh, OK, we'll put a border on it," so we now had this design which was too small and a border being added just to fill up space. I said to the fellows, "What are we selling here, a Beatles album or a centrefold with a design by The Fool which isn't even ready? Hadn't we better get a picture taken of the four of you, and stick that in so we can see who you are?" So they posed for a picture and that went in the middle. The back took some time and had to be left till last because we were printing lyrics and they had to be designed and we had to have a running order and we couldn't have that until everyone had decided on it. I remember Paul and I walking along, I think Kingly Street in the West End, trying to work out some clever word using the initial letter of each song – the first would have to be S for Sgt Pepper and then we'd try and get a vowel, say – but we couldn't get it right, so the running order was decided in another way. But it all worked out and we made it on time.'

Peter Blake recalls:

Robert Frazer, a friend of the Stones, owned the gallery I was with. A cover for *Sgt Pepper* designed by The Fool already existed and was very psychedelic – swirly orange and green and purple – there were a lot of others like it. Robert thought it would be interesting to have the first cover done by a fine artist as opposed to a record-cover designer. A certain amount had already been established: the concept of their being a band within a band, for instance. They'd had their uniforms made already. I think my contribution was to talk a great deal to them about the concept and try to add something visual to it. Paul explained that it was like a band you might see in a park. So the cover shot could be a photograph of them as though they were a town band finishing a concert in a park, playing on a bandstand with a municipal flowerbed next to it, with a crowd of people around them. I think my main contribution was to decide that if we made the crowd a certain way the people in it could be anybody. I think that that was the thing I would claim actually changed the direction of it: making a life-sized collage incorporating real people, waxworks, photographs and artwork. I kind of directed it and asked the Beatles and Robert (and maybe other people, but I think it was mainly the six of us) to make a list of characters they would like in a kind of magical ideal film, and what came out of this exercise was six different sets of people. Robert Frazer chose artists, and I chose Johnny Weissmuller, people like Bobby Breen who was a child star, and Shirley Temple. And then we went to Madame Tussaud's where I heard Sonny Liston would probably be melted down soon. He was no longer world champion, and so I got him and I still have him.'

Sure enough, Sonny Liston stands in Peter Blake's beautiful gleaming-bright white studio in West London: glowering and dangerous in a cream silk dressing-gown piped in yellow, unusually lifelike in effigy. Blake is fascinated by pop curios and artefacts. 'I was interested in pop from the late forties. I mean being involved in it. When I first went to art school, I went to jazz concerts, to wrestling, to all sorts of things.'

Robert Frazer, gallery-owner who brought fine art to the pop world and vice versa. Now dead and much mourned.

33

Already well accepted in the formal world of fine art and as a 'pop' artist, he was crucial to the Beatles' visual leap. Just as George Martin with a background in classical music recording had also been involved with recordings for the Goons and *Beyond the Fringe*, so the formally trained Peter Blake had an innate left-field appreciation of what the Beatles needed to point up their own precise and individual talent. Working in tandem they made the classic album in a classic cover.

Blake was ten years older than the Beatles, but the gap appeared to him not to matter – though the group pre-acid were, I recall, cheerfully ageist. 'It didn't make any difference,' Blake remembers. 'I think it's accepted that there was a certain amount of marijuana-smoking – I mean, not just with the Beatles – it was a social phenomenon, but I've never done any drugs at all. However, there were more links that joined us than separated us.'

Sir Joseph Lockwood, head of EMI in 1967, seemed also to have experienced the Beatles' capacity to engage people rather than throw up barriers:

❝ I knew there was some possible connection with cannabis in the studios – "smells" were noted – but I never pursued it. I had a pretty close relationship with the Beatles, largely because they were so successful. I knew them better than I did most of the pop artists, and the situation developed that where they were refused something by EMI's management, which was quite often – some disagreement about a minor thing maybe – Lennon and McCartney would come to me.'

When the cover, designed to astonish and delight the record-buyers even before they had removed the wrapping, was causing problems, Sir Joseph recalls: 'On this occasion they had been refused approval of their cover design by the EMI music department because there was a mass of important people on it.'

Sir Joseph has said recently that in fact he, too, considered it dangerous to link these important well-known faces – Shirley Temple's, for instance, famous child actress, now a serious Republican politician – with what might be considered 'a drugs record'. On the original album-cover photograph Gandhi was shown.

Paul remembers Sir Joseph coming round to his house near the studios in St John's Wood. 'Sir Joe said: "We can't have Gandhi. We can't offend the Indians ... lots of trouble there, you know ... EMI India...."'

He had a point. India was very important to EMI, which had a virtual monopoly on recording in all of that huge subcontinent, plus all the music from the hundreds of films produced there annually. Big money was on the line.

Sir Joseph Lockwood of EMI.

Paul remembers saying: '"OK. One Gandhi for two Marlon Brandos." We did a swap. It was a laugh actually, because Sir Joe was very good during that time. It must have come as a shock to him, all this stuff. He just didn't know what we were doing – we didn't, either – but I mean we had a better idea of what it was than he did.'

Sir Joseph only agreed on the understanding that Brian Epstein would have each person approached (or, if they were dead, their executors), and would indemnify EMI for 'several million pounds' against a lawsuit.

Paul, according to Sir Joseph, promised that there would be no lawsuit. This was very much in the spirit of the age, the product of the confidence of a rich and famous acidhead at the peak of his powers. 'There is no risk whatsoever,' Paul is quoted as saying. 'Everybody will be delighted.' When Mae West said she wouldn't agree to be on the record and said, 'What would I be doing in a lonely hearts club band?' it was suggested that the Beatles, all four of them, write her a personal letter. They did so and said they would very much like her to be on it, so she relented. Only Leo Gorcey of the Bowery Boys declined and asked for a fee which EMI wouldn't pay, presumably on the basis of 'they'd all want one'. Says Peter Blake: 'A pity, because Leo could probably have used the fee.'

Nobody sued – though, as Sir Joseph says now, with time fast running out and release of the album already postponed, about half the people couldn't be traced (or so he was told) and they went ahead anyway and published without permission being granted by many of the famous faces.

Alan Aldridge, one of the brightest and best of the British designers of the late sixties – illustrator of *The Beatles' Illustrated Lyrics*, and of *The Butterfly Ball* – was commissioned by the *Washington Post* to write about the innovative design of the Sgt Pepper cover. Paul McCartney told him at the time:

❛ We realised for the first time that some day someone would actually be holding a thing they'd call "the Beatles' new LP", and that normally it would just be a collection of songs or a nice picture on the cover, nothing more. So the idea was to do a complete thing that you could make what you liked of: a little magic presentation – a packet of things inside the record sleeve.'

'Not a practical marketing exercise,' says Peter Blake, who remembers the discussion well. 'I think we realised very quickly that it wasn't sensible, so there was the compromise of a flat package in the inner sleeve which slid in easily. I think I'm right in saying it was meant to be a double record, but instead of the second record they got the cutouts, badges, sergeant's stripes and so on.'

Peter Blake describes the building of the collage and the set which young Michael Cooper, a new Beatles favourite, was to photograph. (Cooper was one of the brightest cameramen on the scene, with access to all the artists – Magritte to McCartney.)

‹ All the figures which you see behind the Beatles only filled a space about two feet deep, and then there was a line of figures in front of them which were the waxworks. The actual Beatles stood on a platform about four feet deep in all with the drum in front of them, and in front of that there was a flowerbed which was pitched at an angle, maybe ten feet deep. So that from front to back the whole thing was only about fifteen feet deep. People were asked to put in favourite objects. In a way this didn't work; maybe I didn't explain it well enough, so Paul, for instance, decided his favourite objects were musical instruments and hired a great number of them and came with a vanload of French horns and trumpets and beautiful things, and I think that would have emphasised it too hard, so we only used one or two.'

(George Martin says the Beatles wanted to hold some very un-Beatle instruments: John a French horn, Ringo a trumpet, Paul a cor anglais and George a flute. 'The only trouble was, they didn't know how to hold them.')

‹ John Lennon brought a television set because he felt that television was very important to him at this stage. I had thought they would bring teddy bears, things like that, but it went into a whole other dimension. There are a number of myths as a result. The flowers for instance. My concept was that it was a municipal flowerbed, so that you would have the letters spelled out in flowers like the Boy Scouts' sign of the flowers on the clock at Edinburgh.'

In the event, when the flowers came from the nurseries there weren't enough to do it as Blake had hoped, but they made do with what they had. 'Things happened,' said Blake.

‹ There was a young boy helping who asked if he could do a guitar in hyacinths, and it was such a nice gentle sweet sort of idea that we said, "Yes, certainly," so the sort of white shape at the front of the cover is actually a guitar, and one of the myths that arose is that you could read that as "Paul?" When the stories that Paul had died arrived, this was taken to be a sign that Paul had indeed died, but it was never intended to be Paul; it was simply a guitar.

36

1. Sri Yukteswar
2. Aleister Crowley
3. Mae West
4. Lenny Bruce
5. Karlheinz Stockhausen
6. W. C. Fields
7. C. G. Jung
8. Edgar Allan Poe
9. Fred Astaire
10. Merkin
11. A Pretty Girl
12. Leo Gorcey*
13. Huntz Hall
14. Simon Rodia
15. Bob Dylan
16. Aubrey Beardsley
17. Sir Robert Peel
18. Aldous Huxley
19. Dylan Thomas
20. Terry Southern
21. Dion Di Mucci
22. Tony Curtis
23. Wallace Berman
24. Tommy Handley
25. Marilyn Monroe
26. William S. Burroughs
27. Sri Mahavatara Babaji
28. Stan Laurel
29. Richard Lindner
30. Oliver Hardy
31. Karl Marx
32. H. G. Wells
33. Sri Paramahansa Yogananda
34. Wax Figure of a Girl
35. Stuart Sutcliffe
36. Wax Figure of a Girl
37. Max Miller
38. A Vargas Girl
39. Marlon Brando
40. Tom Mix
41. Oscar Wilde
42. Tyrone Power
43. Larry Bell
44. Dr David Livingstone
45. Johnny Weissmuller
46. Stephen Crane
47. Issy Bonn
48. George Bernard Shaw
49.
50. Albert Stubbins
51. Sri Lahiri Mahasaya
52. Lewis Carroll
53. T. E. Lawrence
54. Sonny Liston
55. A Vargas Girl
56. George (in wax)
57. John (in wax)
58. Shirley Temple
59. Ringo (in wax)
60. Paul (in wax)
61.
62. John
63. Ringo
64. Paul
65. George
66. Bobby Breen
67. Marlene Dietrich
68. Mahatma Gandhi†
69. An American Legionnaire
70. Diana Dors
71. Shirley Temple

* Removed because he was the only one who asked for a fee.
† Removed at the insistence of Sir Joseph Lockwood of EMI.

An out-take from Michael
Cooper's *Sgt Pepper* picture
session in Chelsea in
March.

A who's who of what's
what.

'Another myth is that the plants around the edge were marijuana plants, and for a time I thought someone had played a joke on me and put some in, but they're not marijuana plants at all, just plants from a regular nursery.'

Peter Blake sees the work he did on *Sgt Pepper* as a high point in his life, which by common consent has been one of consistent success as a fine artist.

❛ I couldn't be more thrilled to have worked on it. It was very exciting, of course it was.'

Liverpool inseparables. The Beatles' two road managers through it all: Mal Evans (*left*) and Neil Aspinall flank Paul McCartney in the first flowering of moustache-mania at Abbey Road.

As with everything else that passes through a number of hands, things happen that the artist would dearly love to have changed.

❛ Technically it could be so much better; certainly in the retouching it lost an awful lot because there's an area where Gandhi was taken out above Diana Dors' head and where part of the palm-tree was redrawn, but instead of leaving it at that the retoucher then redrew the whole tree. It might just as well have been drawn from scratch. It would have been a great deal easier to make a flat collage.'

Yes, but . . . it was that painstaking attention to depth and scale and the planes of activity that made the cover breathe. The waxwork of Sonny Liston, the boy Beatles in effigy, the bandsmen dressed not as trendsetters but in daringly silly uniforms, the risks of the terrifically English music, so little of it 'psychedelic', harking back just as much as it reached forward, hardly a blue note on the tracks and nary a one on the cover – all of this made the album's total acceptance in the other worlds of mainstream pop, avant-garde rock, lysergic San Francisco, and the higher reaches of the British establishment the more surprising and yet the better deserved. *Sgt Pepper's Lonely Hearts Club Band*, says George Martin, was the album which turned the Beatles into significant contributors to the history of artistic performance. 'It was the turning-point. Something that will stand the test of time as a valid art form: sculpture in music.'

One Sunday in April, Neil Aspinall drove down to Old Chelsea with the Beatles to launch the album on an unsuspecting, extremely expectant world. No one was to be disappointed. Neil recalls it clearly:

❛ It was six in the morning, and we went down the King's Road in cars to see Cass Elliott of the Mamas and the Papas. We had the album with us, finished at last. She had a great sound system. Her flat was in a block of houses, back to back, really close together, and we put the system on a window ledge and the music blasted through the neighbourhood. "We're Sgt Pepper's Lonely Hearts Club Band...." It sounded great. All the windows around us opened and people leaned out, wondering. It was obvious who it was on the record. Nobody complained. A lovely spring morning. People were smiling and giving us the thumbs up. John and Mal went for a bus ride (something we never usually did) and stayed on the bus until it turned round and came back. John had a new song in his head. I don't know which one, but he said it was OK. '

Ray Coleman, one of John Lennon's biographers, recalls the official playback at Brian Epstein's house at 24 Chapel Street, Belgravia: 'He [John] said he was worried that they had gone too far for public taste. "Will they like it? Will they buy it? I like it, we all feel it's another step up, but will it sell?"'

Reservations had been expressed. The *News of the World*, for example, had declared with much head-wagging: 'Quite deliberately the Beatles are ignoring the oldest mixed metaphor in show business. "When you discover what the people want, don't rock the boat." They're stepping far ahead of their audience, recording music so complex and so unlike the music that made them successful that they could very likely lose the foundation of their support.'

When *Sgt Pepper* was released on 1 June, above and below ground the album was welcomed with real warmth and understanding by the British critics. In *Melody Maker*, Chris Welch, himself a musician, wrote: 'The lads have brought forth yet another saga of entertainment and achievement that should keep the British pop industry ticking over securely for another six months at least ... it is a remarkable and worthwhile contribution to music.'

In the *International Times* (*IT*) an unsigned appreciation declared:

❱ Too many groups have been writing "psychedelic" music before they have achieved sufficient insight into its possibilities. The Beatles stayed cool until they had thoroughly explored the potential of freak-out sounds.... Tripping with this record is a mind-blowing experience. The record is a continuum of fantastic sounds.... Musically it is highly sophisticated.'

In these tripping times, the writer recommended eating the cardboard cutout moustache from the sleeve insert 'to see what might happen'. He said he had heard there might be interesting results, though he admitted nothing had happened to him after eating the one in his copy. George Harrison said later: 'As if EMI would impregnate every album insert!'

The *New Musical Express* reviewed the album track by track, describing the whole as 'a sort of concert', and nominating George's 'Within You Without You' as the most memorable. Their critic Allen Evans summed up: 'No one can deny that the Beatles have provided us with more musical entertainment which will both please the ear and get the brain working a bit too!'

He said he would not like to say whether it was their best yet, and he would argue that it might not be worth the five months it had taken to make, but it was 'a very good LP and will sell like hot cakes'.

Paul McCartney says today that other Beatles albums outsold it, George Harrison is not at all sure it was their best LP, and I remember Ringo saying years ago that he preferred *Abbey Road*. But out of the twelve of their basic *œuvre* it is still *Sgt Pepper* that speaks loudest of its era. Ray Coleman was editor of *Disc and Music Echo* at the time and today considers the album the 'very zenith of rock 'n' roll. It ushered in the prime era of British psychedelia which others were still trying to equal well into the eighties.'

Coleman remembers the then unique 'listening party' to launch the album. He and other editors, music journalists, columnists and critics were invited by Brian Epstein to his house in Chapel Street, Mayfair. There was an enormous amount of very good food and a whole mess of drink for a press corps who had waited impatiently and none too silently for the first hearing of the album. Coleman says today: 'Few of the guests, including me, expected the album to be so revolutionary.'

Since then, listenings and revolutionary albums have become commonplace in the record business. I conducted dozens of listenings in the years that followed. In time, as feet shuffled restlessly, I learned to dread them. In 1980 I presented George's album *Somewhere in England* (first version) to Warner Brothers in an afternoon session, following a morning event that had featured John and Yoko's *Double Fantasy*. Comparisons became odious that evening. What, you may ask, has this to do with the price of fish? To which I reply: Nothing, I just thought I'd mention it.

Sgt Pepper was released on 1 June. It was a critical and commercial triumph. In Fleet Street, all over Europe, far away in San Francisco, in the first, second and third worlds, people were brought to the point of smiling as the spirit reached across the world.

Allen Ginsberg says:

> There was this element of adolescence opening up and discovering the universe. There was an individual life in the life of friendship or imagination that was cheerful and uplifted or humane with some rediscovery of humour.
>
> 'After the apocalypse of Hitler and the apocalypse of the Bomb, there was here [in *Sgt Pepper*] an exclamation of joy, the rediscovery of joy and what it is to be alive.... They showed an awareness that we make up our own fate, and they have decided to make a cheerful fate. They have decided to be generous to Lovely Rita, or to be generous to Sgt Pepper himself, turn him from an authority figure to a figure of comic humour, a vaudeville turn.

The circus poster that provided most of the lyrics for all but one verse of 'Being for the Benefit of Mr Kite'. The poster was 'liberated' from a café during the filming of the 'Penny Lane'/'Strawberry Fields Forever' clips.

'Remember, this was in the midst of the sixties; it was 1967 when some of the wilder and crazier radicals were saying "Kill the pigs". They were saying the opposite about old Sgt Pepper. In fact the Beatles themselves were dressing up in uniforms, but associating themselves with good old-time vaudeville authority rather than sneaky CIA, KGB, MI5 or whatever. It was actually a cheerful look round the world ... *for the first time, I would say, on a mass scale.*'

McCartney himself, around the time of the worldwide acclamation of the album when people were reading into it all manner of psychedelic ideas, was explaining just such a positive attitude to Alan Aldridge. In less complex terms, he set it out: 'I was just thinking of nice words like "Sgt Pepper" and "Lonely Hearts Club" and they came together *for no reason.*'

Lovely Rita, McCartney saw as a friendly soul: 'And the kind of person I'd be to fall for a meter maid, would be a shy office clerk, and I'd say "May I inquire discreetly when you are free to take some tea with me?"' (That *is* tea, not pot.)

Very dry people, just as much as crazy adventurers in the streets, loved *Sgt Pepper*. Such a man was William Rees-Mogg, then editor of *The Times*, since knighted. His sense of natural justice and honour was to lead him later that year into choppy seas with hard right-wing eyes trained on his unwelcome libertarian stance.

Sir William now says:

‹ It was a period of great change. It was a time when the so-called generation gap suddenly seemed to become much wider; it was of course before the 1968 riots in the universities and all of that. I was very conscious that something was happening and that people were just coming out with new ideas, a new vision of the world. The Beatles were at the beginning of it, and *Sgt Pepper* was a great recording which everybody enjoyed. It went right across the age groups, right across society, and it was perfectly apparent that this was music of real quality. It was the first Beatles record I bought. It summed up the Beatles' coming into the consciousness of non-pop-music people. As the sixties went on, the years were like a wave; there was a great optimism: 1967 was the last "bull year" in that the quality of the optimism of that year appeared to be undimmed. Human nature appeared to be changing. Flower power was here. But it spluttered out in the violence of 1968, and you got a decline from the optimistic idealism of the generation of youth to an almost despairing attitude.'

The music critic of *The Times*, William Mann, remembers:

The gypsy-caravan Rolls-Royce. What else ...?

❝ I was certainly older than the audience for whom they were writing, in my forties, but I was delighted. The sixties were for me a wonderful decade, a golden age for music and I suppose for lifestyle as well.'

Mann has been somewhat ribbed – even reviled – by fools in ivory towers for liking the Beatles.

❝ Of course you don't expect to be appreciated if you write about something that's unconventional, and it was in those days fairly unconventional for a serious music critic to write about popular music. (They do it all the time now.) I had one colleague who refused to believe that there was any musical value whatsoever in any piece of popular music – and this is a person who idolises Mozart, who wrote plenty of popular music.

'As for *Sgt Pepper*, it was, I think, possibly the first rock LP that was held together, however speciously, by a thematic device – namely the first song which is reprised towards the end – and this gave it a sort of unity which I mentioned in my story.

'*Sgt Pepper* was a surprise. I suppose all the Beatles LPs had surprises in them, but this one contained a good number of unusual songs. I think the literary interest was unusual at the time ... all told, it seemed to encapsulate the spirit of 1967, the flower-power period and all that. And it still, when you hear it again, conjures up a period which has now gone, of course. And that is actually what music is about, isn't it? You want a piece of music to encapsulate the period it was written in, and *Sgt Pepper* does seem to do that.'

Wilfred Mellers, the musicologist, agrees. 'It doesn't seem to me to have faded after twenty years, and that's the test, isn't it?' As an academic thought to be a bit odd to like the Beatles so much that he lectured on them and wrote a great book, *Twilight of the Gods*, Wilfred Mellers declares:

❝ When they asked, "Isn't it odd ... a university lecturer, etc....," I *always* gave the same answer: "No, I don't think it's odd at all. It seems to me perfectly natural; some things are alive, some things are dead, and this is one of the things that is quite definitely alive." The essence of [the Beatles] was this guileless honesty, the spirit of Beatle genius is what we call its adolescence, this pristine verbal consciousness.'

Wilfred Mellers has much to say on the music of Lennon and McCartney and George Harrison, and is particularly impressed that they have 'come through this world'. 'Maybe that is what they are about,' he says. 'Coming through this world that is too much for lots of people.'

Sir Joseph Lockwood recalls:

❝ Just about the time the record was issued I got an invitation, and I went, rather unusually for me, to a dinner-party with a very rich group of middle-class older ladies, and I never met with such an atmosphere – they were absolutely thrilled with this record. Most of us sat on the floor for hours after dinner singing extracts from it. This to me was a new experience – the music had spread so widely!'

Prince Charles, still at school, was very keen on the music and used to write letters to Sir Joseph. Similarly, on the other side of the Atlantic, apparently square Hugh Downs, presenting the news on American

Al Kooper

television, described the album as 'one of the world's great treasures'.

On a flying visit to England, Joan and I heard the album at John Lennon's house in Surrey in May 1967, by which time he had grown so used to the work that he was eager to play us a new song – 'Baby You're a Rich Man' – and pieces of another. It was said that they had spent thousands of hours and £25,000 on the album, and my recollection is that John was talking over it as it played, anxious to get to the next place in music. We had the record with us when we got back to Los Angeles, after a remarkable weekend of LSD, music, love, flowers, bells, incense candles, and many wild rides in John's Rolls-Royce, newly painted that weekend to look like a Romany caravan.

I took the record back to Los Angeles to the Monterey festival offices, and people were brought to a state of grace at the first hearing one lunchtime in May. Michelle Phillips remembers: '*Sgt Pepper* was what we listened to for the next days and weeks: that record, played over and over again. It was the theme of the people working for the festival.'

The great Al Kooper, a true musical instinctive with an honourable background as organist, guitarist, producer, arranger and founder of bands, was there at the first listening.

❛ I was a very big Beatles fan, and each album they made they upped themselves, especially with and after *Rubber Soul*. *Sgt Pepper*, for one thing, was the album that changed drumming more than anything else. Before that album, drum "fills" in rock 'n' roll were pretty rudimentary, all much the same, and this record had what I call *space fills* where they would leave a tremendous amount of air. It was most appealing to me musically. Also the *sound* of the drums got much better. What I had to figure out now was: What am I going to do to get drums to sound like that? As for the other aspects of the album ... there are millions of things! It was incredibly well done, sociological opera for its time. I mean, it was the kind of record you would get up in the morning and put on, start your day off with it. It will always be a great record. Timeless.'

Steve Gaskin, who now organises a Tennessee commune but who, back then, was a 'senior hippie', says:

❛ The album is engraved on my memory. So many of us came to the big hippies' communal house we lived in in San Francisco and we each had multiple copies of all the Beatle records. We used to stack them up so we could put on side one, side two, side one, side two ... hours at a time, just leave it all day long, you know. And we always felt we were talking about Sgt Pepper as if he were really

John Sebastian

some sort of mythical band leader for *all* hippies. We were really talking about worldwide transformation – and we weren't just talking about music but about everything.'

Ben Friedman kept a record shop in San Francisco.

 We had a shipment of the album from Capitol Records. We emptied all the other records out of the racks. The entire window was covered by racks which would hold twelve records in each section. We placed *Sgt Pepper* in each section of each rack and filled the windows. We covered the entire space with *Sgt Pepper*. It was such a great record. Now, some of the wholesalers didn't think it could be that great, but we insisted that we wanted 1,000 records and we put them all in the window and we sold them all.'

Friedman's shop was a special hangout for artists now famous, and designers later to be well known for their work on posters and San Francisco artefacts.

We had fun because you get immersed in the records and in the posters and people and we were open till twelve or one o'clock in the morning generally. And all people who are now so famous were just ordinary people, and they were all in the store. All friends.'

Dr Timothy Leary, whose extravagant references to the Beatles as 'avatars' had impressed so many of us, does not feel that the description has survived the passage of the years. He stands by *Sgt Pepper*'s impact on that generation, however, and states that in that moment the album 'gave voice to a feeling that the old ways were over … it came along at the right time in that summer'.

John Sebastian of the Lovin' Spoonful said that *Sgt Pepper* sent writers and arrangers and band members scattering.

❝ It was like throwing down a hat in the centre of a ring, it was a tremendous challenge. I remember having just finished an album that was fairly compact in its arrangement and then hearing this incredible pile of tracks with stuff going backwards, entire orchestras playing very unconventionally, mechanical tricks which we'd never heard before and it seemed like an almost insurmountable task to come up with anything even in the same ballpark.'

Sebastian remembers Brian Wilson, writer and quasi-leader of the Beach Boys, being very funny on the subject of the Sgt Pepper Effect. 'It sent him running up to his room practically for a thumbsucking episode. He didn't know what to do about it.' Both Sebastian and Wilson were among the best, maybe *the* best, in their fields, but *Pepper* to them was a frightener and a joy. Says Sebastian: 'After you got over the sheer delight of listening to this wonderful album, you then had to think in terms of staying in the same market-place.'

The man who is now named Ponderosa Pine (after America's most threatened great tree) was, in 1967, plain Keith Lampe. He heard *Sgt Pepper* with Abbie Hoffman and about ten others. Ponderosa Pine, though still as cosmic as a sunbeam, is no panty-waist. He was an artillery officer in the Korean War and later burned his campaign ribbon and discharge papers in the cause of peace. He was an early dropout but nobody's half-witted pothead. None the less, after hearing *Sgt Pepper* by these bad-boys-next-door, leathery Keith Lampe was 'blown away by the music'. He says now in Ponderosa Pine reflective mood:

❝ When "Day in the Life" ended there was silence for a long, long time. It increased our confidence in the future a great deal. It was as though the millennium was at hand, and so the music was necessary to us as activists. It was something that allowed us to keep building momentum rather than exhausting ourselves in repetitive exercises. And I still think of it as a tremendous cultural importance, and its effects are still to be seen here and there today.'

Donovan was a friend of the Beatles. He was himself very successful by 1967, and much admired and treasured by people who looked to him for part of the soundtrack for mind-broadening. He remembers hearing *Sgt Pepper* with Ronnie Lane and Steve Marriott of the Small Faces – also prized trips accompanists – and Marianne Faithfull. Donovan recalls:

❰ Ronnie shouted, "I've got it," and I said, "Let's *play* it," and it was astounding. The breadth of its vision and the quality of its sound and the way it followed the singles ["Penny Lane" and "Strawberry Fields Forever"], and the new direction that had been carved by this band and the excitement that had been created, seemed to culminate in this classical rock "movie". It evoked so many images, and the mind opened and you didn't have to be high to dig it.'

But it helped?

❰ If you could only dig it when you were high, then it wouldn't have been so popular because not everybody was getting high, but if you *were* sitting smoking something there was definitely an opening up. It was astounding.'

The album certainly opened up a new world for Peter Fonda:

❰ I had been told "You have to play the game that Hollywood's designed". But I decided that I had to make my own movies and on hearing the song "I'll get by with a little help from my friends" I wondered what would happen if *I* got up and sang out of tune. Would it make the audience get up and walk out on me? I knew that if I had a little help from those friends (just in terms of encouragement, if not direct input), then I could get by. And I felt that if *they* could go off and be so outrageous and make it work, then I could, too. And I did. And with a lot of help from my friends, like Dennis Hopper and Terry Southern, I came up with *Easy Rider*. Twenty years later it's still cooking fine for me. And I'm still singing out of tune.'

So the album that had taken so long had shown that the time was worth the taking. Indeed, if it came to that, it was no longer appropriate that an album should be seen as due or overdue. Don Short of the *Daily Mirror* had written in the spring: 'The Beatles ... obviously aren't worried about the mounting impatience of their public.' No. Why worry when something as transcendental was on the way from inner space to the world at large?

In *Sgt Pepper* it seemed there was an agent for bonding humanity like no other in the secular world in peacetime. The writer Langdon Winner said it was the closest Western civilisation had come to unity since the Congress of Vienna in 1815:

❛ At the time *Sgt Pepper* was released I happened to be driving across country on Interstate 80. In each city where I stopped for gas or food – Laramie, Ogallala, Moline, South Bend – the melodies wafted in from some far-off transistor radio or portable hi-fi. It was the most amazing thing I've ever heard. For a brief moment, the irreparably fragmented consciousness of the West was unified, at least in the minds of the young. ❜

Meeting the press in Brian
Epstein's house for the
launch of *Sgt Pepper*. There
was much comment on
their 'unconventional'
clothing.

50

The Charlatans in the
Panhandle, Golden Gate
Park, San Francisco. They
were the first 'fancy'
dressers in the old West.

TWO

MUSIC, LOVE AND FLOWERS

'Strawberry Fields Forever' had suggested that living was easy with our eyes closed, misunderstanding all we saw. Nothing was real, and there was nothing to get hung up about. The Beatles' newer, more expectant and excitable supporters, eager for change, could see, however, that the more some things changed the more others appeared to be just the same. Popular music was all over the place. There was, to the purists, plenty to get hung up about.

Unreflected in the charts, the product of real undercurrents of change in not-so-secret halls of romance and wonder such as the UFO Club in London and the Fillmore and Avalon ballrooms in San Francisco, were all manner of strange and exotic happenings based on a healthy progressive response to the new possibilities: underground attitudes, abstract lyrics and magical lighting techniques, newly fused music called by all sorts of labels – folk-rock, raga rock, acid rock, good-time music or the generic 'San Francisco sound'. Whatever the labellers chose to call it, there *was* something good and new and very dance-based happening. Anyone who had eyes and ears could sense the changes.

However, the commercial audience was still avid for old-style romantic ballads. Harry Secombe was at number one in Britain in the April *Disc and Music Echo* chart with 'This Is My Song', and Petula Clark on top of the trade chart in England and number five in the United States with her version of the same song. Vince Hill had 'Edelweiss' in the top five; the Seekers were in the American top five with 'Georgie Girl'; Ken Dodd was in the British hit parade together with Val Doonican, Cliff Richard and several 'safe' groups: the Troggs, the Tremeloes, Herman's Hermits. There was much letter-writing to the music papers: 'How dare people prefer Ken Dodd?' countered with 'Who do these so-called knockers of "real singers" think they are?' Nothing was real: nothing had changed, it seemed. And where *were* the Beatles? In Abbey Road studios, making history.

It was because there was clearly so much room for *everyone* – Harry Secombe or Pink Floyd, the Monkees or the Beatles – that I was out of patience with the war of words that raged in the music papers and on the streets. The old guard, the new guard, they were all of a frenzy, the question the eternal one of 'street cred': Who really guards the Gate of Integrity in the music business?

If we look at the evidence of the charts, we will see immediately that there was no one clear directional trend by which pop newcomers might be judged. A study of number one records both in Britain and in America reveals only some very basic general truths, foremost among them the fact that after the temporary British invasion of the American Top 100 in 1964–5 the charts on both sides of the Atlantic had begun to settle down until by 1967 each country seemed determined to place its own artists at number one.

Of the fourteen top British records in 1967, only three were by American performers: 'I'm a Believer' by the Monkees, 'Somethin' Stupid' by Nancy and Frank Sinatra, and 'San Francisco (Be Sure to Wear Flowers in Your Hair)' by Scott McKenzie.

Of the nineteen top records in the American charts that year, only five were by British artists, and three of those were by the Beatles: 'Penny Lane', 'All You Need Is Love' and 'Hello Goodbye'. The other two were the Rolling Stones' 'Ruby Tuesday' and Lulu's 'To Sir with Love', the title-song of a film in which she also acted.

It was a bad year for soloists – particularly men. Only three men went to the top in Britain: Scott McKenzie with his one-off 'San Francisco', Long John Baldry with 'Let the Heartaches Begin' and then Engelbert Humperdinck (formerly Gerry Dorsey), who came in out of the cold with a new name and two number one hits – 'Release Me' and 'The Last Waltz'. In America there were *no* male soloists at number one that year and only two women: Aretha Franklin (with 'Respect') and Lulu. The American charts had only three number ones by black artists – Aretha Franklin and the Supremes (two). The British had only one – the Foundations, a mixed black and white group.

There was quite a discrepancy between British and American top singles, though we were never again to return to the pre-1964 situation where there wouldn't be any British artist in the American Top 100. In 1967, only four records were top in both countries, two of them again by the Beatles: 'All You Need Is Love' and 'Hello Goodbye'. Also the Monkees' 'I'm a Believer' and Frank and Nancy Sinatra's 'Somethin' Stupid'.

So groups were still predominant, male singers rare as soloists in the charts (why go it alone when you could have fun in a group?), women could still make it alone but tended not to be members of groups (the

Mamas and the Papas in Los Angeles, and The Great Society, Jefferson Airplane, and Big Brother and the Holding Company in San Francisco were among the exceptions that proved the rule. These were pre-feminist times). Lulu, at number one in America, had no success with that same record in Britain; while the consummate British pop star Sandie Shaw, a success in Britain from 1964 onwards with a steady flow of chart hits, never could keep a foothold in the American market.

The British invasion having peaked in 1965 with the male groups from the Beatles to Freddie and the Dreamers through Herman's Hermits, Chad Stuart and Jeremy Clyde, Peter and Gordon, the Americans fought back with the Byrds, breaking through in July 1965 when 'Mr Tambourine Man' became number one in Britain. It was a natural organic Dylan-written response to the Beatles. (The door had, however, been opened by the Righteous Brothers with 'You've Lost That Lovin' Feeling' at number one in both countries in February 1965.) By 1966 there was much communication and travel between young British and American musicians and their satraps. The older artists hung in there, too, so that by 1967 just about anything might happen. Few people thought the 'old' crooner Sinatra and his pert daughter could walk all over the hit parade, but they did with 'Somethin' Stupid'.

Engelbert Humperdinck obliging fans and cameramen in traditional discomfort. He was a dominant pop star in 1967.

Engelbert Humperdinck was the new British rage after being neglected for years as Gerry Dorsey. He would eventually make a highly profitable career in America as a live performer in Las Vegas though he never achieved number one in the singles charts, which would soon be dominated by rock-orientated acts. Britain by contrast, even in that hippiest year of change 1967 (even in multicoloured bangles, baubles and beads, with feathers and bones and pockets full of God knows what chemical madness), would still sustain a 'mums and dads' market.

There was much confusion in the minds of pundits that year, with all sorts of strange things happening. In San Francisco – as in Liverpool five or six years earlier – there were many hundreds of bands playing a distinctive sort of music for the people immediately around them. Their music was immensely personal and became very powerful in the alternative way of life known as the 'counter-culture', which was being pursued with real diligence by all sorts of little tribes within the great Bay Area. If very little of it showed in the charts or on the radio – and very little of it did – that didn't mean it wasn't happenin', baby. It was! Haight-Ashbury, those two streets at an intersection on the edge of the 'Panhandle' by Golden Gate Park, had been flourishing as a centre for real cultural change since early 1966 (though, as we'll see, the roots went deeper and had been planted by others in another time), and the promulgation of a New Music by the Beatles had been answered with knobs on by such as the Grateful Dead, Jefferson Airplane, Country Joe and the Fish, and the Quicksilver Messenger Service. The bands survived, mostly without record contracts, because there were fans to support and cherish them, and benign promoters and friendly halls to give them their venues. While this cauldron was bubbling in the backroom, attracting newer and more exotic herbal and metaphysical additives, there was a welter of moneymaking in the music business in another centre, the Hated Hollywood, a fascinating township of greater Los Angeles much despised by the people of San Francisco, which though smaller than LA is no less self-adoring.

The Monkees were now an established worldwide junior showbiz sensation, a nicely calculated financial operation turning a pretty penny while the press was busy making a dog's breakfast out of the trumped-up beauty contest: Monkees v. Beatles. Formed by some very sharp Hollywood types, the Monkees foursome now had a place in the sun; their rejection by 'hip' America and Europe notwithstanding, their records were making a fortune and the television show was a smash hit. Mike Nesmith, Mickey Dolenz, Peter Tork and Davy Jones (three Americans and an Englishman) had been chosen out of hundreds of aspirants (including Stephen Stills and Charles Manson) to be 'American Beatles' and 'clown around by numbers' on television, singing songs carefully crafted for chart success.

The Monkees always seemed to me to be a perfectly legitimate exercise in showbusiness, and I always said so – to support the 'boys' themselves and to annoy the puritans. I still believe that. The Beatles themselves were always happy to acknowledge the Monkees, and Paul invited Mickey Dolenz, the drummer, around to his house to underline the point – an overture heralded in the press: 'Beatle Paul welcomes Monkee Mickey to St John's Wood home.' For a while it was only the uptights who, as usual, took offence at this manufactured group. Then the four Monkees, themselves unhappy at not having been allowed to play on early records, started to demand real musical status within their recording arrangements.

In an article I wrote I insisted: 'Let's hear no more of the Monkees vs Beatles rubbish. . . . Let us say the Monkees are OK and valid and real and good and honest and hopeful. Let us welcome them to "the Scene". Let us enjoy them. Let us pray that *they* enjoy themselves for I hear that there are times when they do not enjoy being Monkees.'

The Beatles, secure in their conquest of the world and now 'off the road' for ever, knew that whatever the press made of the new American pretenders they held the crown, the throne room, the orb and the sceptre. The Beatles were so serene that they didn't even mind that Humperdinck had kept them off the top of the British charts throughout the long and successful run of 'Penny Lane' and 'Strawberry Fields Forever'. For as long as that record was at number two, the Hump (as he was known in

Beatle Paul at home to
Monkee Mickey. A
comfortable coalescence.

the British musical press) held on to number one, and by the time 'Release
Me' slipped down the charts 'Penny Lane' and 'Strawberry Fields Forever'
had spent their energy. And what a fuss there was in the British music
press and in the Schadenfreudian columns of some of the regular press:
'Beatles Fail to Reach the Top', 'First Time in Four Years', 'Has the
Bubble Burst?', 'Could the End Be Nigh?'

Nigh? No. *High?* Yes – very. They were getting ever higher in the
Abbey Road studios making *Sgt Pepper's Lonely Hearts Club Band*. And,
while the world waited, Harry Secombe got to number one to replace
Humperdinck in the *Disc* chart, and visiting Americans wondered how
this could be the Swinging London, the Mecca of Pop, the home of the
Sultans of Style they'd read about. They said: 'The boutiques are *great*,
but that radio. Jesus! It's so *square*. Only one regular station and something
they call pirates.'

The BBC was still the only legal British-based broadcasting outlet for
records, but Radio Luxembourg, coming from mainland Europe, had
been around for thirty years, though interrupted by the Second World
War. But change was in the air. Pirate radio ships out at sea were giving
the BBC a real battering in their illegal response to the public craving for
pop music in the mid-sixties.

I was living in America and only visiting England with Byrds ('Mr
Tambourine Man') or Beach Boys ('Good Vibrations') or Beatles (Brian
Epstein's housewarming), so what I was picking up was gossip, lightning
images, and Insights from the Charts. On matters strictly pop, I was sorry
that the Beatles hadn't reached number one. Epstein had been right: the
'Penny Lane'/'Strawberry Fields Forever' work *was* definitely their best
yet, and I dare say it is played more often than 'Release Me', though as

Humperdinck never, ever said an immodest word about *his* triumph it is for me to trumpet now that they survived him on radio. I wrote happily that there was plenty of room for 'Penny Lane' and 'Strawberry Fields Forever' and the Monkees and other contenders for the crown.

For about three years in the mid-sixties I had a column in *Disc* newspaper in Britain. It was first called 'Our Man in America', later 'Hollywood Calling', and had its followers among fans and groups. The Beatles loved it, finding all sorts of secret messages in it – Brian Epstein was a keen reader between the lines. (John was interested in the activities of two invented Lennon relatives, Uncle Stan and Auntie Flo, whom I described encountering various embarrassing situations in Los Angeles. Readers never questioned their existence. Nor, in a way, did I. I believed in them. It was a relaxed time.)

In *Disc* on 18 February I wrote:

> "Penny Lane" is the most requested song in Los Angeles this week and it is the best. It is the best of the best of the best group in the world. "Strawberry Fields" is the next most requested song and seems to be the one the groups like best ... the margin of preference is slight however and against the total musicality of the Beatles the choice is academic and of little consequence.'

Battle-lines were now clearly drawn between hip and square, hippie and straight musical tastes. The underground press had a growing readership, and the 'straight music' press was increasingly divided into committed and impartial journalists. Hugh Nolan and Nick Jones (of

Janis and Grace – Joplin and Slick at the Fillmore

Disc and *Melody Maker* respectively) nailed their 'flower power' colours to the mast, and among the 'straights' Bob Farmer of *Disc* was constantly up to mischief urging people to protest against the New Movement in music. The musicians were a sort of mad cavalry, mounting their instruments and riding off in all directions.

There were now those whose songs/records/performances/clothes were indivisible from their perceived beliefs or attitudes, or state of mind: the Beatles, the Rolling Stones, Donovan, the Who, Buffalo Springfield, Jefferson Airplane. Then there were Petula Clark, Engelbert Humperdinck, Vince Hill, Ken Dodd and Tom Jones, happily going about their chart business without trying to give or take offence. Fans, often immature, supported them vociferously from either side of the divide.

On the sidelines were some major artists who took public attitudes: Paul Jones was very pro-Beatles and angry about Humperdinck's success in keeping 'Penny Lane'/'Strawberry Fields Forever' out of the number one spot. The press worked hard on this, and Paul Jones stood firm: it *was* a disgrace. Humperdinck refused to join the fight. Paul Jones's old bandleader, Manfred Mann, received some gratuitous long-distance remonstrations from the American columnist for *Disc* – 'he is a man with uptight lines at the corner of the mouth' – for presuming to comment on the Beatles without acknowledging their endless grace.

And still quite outside and beyond all this were the bands who didn't make records: they played music live for their fans, who danced and were to be found – as we've seen – in the UFO Club in London and in the ballrooms of San Francisco.

There might never have been a 'San Francisco sound' if not for the pioneering energies of two key figures: Bill Graham and Chet Helms. In the melting-pot that had become the San Francisco Scene, they controlled the key concert and dance venues – Chet the Avalon and Bill the Fillmore. Between them they inherited the scene set by Marty Balin's Matrix, 'Big Daddy' Tom Donahue's short-lived Mother's, and the Family Dog's Longshoremen's Hall (see Chapter 4, no relation to the British Family Dogg). The men around Bill and Chet, and the women behind them – remember, feminism was some years away from a real flowering – were at the fulcrum of a counter-culture now finding its own fearless informed voice.

The two ballrooms were patrons of new trends in the visual arts – weekly, innovative young artists competed for the honour of designing the ballrooms' latest poster – and sponsors of the new music and dance, yet Bill and Chet could not have been more different.

Both were spiritual devotees of the American Dream, but where Graham, a Jewish refugee, thought that it was still possible to achieve

it Helms, a free-floating Drop-Acid-and-Set-the-People-Free believer in
the power of dance, was appalled that the dream was fading in the heat of
repression. Yet Bill the great straight promoter and Chet the acidhead
with a heart of pure thistledown were equally determined to make
America more beautiful – and where better to begin than in the Theatres
of Joy, the ballrooms?

Paul Kantner of Jefferson Airplane saw a new intimacy in the way
audiences in San Francisco were able to relate to their musicians. They
were all young together.

❛ The Beatles helped that, but at times *our* audience was more
outrageous than the people on stage. There was a very large
interaction between us. We were only "little stars", and people
would just say, "Oh, hi, Paul," or "Hi, Marty. How you doin'? Nice
songs you did the other day, nice glasses," and so on, and it was a
mutually respected and shared sort of experience rather than just a
performer–audience situation, and that translated over into every
aspect of the music. ❜

Chet Helms remembers the Avalon ballroom relationships well:

❛ It was mostly an organisation of peers, people on an equivalent
level. The Grateful Dead were accessible. For example, Jerry Garcia
would lean off a two-foot stage and say, "Hey, Pete, how's the old
lady and the kids? Haven't seen you in a month of Sundays." ❜

Helms believed that young people went to a show not just for the
music but to be with others, be seen by and see other people. 'Music is
a medium for that happening. Light shows are a medium for that
happening. Costumes are a medium for that happening.'

David Simpson, one of the sages of Haight-Ashbury who assumed
responsibility for some of the caring tasks of the era, saw the local music
as the backbone of the community:

❛ It is very important to know how closely the alternative community
of San Francisco identified with the music and specific musicians –
the Grateful Dead, the Jefferson Airplane, the Messenger Service,
and Big Brother and the Holding Company. They were our bands,
they were our musicians. Neither they nor we felt the distinction
between the artists and the people, and it gave the music great
strength. By 1968 nobody danced at rock concerts any more, but in
1966 and 1967 nobody sat down. It was quite impossible. The
concerts were a mêlée of bodies. It was a wonderful inspired sense
of oneness. ❜

Chet Helms is still an unreconstructed believer in the values of the Avalon as the place where people spontaneously *gave*. He is proud, too, that the music played there and in the other centres where San Francisco music was played had a basic character of freedom and improvisation, which was itself a reflection of what was going on socially. Jazz was very influential, too. The 'San Francisco sound' he believes to be a misnomer. 'The aspect of jazz that was improvisation was brought over into the rock medium. And improvisation which was a large factor in Indian music was brought in and fused. There was an environment which was crossover, a lot of variations on old themes, and it was a very constructive and creative period.'

Joe Boyd, doing his own similar thing in London at the same time, agrees with that theme of aware audiences and innovative bands. That they fused on the same level was the acme of the many achievements of UFO, the club he helped to run, and he saw Pink Floyd and the other

The Dreamchild: Marianne Faithfull

bands he promoted there as part of a happy ambience of equals – all creative people with the bands of joyful minstrels providing the soundtrack and the lighting. (The lighting was crucial, and Pink Floyd always said that their lighting people were band members.)

The record business was now said to be worth a billion dollars a year, but the only thing that people knew for certain about it was that things were in a right old muddle. Dave Dee, Dozy, Beaky, Mick and Tich, and the Walker Brothers were making a lot of hits in England, but though the Walkers (not brothers, incidentally) were American they didn't amount to a hill of beans in their own country. On another planet, the young black from Seattle with the strange trick of playing his guitar behind his back or with his teeth, Jimi Hendrix, was ripping them up in England. Gene Pitney, another American, was also very popular in England but in trouble with some fans for saying silly things about the Beatles being 'too far out'. Cat Stevens, it was said, 'really deserved a hit'. Harry Secombe spoke out on 1 April 1967: 'Stop slamming the squares. Surely there's room for anything that's good. I go for pretty well everything in the charts.'

I was interviewed early in the year by Al Aronowitz for the *Saturday Evening Post* and went into a terrible rant about the state of popular music. In the first paragraph of his five-page words-and-pictures supplement, Aronowitz wrote:

❮ Taylor was beginning to feel that the pop music world that had been so conveniently at his finger tips seemed to be moving beyond his grasp. In London there were rumours the Beatles would never perform again in public. In New York Herman was said to be looking for a TV job without his Hermits. The Young Rascals, once heralded as the American group most likely to succeed the Beatles had just returned from a European tour that lost $20,000. Mod shops

Whomania. Lock up your daughters.

were thinking about stocking cowboy shirts. Groupies were torn between Herman Hesse's mystical *Siddhartha* and the monosyllabic teenybopper bible *16* magazine.'

Having referred next to the expected Sunset Strip riots (see Chapter 5) when 'the Strip would become a battleground, the cops versus the mini masses, long-haired, bellbottomed teenagers who have become the shock troops of Hollywood's psychedelic revolution', Aronowitz went on to say: 'Once upon a time, Taylor knew the pop music world as well as anyone, but still confessed his bewilderment. "The industry", Taylor said, "is booming. It should do a billion dollars this year. But it is not in good shape."'

What I didn't realise then was that the centre had shifted from the Top 40 to a new music beyond the charts. I was to find this out in the coming months, during which I dropped all my clients and then, in the mood of those times, decided to 'drop out' myself. Hadn't that been the advice on high: 'Turn on, tune in and drop out'? And when I had done it I told Al Aronowitz, whose article was eventually published in July 1967, having been six months in the making:

❛ I became bored. I became bored with a performer's pet hates and pet loves and what he eats for breakfast. The best artists in the business – the aristocracy – are moving into positions of power. They're making fewer and fewer compromises with commercialism. There's hardly anything interesting happening outside this exclusive circle. But what's happening inside may be the most remarkable story of our time.'

It's instructive to note the pictures used to illustrate Aronowitz's article. On the cover, Herb Alpert and the Tijuana Brass, Nancy Sinatra and the Supremes. Inside, Herman of the Hermits, a huge double-page spread of the Grateful Dead, who by the high summer were receiving their first attention outside San Francisco, having released an album on the Warner Brothers label (courtesy of Joe Smith, one of the very few Los Angeles executives to take the trouble to hang out in San Francisco). On another page there's a picture of the Byrds and me, Petula Clark, then Bob Dylan – full-length, eyes closed, in majestic silhouette – Simon and Garfunkel, Paul Revere and the Raiders, and the Lovin' Spoonful, all with equal space. Finally, with two-thirds of a page to himself, in full hippie drag with hands together, staring contemplatively into a rock-pool, Donovan.

In that selection of pictures you have the span of popular music as perceived in main-street America in mid-1967. The magazine was at the

The Doors sharing a joke

printers, and Aronowitz therefore did not report on the bands seen for the first time outside San Francisco during what Tony Palmer described as the most important event in the seventy-year history of popular music, the first (and last) Monterey International Pop Music Festival, which took place in June of that year.

At the year's end, Frankie Vaughan, the Troggs, Des O'Connor, the Seekers, Shirley Bassey & Co. were all in the British charts alongside a very psychedelic Traffic, Procol Harum, Eric Burdon, and the Beatles. *The Sound of Music* was the top album over *Sgt Pepper*, which couldn't sustain its reign despite having outsold every previous group album, including the Beatles' own.

Earlier in the year, the July edition of *Record World* had awarded their own disc-jockey pollwinners as follows: Top record of the year 'I'm a Believer' by the Monkees and 'Somethin' Stupid' by Frank and Nancy Sinatra. Equal runners-up were 'Strangers in the Night' and 'Born Free' by Frank Sinatra and Roger Williams respectively. Top female vocalist honours were shared by Petula Clark and Nancy Sinatra. The Beatles came third in the group section, sharing their place with Tommy James and the Shondells. The most promising male vocal group were not the Grateful Dead or any of the Monterey contenders but the Buckinghams. Sonny and Cher were rated top duo over Simon and Garfunkel. The top male group was the Monkees, and nowhere was there a mention of Janis Joplin or Janis Ian. The most promising female newcomer was Aretha Franklin with 'Respect'. (The term 'promising' was a bit rich coming as it did after twelve singles in six years, but she had to come to Atlantic and their star producer, Jerry Wexler, to make it.) Most promising male newcomer was Neil Diamond, and in the light of his longevity the award was probably justified.

And yet we were in a time of great change. With dancing in San Francisco, the secret and not so secret mind expansion, the balladeering and the new confidence of Soul (through the continuing power of Atlantic Records, the Motown artists and Otis Redding – alas, to die in December of that year aged twenty-six), there was a whole lot of shaking going on.

I would say that the great sea-change in pop was that after 1967 it became ever so slightly serious. The lyrics now really had to be listened to. There had of course always been lyricists of wit and charm, but now there was surrealism, seriousness of purpose, earnestness, even – dare we say it? – silliness in the attempted sending of messages of social import, or in the search for change. In due course all lyrics would be examined in painstaking detail for meanings behind meanings, and false motives would be imputed, reputations impugned and records banned. But where it had once been only folk-singers and blues singers who sang of the search for a better life it was now white boys in funny clothes with even stranger names.

It was not a change welcomed by all, and of course many pop singers prattled on as usual about moon and June. But from now on another Us and Them had emerged: Hip and Straight pop stars. By the year's end the Beatles had had two more hits in Britain and America: 'All You Need Is Love' and 'Hello Goodbye'. They were revered and loved for it, but to this day there are those who say that in 1967 pop music lost its innocence and has never recovered. The truth is it was always a bit of a shambles.

Some of the American groups with followings built on good old-fashioned American rock 'n' roll – fanmags, 'American Bandstand', and one-night stops on the concert circuits – sailed through 1967 unaffected by changes in consciousness, inner space travel, necklaces on men, or other irrelevances. One such was Paul Revere and the Raiders, who had four singles out that year. They kept right on earning and appearing on 'youth' television, and nervous citizens felt reassured that some good safe things never changed.

Others changed their names, like the Pulsations who had become the Buckinghams during the British invasion. They had a number one on 18 February, giving way to the Stones the following week. They were good, but not really part of what would soon be 'happening'. They were, in a way, just too late: neither *then* – well trained, old guard, built to last – nor *now* – avant-garde, sure of a jetstream of hip acceptance.

The Beach Boys and the Doors were respectively the old and the new, and both were to succeed in interesting ways in 1967. The Beach Boys entered the year as very real contenders with a huge modern hit in 'Good Vibrations', number one all over in late 1966. Their album *Pet Sounds* was not a big seller in America, but musically it was a great treasure – a mighty good response to what the Beatles had been up to with *Rubber Soul* and *Revolver*. The Beach Boys were nobody's fools and always had to be watched by their peers.

McCartney took time on his April 1967 trip to see what Brian Wilson was up to in the studio. They met in our house over on Grandview Drive off Laurel Canyon, and I made them listen to Glenn Miller while they settled in. They each brought out demos of new stuff – I forget what – and after broadening our minds we went off to hear the Beach Boys rehearse a song called 'Vegetables' before hastening west to Bel Air to join the Phillipses, John and Michelle, and Scott McKenzie (then an unknown tenor) where, in Jeannette McDonald's old mansion, we all did a lot of ganja and listened to the stars singing oldies to acoustic guitar with Wilson playing wine-glasses filled with varying amounts of water. It sounds like fun, but actually I've had many better evenings. (I never liked the song 'Vegetables'. It seemed daft.)

The Beach Boys – all substantial pop performers, Wilson family and friends – finally released the wonderful 'Heroes and Villains' and later 'Surf's Up', both with lyrics by Van Dyke Parks, set to brilliantly constructed melodies by Brian Wilson and arranged by Brian with an uncanny sense of what the very best pop music can attain. Brian Wilson was quite a giant and by 1967 he had attained his full height. Living in alarming ever-changing luxury and eccentricity, with sandbox and tent and God knows what else inside his Bel Air house, he was both a care and a joy to his nearest and dearest.

The Doors, however – Jim Morrison, the beautiful Californian romantic who became a sad self-impersonator, and his three very talented colleagues, Ray Manzarek, Robbie Krieger and John Densmore – were about to leave their very hungry beginnings behind them. (I first saw them in late 1965 or early 1966 doing strange things with sounds and words, Morrison playing with the microphone up against the speakers and singing some very finely aimed, original songs. They were a support act for Captain Beefheart at the Whiskey A Go Go in Los Angeles; the place was not full.) By July 1967, as much treasured Elektra artists, they had a famous and brilliant number one, 'Light My Fire', which must be in everyone's top ten great pop records of all time.

We all thought that barring accidents (and up to then there hadn't been many – almost everyone influential in the music business was still alive and likely to remain so, we thought) the Doors would be around for years to continue weaving their strand in the fascinating fabric of the new music, and when after 'All You Need Is Love' (which replaced 'Light My Fire') left number one we welcomed the fascinating Bobbie Gentry with 'Ode to Billy Joe' it did seem as if pop had never been more interesting.

We should pause for a moment in order to do justice to 'All You Need Is Love' – a cornerstone of the era, a turning-point in communication. The song was Britain's contribution to the first worldwide satellite television broadcast and it was thought to have been seen by 400 million people. It went around the world live from EMI studios in Abbey Road on the evening of Sunday, 25 June. Joan and I were watching with the family in Los Angeles around midday. Brian Epstein had telephoned from the studios to make sure we were tuned in to the Los Angeles educational channel, waiting as the earlier items were bouncing off the satellites – babies being born, new discoveries in science explained. 'The boys' song is just beyond belief – quite the loveliest thing they've done. And absolutely the right message,' he told us.

When the song had reached the top three in Britain he told *Melody Maker*: 'It is a wonderful, beautiful, spine-chilling record. It cannot be misinterpreted. It is a clear message saying that love is everything. It is the best thing they've done and I'm not surprised that it is such a great success.'

The record was completed in ten days, the song written only three weeks before the show went on the air though they had committed themselves to the programme months before. Paul says today:

◄ If we had anything to say to the world, I think that would be it. It

Nancy and Frank – solidly
into the old ways and
traditional beverages

was a way of putting this philosophy to everyone, and it was an exciting evening anyway because we'd worked on it for a few days, rehearsing it and knowing what we were going to do, and then we piled all our friends into the studio, which was great.'

George agrees it was a great thing to know there were all the hook-ups available for the first time:

❮ Doing something live is always exciting and creates a lot of nerves. We did it in a way to get over the message, and it was right for the time. All the people who wanted to hear that sort of thing heard it, and all the people who thought it was a lot of old cobblers still thought it was. It was harmless, though, and it didn't kill anybody, did it?'

From 'Light My Fire' through 'All You Need Is Love' to 'Ode to Billy Joe'. . . . How different in mood the three songs were – but they were all clever.

Having become completely electric, we were getting eclectic, too, which is really what I had welcomed when the Byrds turned up the cerebral level of music with 'Mr Tambourine Man'. Then came 'The Letter' by the Box Tops, a catchy hit which stayed a month until Lulu knocked it off. The arrival of 'The Letter' proved to me that Bix Beiderbecke was right when he said: 'Just because I ain't receivin' don't mean you ain't sendin'.'

I was by now far too psychedelic for the Box Tops and much else, and my previously rather tame column in *Disc* had started to attract hate mail from within the mainstream of British pop. Someone persuaded Dave Dee of Dave Dee, Dozy, Beaky, Mick and Tich, to contribute some few hundred words to *Disc* adjacent to a double-column picture of Dave, headed 'Dave Dee Launches an Amazing Attack on the "Hollywood Hippy" Scene'. The text was awfully cross, very un-Dave Dee, obviously ghost-written. One passage read: 'I cannot comprehend how in a week that sees the world stumble to the brink of warfare and destruction [the Six-Day War, I presume], Mr Taylor can write: "When an album like *Sgt Pepper* and a single like Procol Harum cascade across the world everything else seems ordinary."'

There was much more of the same, and in the next week I replied acerbically, and there was a brief fury of side-taking and then the thing died away. But the exchange showed one thing clearly. Pop music was now a real battleground. If you were not for us, you were against us.

There was one very good new group in the charts that showed great promise and, interestingly, appeared not to anger either side. They were from Australia and called the Bee Gees. In 1967 they released four singles in Britain and the third, 'Massachusetts', became number one. Brian Epstein and Robert Stigwood managed them; each forecast great, even gigantic, success for the group, and events have shown that (as Australians say) they were not wrong. The young Bee Gees had had hits in Australia before coming to Britain, and after breaking into America after 1967 they were by 1978–9, in terms of sales, beyond all previous records.

They would themselves concede that they were *not* the Beatles, though there were those who thought they *were* the Beatles, disguised under a trick name (Bee Gees, BGs, short for Beatles Group), and those who said they would be bigger. The Bee Gees, I always thought, proved that the hits will keep on coming.

In 1967 some things came to an end. The Byrds finally lost David Crosby, long dissatisfied, wanting always to move right along, jamming with Buffalo Springfield or looking for fresh liaisons in harmony. Ahead of him lay Crosby, Stills, Nash and Young, but that is another book. Al Kooper left the Blues Project, and the Mamas and the Papas gave their last Los Angeles concert at the Hollywood Bowl that summer.

But Al Kooper formed Blood, Sweat and Tears at the end of 1967 and thus began the first great rock band to feature big horns. 'God bless you, Maynard Ferguson,' he wrote later. The excellent Move became a wild 'psychedelic' band in England, had hits, smashed up things on stage and played a very unpsychedelic joke on the Prime Minister – for libel reasons it cannot be outlined here – who successfully sued them.

The Move, cheerful and fearless, were in fact anxious not to be categorised as psychedelic but were nevertheless so labelled because of their choice of venue – UFO and the other naughty clubs – dress, and some special ingredient in their music which said: 'We may get hits but we aren't mainstream.' Two particularly innovative members of this pretend-violent group were Roy Wood – who went on to paint his face, tease his hair and become a pre-Kiss fright – and Jeff Lynne who later left the Move with another band member, Bev Bevan, to found ELO. Right now, Jeff Lynne is working with George Harrison on the latter's new album.

England had taken fairly quickly and warmly to the catch-all term Flower Power. With a national press eager to build it up, exploit it and knock it down, and a country sufficiently small and densely populated to move new fads up, out and down very quickly, it was not surprising that groups sprang up in funny clothes, snatched a hit and then vanished. The Flowerpot Men were one. The Move – though they were very good and lasted longer than the vogue – were *categorised* as another. Pink Floyd, adventurers in electronics and brilliant light shows, were of course in

A brighter shade of male: Gary Brooker (*right*) and members of Procol Harum

the vanguard, though aware of the pitfalls of dying with a fashion. In an article in *Melody Maker* headed 'Who Killed Flower Power?' their producer, and UFO organiser, Joe Boyd said:

⟨c⟩ The flower power scene hit much quicker than anyone imagined because it got turned into a clothes fashion. And now for the same reason everybody is predicting its even quicker demise ... however the simple fact that psychedelic music is a major part of the British scene nowadays shows that since the Beatles, the scene is now in another stage of its progression.'

The Floyd, of course, were to survive.

Certainly dressed in pretty clothes, and very non-aggressive, Cream were formed in late 1966 primarily as a *music* band to whom fashion was irrelevant. They were probably one of the first (*the* first?) supergroups in that they took their members from established outfits – the *cream* of the crop. They became influential and much respected in 1967 with the album *Fresh Cream*. Ginger Baker, Jack Bruce and Eric Clapton are still formidable figures today in separate configurations. The year 1967 was a good time for people like Cream, Traffic, Small Faces, Hendrix and others both to take their music seriously and to profit from it. Look what happened to Procol Harum, that strange five-man band with a special lyricist and adviser in attendance. Many of the band had previous, quite settled musical associations (the Paramounts, backing up Sandie Shaw, whatever), but what was to happen when they sent out into the world a wondrous sound with a stranger-than-strange title was unprecedented. Within days, even minutes, of the record's release Procol Harum left Britain in the wake of what *Melody Maker* called a 'Beautiful Dream'. The public were truly stunned, thrilled and transported by the loveliness of the melody and the texture of Gary Brooker's voice in 'A Whiter Shade of Pale'; enchanted by whatever it was they read into the words. The record came right out of a very blue and lucid sky with diamonds in late spring and stayed five weeks at number one, selling $2\frac{1}{2}$ million copies. Keith Reid, barely twenty-one, wrote the words; Gary Brooker the music, after Bach. Were they men or elves? Gods or psychedelic dreamers, poets or peasants, *what?*

One morning in May 1967, on the way to Brian Epstein's housewarming in Sussex, Joan and I heard the record in John's Romany Rolls-Royce/Art Nouveau luxury car/Psychedelic Limousine (it was severally described, so take your pick) a few days after both the record and the newly painted car had been unveiled before a nation still not fully inured to sensation even in this sensational year. John placed the stylus of a then very modern record-player on the magical Deram (Decca) single

Some (*one*) of Cream in waiting (Ginger Baker)

The Move

and waited for a cosmic response. But we weren't concentrating, being rather 'zonked' after the long flight from Los Angeles. Later, after a terrifically illuminating bout with a double dose (500 micrograms) of the best LSD available from Augustus Owsley Stanley III (aka The Bear, The Naughty Chemist), I realised that 'A Whiter Shade of Pale' was *the* great Bachian anthem of the early Summer of Love, and at the end of a great British weekend of lysergic initiation I took the record from the car and back in Los Angeles handed it to Lou Adler, who had a dozen acetates run off for himself and our mutual friends. We pushed it round the offices of the pop festival which we were planning and then to A & M Records. Herb Alpert, Jerry Moss and Gil Friesen at A & M signed Procol Harum, did a special label deal with their producer, Denny Cordell, and a very profitable time was had by all for some years until business differences stepped in and spoiled the party.

Still in Britain, and poised to take on the world, there was Traffic with Stevie Winwood, a delightful young man, all of nineteen years old, who had earned much success and respect with Spencer Davis, in his new incarnation. Winwood and the rest of his new band (Dave Mason, Jim Capaldi and Chris Wood) went off into the country to get their heads straight, one of the very earliest bands to do such a thing in Britain – later it became a cliché and a matter for much parody and jest – and talked of peace and serenity and wore a lot of beads and did, I should think, a

Cass Elliott at Monterey

lot of nice things. Nick Jones in *Melody Maker* was well tuned in to it all, writing of the 'gentle natural inspiring peace of their small cottage nestling in the Berkshire Downs' and 'the city where traffic is nothing but hot sweating metal and signs that say "no" instead of "go"'. Winwood himself spoke of exploring the temple of his mind.

Despite a difficult year with the gutter press and police contriving to bring them to heel, the Rolling Stones produced two albums and some notable singles. January 1967 had the highly praised, bestselling *Between the Buttons* gracing record-racks everywhere, and they 'bookended' the year by releasing *Their Satanic Majesties Request* in December. The cover of this album was a departure from their mutually rewarding relationship with the excellent Gered Mankowitz, photographer and innovator. For the exotic 'three-dimensional' *Satanic Majesties* sleeve the Stones roped in Michael Cooper, who had done the Beatles proud on *Sgt Pepper*. It was a rousing end to a carousing year for the Rolling Stones. They had two singles in Britain, separated by the Jagger–Richards drug busts, sentences and appeals, but both were hits. The first single, 'Let's Spend the Night Together', ran into difficulties over 'suggestive lyrics' but it did well. On 18 August, 'We Love You' was released with overlaid but distinct sounds of the Beatles singing in the background, and – or so the *Daily Sketch* reported – 'you could also hear the sound of a prison warder's footsteps accompanied by the clanking of chains and the banging of a prison door'. In July handcuffs – 'Jagger links' – were on sale in Carnaby Street at a pound a set and the Who, good allies, were releasing two Stones songs, 'The Last Time' and 'Under My Thumb', to keep the Stones' work before the public.

They were off the road that year. Bill Wyman was quoted as saying: 'Touring would be just a drag now. It's all right leaping on to the stage when you're 20, but when you get to 25 or 26 it gets a bit embarrassing.'

Pink Floyd were now spreading from the UFO into the mainstream of the British charts, first with 'Arnold Layne' and then with 'See Emily Play'. They had a wonderful album called *Piper at the Gates of Dawn*, a title taken from a chapter of *The Wind in the Willows* – a move which many of us thought to be a Very Good Thing. My boyhood innocence seemed to have been returned to me by LSD. Some found only God. I also found Piglet and Pooh and Mr Toad.

We were not afraid to be young again. Wilfred Mellers avers in 1986:

> ❝ Adolescent art is important for people of all ages. It has always existed, but it's comparatively recently that people have begun to take it seriously. Now of course, *all* children create. This is a perfectly natural thing to do, but it is stifled in you by education in our Western world. The values we live by do not, on the whole, allow for that kind of spontaneous creativity. Except for exceptional people like artists and madmen. And children come into that category.'

Mellers agrees that the Beatles had made adolescent art something not to be sneered at – not by any means!

In 1967, too, the 'straight media' were really waking up to the power of the music. In a five-page study of the Beatles, *Time* magazine concluded:

Three of the Mamas and the Papas on a London 'bummer' after Cass's arrest on charges of pinching two blankets from a hotel. The case was dropped. *Left to right:* Denny Doherty, and Michelle and John Phillips.

> ❝ The Beatles, along with other British groups – the Rolling Stones, the Animals – revitalized rock by closely imitating (and frankly crediting) such Negro originators of the style as Muddy Waters, Chuck Berry and Bo Diddley. Soon the Negro "soul sound" surged into the white mass market....
>
> 'As the Beatles moved on, absorbing and extending Bob Dylan's folk-rock hybrid and sowing innovations of their own, they were like musical Johnny Appleseeds; wherever they went, they left flourishing fields for other groups to cultivate.... Yet the Beatles' example is not limiting but liberating, as other rock musicians have attested with generous praise. Says hefty Cass Elliott of the Mamas and the Papas: "They're untouchable."...
>
> 'Blues, folk, country and western, ragas, psychedelic light and sound effects, swatches of Mahler, jazzlike improvisations – all are spaded into the mulch by such vital and imaginative groups as the

71

Doors, the Grateful Dead, the Jefferson Airplane, the Paul
Butterfield Blues Band, the Byrds and the new British trio, the
Cream. Like the Beatles, most of these groups write their own music
and thereby try not only to arrive at their own peculiar mixture of
elements, but also to stamp their identity on whatever they do.'

The United States was awakening at all levels to the importance of pop
as a form to be recognised. Leonard Bernstein in a 1967 CBS news
documentary which he hosted stated:

❬ For a long time now I have been fascinated by this strange and
compelling scene called pop music. I say "strange" because it is
unlike any scene I can think of in the history of all music – it is
completely of, by and for the kids, and by kids I mean anyone from
eight years old to twenty-five. They write the songs, they sing them,
record them; they also buy the records, create the market, they set
the fashions in music, in dress, in dance, in hairstyle, lingo, social
attitudes. And I say "compelling" because it shows no sign of
abatement. The fads change, the groups change, but the songs keep
on coming: increasingly odd, defiant, and free. This music raises
lots of questions but right now, for openers, here are two that concern
me most: (1) Why do adults resent it so? and (2) Why do *I* like it?'

Bernstein went on:

❬ I came to these songs naturally through my children but I have a
sneaky feeling that I would have heard and responded to them
anyway – after all, they are part of music, which is my world, and
a part that is so persuasive as to be almost inescapable. Many
parents do try to escape this music, and even forbid it on the grounds
that it is noisy, unintelligible and morally corrupt. I have neither
escaped nor forbidden it, neither as a musician nor as a father.
'I think this music has something terribly important to tell us
adults and we would be wise not to behave like ostriches about it.
Besides, as I said, I like it. Of course what *I* like is maybe 5 per cent
of the whole output which pours over this country like the two
oceans from both coasts and it is mostly trash, but that good 5 per
cent is so exciting and vital and, may I say, significant that it claims
the attention of every thinking person.'

And after that very powerful endorsement the great Bernstein went on
to illustrate his point with a cheery extract from 'Good Day Sunshine'
by the Beatles, played by the Beatles, followed by much praise for its

construction and a further energetic rendering of the song by Bernstein on piano. And so the programme went – from endorsement to real joy. With such attention, it is not surprising that pop music was deemed, in that great year, to be worthy of its very own and very first *festival*.

The Monterey Pop Festival had small beginnings indeed. The first the British public knew of it was in my column in *Disc* when I wrote: 'We are having a large pop festival here in June, and we hope you can come.' The announcement was made under the banner 'Our Man in America' and continued:

❮ Tea and cakes will be served and there will be lots of fun in the open air (if wet in the church hall).

'Styled "Monterey International Pop Festival – '67" the event starts on June 16 (a Friday) and ends on Sunday night, June 18, with a concert by Ravi Shankar. Already booked: the Byrds, the Buffalo Springfield, the Jefferson Airplane and numerous of the Tomorrow groups now flourishing on the psychedelic San Francisco scene (what DOES psychedelic mean?).

'It is hoped to arrange a charter aircraft from England. Monterey on the Pacific coast is already the beautifully located arena for international folk and jazz festivals; about 30,000 people can be accommodated over the weekend.

'Beach Boys, Stones, Who, Kinks, Donovan are soon to be asked to participate. Fees paid to groups will be moderate to high and ... it should be great because nothing like this has ever been done and if ever pop music was ready, it is now and there never was a time like the present anyway.'

Scott McKenzie, informal in London on the crest of his hit

That was not only a column item: it was also a press release. I had been waylaid in my attempt to 'drop out' by the man who had the vision and the drive first to think up the festival, to book the fairground, sign up the first acts and raise $60,000 capital to get things moving. His name was Alan Pariser, a man about the scene with a good conscience and a great love of the progressive music then abounding. He had tasted a small triumph producing his first concert in late 1966 for an activist cause which featured the Byrds, Buffalo Springfield, the Doors, Hugh Masakela, and Peter, Paul and Mary. It was held at the Carousel ballroom in Los Angeles. I had been the MC, and Pariser and I had become friendly.

Pariser had also been at the 1966 Monterey Jazz Festival at the fairground 150 miles south of San Francisco, and when that was all over it came to him that maybe there could be a *pop* festival! Why not? Weren't the time and the mood right? Up ahead he could see the full flowering of the Scene in San Francisco, knew it was the same in Los Angeles and

73

Monterey

London. He went for investment and positive attitude to the record
industry, which was discouraging, so Pariser raised money outside it:
thirty thousand dollars from his sisters and his mother. Ten thousand
from Harry Cohn, Jun. (son of the late boss of Columbia Pictures), ten
thousand of his own money, and ten thousand from Bill Graham of the
Fillmore who wished to remain anonymous. Pariser booked the
fairground and some acts. He found a partner, Benny Shapiro, an old
hipster who had promoted a lot of good fifties and early sixties action,
and together they persuaded me to come out of dropout. Pariser had a
mission to explain and to get people together, and it is to his vision, and
that of many generations of young people, that the world should pay
tribute for the creation of festivals of pop/rock music. Alan Pariser
thought of it first, got it together and held it there for three months before
the festival changed shape, becoming a charity endeavour under the
management of two supremos, Lou Adler and John Phillips, producer
and leader respectively of the Mamas and the Papas.

Pariser was retained as co-director, and today he acknowledges that
'Lou and John brought a lot to the festival', but has not quite forgotten
that a festival that took as its motto 'Music, Love and Flowers', and
which turned out to be a majestic and triumphant beacon to youth and
new music at its best, was also the cockpit of some very dodgy infighting
for a few desperately difficult days in the spring of 1967. Pariser lost his
partner Benny Shapiro, aced out and bought out for $8,000. The original
investors had their money returned. It was a classic Hollywood palace
coup.

74

Shapiro's former Renaissance Club was used as festival offices, at 8424 Sunset Boulevard almost opposite Gene Autry's Continental Hotel, an ideal place. I became full-time publicity director on a salary of $250 a week. It was agreed that the festival would be held for a charity. Full expenses would be paid, but there would be no fees. The Mamas and the Papas had made their appearance contingent on the charitable status and they were supported by Simon and Garfunkel, then approaching the beginning of their long stay at the top of the heap. Pariser recalls that despite the strength of the people he had signed – the Doors, the Byrds, Jefferson Airplane, the Grateful Dead and Ravi Shankar – there was a real sense that he would need *top* top-liners and that without the Mamas and the Papas there could be no festival. To everything there is a season, and that was the high season of the Mamas and the Papas.

The musicians of San Francisco, always independent from the Los Angeles way of looking at things, saw the Monterey Pop Festival through fairly sceptical eyes. One of the many acts who contributed to the unparalleled success of the event was Country Joe Macdonald. He says now: 'I think the festival changed *our* dream [that is, San Franciscan musicians'] for ever. The south Californian and Los Angeles entertainment business entered into the scene with the "San Francisco Wear a Flower in Your Hair" attitude.' This was a rather angry reference to Scott McKenzie, who that summer had a worldwide number one record, produced by Lou Adler on his own label, and written and co-produced by John Phillips. Scott McKenzie came on during the final performance of the three days – the Mamas and the Papas spot – and, depending on your attitude, was either a wonderful piece of icing on the cake or, as Joe Macdonald still fiercely sees it, 'a total ethical sellout of everything that we had dreamed of'. (Me ... I thought it was a great pop record.)

Country Joe had always been more than a very psychedelic musician (though he was certainly that). He had also been in the American navy, had seen action overseas and was not playing around when he opposed the Vietnam War. He was politically educated on the left and knew that life was for real. Today he still regrets the chaining of the dream at Monterey, but adds:

❝ When I look back on it now, I think it was something that we desperately needed because we were totally isolated [in San Francisco]; we did not understand any of the business, and it was the beginning of all our careers and the beginning of the spreading of this message in a very professional and natural business/entertainment way throughout the world, and the film stands as a testament to that.'

The film was *Monterey Pop*, made by D. A. Pennebaker of New York, then and now a wonderful film-maker (*Don't Look Back* is among his successes). It was filmed by Pennebaker himself and about nine other cameramen using hand-held equipment, and is a wonderful visual record of a great time.

Paul Kantner of Jefferson Airplane thinks: 'Monterey was totally ruined by Los Angeles interests in terms of money, though money wasn't what everyone was there for. Being there was just a huge brotherhood of people.' He concedes: 'It's a corny word now, you know, having gone through the sixties, but everybody was there very positively to enjoy themselves, to meet other people, to find new friends, old friends, old drugs, new drugs.'

Feuds between the Los Angeles and San Francisco interests notwithstanding, the events of that weekend were manifestations of pure joy and enormous organisational drive. Never a great administrator, I nevertheless took care of about 1,100 journalists, squeezing them into a horrendous compound just below and in front of the stage, and from there words went around and around the world that something *was* happening here, and what it was was exactly clear. Music, Love and Flowers – Monterey had plenty of all of it.

In the first flowery press release, issued after the quick burst in the *Disc* article, I stated that the 'Festival plans to attract tens of thousands of pop followers – the young and those who remember, the free and those who would like to be, to watch and hear and absorb and enjoy some of the world's best young entertainers in the happiest surroundings'. And so on. At the final press conference, Police Chief Marinello, a man of infinite pessimism before the festival began (who had brought far too many police to the grounds to prepare for what the locals feared would be the worst orgy of drugs and sexual frenzy yet seen in northern California), was happy to say that many of his men had been sent home.

There wasn't any trouble at all. 'I like these hippies,' he said. 'They're going to show me round Haight-Ashbury.' I thanked Marinello for the quality of his concessions and his openness, and took from my own neck a leather and glass-beaded ornament and placed it round his neck, saying: 'This is from us to you and it makes us one.' Lou Adler beamed. Marinello beamed. The watching press, sitting many rows deep in the press-hall, were surprisingly unembarrassed by this 'hippiness'. I was later charged under section 4:12 for overacting.

The final press release to prepare the mood for the three days of concerts read in part:

❦ Throughout the extraordinarily complicated planning period none of us in the Festival Office in Hollywood exchanged a harsh word

and we know we can pass the weekend peacefully because we've learned to remind ourselves in moments of pressure that it's a festival we're having, not a war. We're having fun and we know that you will. There will be no problems. There will only be dilemmas capable of resolution. It's all so easy. Isn't it?'

There was much more in the same vein. It was written in a tone of dewy-eyed friendliness and, though every kind of newspaperman attended, underground, overground, weekly, daily, monthly, from all over the world, *The Times, Daily Mirror, People, Ramparts,* the *Oracle* (I never saw so many people from one newspaper as there were from the *Oracle* – not until the *Sun* covered Pat Phoenix's funeral nineteen years later when I was preparing this book), not a single member of the musical press openly criticised us for being naïve. We were running a festival, and it succeeded. *That* was the point. There were all sorts of people involved: the inhabitants of Monterey on one hand – arch-conservatives, and very very tight – and the Diggers on the other – arch-free-space cowboys and very loose – together with the Hell's Angels, Augustus Owsley Stanley III dispensing acid, and many of the greatest pop acts in the world. Yet the elements mingled so well that nobody cried for attendance upon their own ego and a good time was had by all – all except one poor bastard called MacBowe who worked for one of the wire services and who saw a button that said 'Reagan Eats It' and tried to get the button arrested.

Rock Scully of the Grateful Dead persuaded local bureaucrats and educationists to open fields and buildings to accommodate the overflow of visitors. Despite the many areas of potential for violence, hassle, scams, fire, pestilence, or just bad vibes and negative press reviews, there was none. The media were unanimous: a big big hit. Ralph Gleason, jazz critic of the *San Francisco Chronicle,* accustomed to being treated with the utmost respect for the respect he showed the young, was measured and positive: 'Even if the performers may not all realise how seriously their words and this music are taken by the youth, the Monterey Pop Festival was a beautiful thing.'

Gleason had been one of the barriers to our putting the festival on, back at the end of the winter. He needed much convincing that we from Hollywood were capable of singing in tune with the San Francisco notion of 'free'. How could the concept of music, love and flowers be entrusted to people from Tinsel Town? As I was from Liverpool, by way of West Kirby, I felt very clean, very un-Hollywood. How could anyone think of me as anything other than sincere? Why, I was a dropout myself, a father of four on $250 a week, so I stuck it out and battled through, blazing with sincerity. Through all of it I loved the Movement, the

Ralph J. Gleason, now with the Great Majority but not forgotten

changes in music, the new freedoms and indignation. In the end, the love one takes equals the love one makes, as the Beatles indicated much later, so if we meant well – and we did – we were vindicated. A splendid time *was* had by all.

The reports continued to surface as the months passed. Jann Wenner, formerly of the radical *Ramparts* magazine, was at the festival as a journalist. Asked today to express his feelings on Monterey he says: 'Monterey was the nexus – it sprang from what the Beatles began and from it sprang what followed.' He was a freelance by the time the festival was launched. Crazy about *Sgt Pepper* and the festival, he tried to get *Look* magazine and one other to take a report on Monterey and failed. *Hi Fi* magazine, who *had* commissioned a piece on *Sgt Pepper*, turned down what Wenner submitted, because they said it contained too much hyperbole; nothing could be that good. So Jann Wenner founded *Rolling Stone* to give himself a platform for his enthusiasm, linking with Ralph Gleason as partner. Gleason, who died in 1975, is still named on the masthead.

He ran his first review in the *Chronicle*, two columns' width and a full page long, on the day following the festival, Monday, 19 July. It ended with the words: 'The Sgt Pepper buttons set the theme.' The splendid time guaranteed for all was taking place. The column had opened up with an unequivocal rave: 'The festival was a beautiful, warm, groovy affair which showed the world a very great deal about the younger generation . . . the music was fine, the staging was excellent and the shows were good . . . but beyond that it showed something very important – you can have 35,000 long-haired, buck-skin and beaded hippies in one place without a hassle.' Assistant Chief of Police Bob Trenner put on a wig, decked it with flowers and said: 'I'm joining 'em.'

In his Wednesday column, again a full-page double column aflame with real fiery love, Gleason opened: 'The repercussions [of the festival] are really only now beginning to be felt and there will be a discussion and re-evaluation for a long time. The weekend went out in a blaze of glory.'

After a very detailed review of the music, some of which he hadn't liked – Hendrix, the Who, Masakela, and in this he was ruggedly out of

Otis Redding at Monterey, with but a few months to live. It's still unbearable and almost unbelievable.

line with many other critics – Gleason compared the frankness of the musicians with previous generations: 'This ability to state personal views characterises this entire musical movement. This generation speaks out.'

In conclusion Gleason stated:

‹ Early on Monday morning, a solitary guitarist was playing and singing on the grounds as the clean up crew was working. He sang of peace and brotherhood and I thought of David Crosby's words after the show's conclusion. "I hope the artists know what they have here; the power of it to do good. It's an international force." '

Jann Wenner wrote a *Melody Maker* report on the Monterey Festival and said:

‹ It was a superb moment for rock 'n' roll – an example of the style for which Californian music has become famous. This the first music festival of its kind, and the first to be run by the artists themselves was a general success. The star of the show was San Francisco and the sound of that city.'

He also had much praise for the British acts. Wenner was an anglophile.

Al Kooper, who was between bands, was an assistant stage manager to Chip Monck at the festival, performed with a pick-up band and had good reviews. In his very good and funny book, *Backstage Passes*, he described the festival as three days of paradise. He had come out West to 'keep in perpetual motion from a nervous breakdown', having just left the Blues Project. He says now:

‹ There were many things [at Monterey] that had never been done before; they never put on these many people with long intermissions between each act. The shows I played as a kid they'd have twenty acts but you played three songs and then ran off and the MC would come on and say: "Now here's the next one." But here they were having blank spaces while they set up for the next act, and they just played canned music and everybody whacked out of their heads and just enjoyed the canned stuff until the next set up was ready and it really went amazingly smooth for such a tremendous undertaking. Everyone had worked really hard in the preparation of it to see that that happened. It was just a moment in time when it could happen like that. In terms of significance for the future, it put together a lot of different music – it encompassed the widest umbrella under which all this music called pop could flourish. Amazingly so.'

The cast was as broad as it was long, and alphabetically:

My own sense of elation was very overwritten – and why not? I thought – in the piece I phoned through to *Disc* from the motel in Monterey that Joan and I and our four children used as home during the festival. Hours after the Mamas and the Papas had closed the festival dressed like Ruritanians, I concluded in purple prose worthy of Very Great Owsley: 'All of us were back in the light, the colour, the music and the people ... flowing out of the universe into what began as rock 'n' roll and is now The Happening. I have nothing more to say, just that it happened in Monterey and it mightn't have done.'

Writing in the August 1967 edition of *Jazz and Pop* magazine, a San Francisco jazz writer put it more prosaically but said a mouthful:

> **The fact that this festival was, in truth, a selective *rock* festival with little nodding towards pop may mean that all pop is rock, but I think not. I think creative pop is rock, just as creative pop thirty years ago was jazz (or swing).**
>
> **'With all its limitations and faults it [the festival] broke ground for a whole new area of musical expression in America. And it made it quite clear that today's younger generation are not just going to create their own music – they are going to teach an older generation a few things about how to appreciate it besides.'**

And so the festival settled into a radiant glow, bathed in a beautiful light which never really went out. It *did* happen in Monterey, and the flame still burns. It was one hell of an idea Alan Pariser had, one hot torch Lou Adler and John Phillips picked up. 'An attraction, a challenge, a coup' – those are the words Adler offers to describe what led him to get into the festival.

At this distance, I'm fascinated by the good, great and/or famous groups who didn't play Monterey. Aretha Franklin, as we've seen, was number one with 'Respect' in the first week of June. In the previous week the Young Rascals had 'Groovin' '. The Supremes had just had their tenth number one single. (Otis Redding the writer of 'Respect', however, was at Monterey and *was* one of the festival's sensations. Michelle Phillips says that for her, as a prime organiser, he was *the* reason she wanted a festival at all. He did not have his first number one until three months after his death in December 1967.) The Doors, whose 'Light My Fire' was at number one in July 1967, and who had featured on Alan Pariser's original list, were not at Monterey. The Beatles, of course, were not there – too hot to travel, too out of concert practice. They had

The Association
Beverly
Big Brother and the Holding Company
Blues Project
Booker T and the MGs
Buffalo Springfield
Eric Burdon and the New Animals
Paul Butterfield Blues Band
The Byrds
Canned Heat
Country Joe and the Fish
The Electric Flag
The Grateful Dead
The Group With No Name
Jimi Hendrix Experience
Jefferson Airplane
Al Kooper's Band
Scott Mackenzie
The Mamas and the Papas
Hugh Masakela
Steve Miller Blues Band
Moby Grape
Laura Nyro
The Paupers
The Quicksilver Messenger Service
Otis Redding
Johnny Rivers
Ravi Shankar
Simon and Garfunkel
The Who

The board of governors was as follows:

Lou Adler
Donovan
Mick Jagger
Paul McCartney
Roger McGuinn
Terry Melcher
Andrew Oldham
Alan Pariser
John Phillips
Johnny Rivers
Smokey Robinson
Abe Somer
Brian Wilson

Monterey

McCartney on the board of governors and they contributed a self-painted advertisement to the souvenir programme-book, and were widely thought to *be* at Monterey anyway, such was the power of rumour. The myth, 'Three of them are here, dressed as hippies', persisted through the weekend. It was not my rumour, but I might as well have told that to the Marines, for the more I tried to deny it, the stronger it got, so in the end I conceded they *might* have been there. In an editorial note in *Fifty Years Adrift* George Harrison says: 'I wasn't there. . . . We just took acid at St George's Hill [where John lived] and wondered what it could be like.'

The Rolling Stones were not at Monterey as a group, though Brian Jones attended as a private citizen, in satins and furs, came on stage on the final night and introduced Jimi Hendrix. In Britain, Mick Jagger and Keith Richards were having a long wait to appear on trumped-up drug charges. Donovan, similarly, was hamstrung by drug/visa problems but was, like Jagger, on the board of governors in tribute to his musical qualities. Unhampered by anything at all, the Turtles weren't there. God knows why. Quite psychedelic and jolly enough to qualify, they had had a number one in March called 'Happy Together'.

The Monkees? In hippie terms it seemed like an impossibility to include the Monkees, but in a *really* balanced pop festival they would have been there. They had it all: inwardly, they were quite as 'hip' as anyone else, some of them just as interested in expanding their minds as the next acidhead. As for acid cred, Mickey Dolenz had genuine ancestral links with American Indians. Indeed, he was at the festival for all three days, dressed without embarrassment as a chief in full headdress. Joan and I had become friendly with Monkee Peter Tork, who was quite a flower child, and I invited him to write a piece for the souvenir magazine. (I had to cut it for lack of space, and he hasn't spoken to me since.) He was also encouraged by Lou Adler to MC one of the concerts. The Monkees could, by June 1967, all play in concert very well (and would later that year tour with, incredibly, Jimi Hendrix) and were working with Jack Nicholson (a huge upcoming hero of the counter-culture) in his role as writer of their first feature film. But there was never any question of their performing at Monterey. Were they any less appropriate than Lou Rawls or Johnny Rivers, who *did* appear and – never mind some hipsters' doubts – did well? No. But it is, alas, always the case that fears of not seeming to have whatever cred is currently the fashion can make yellow-bellies of most people (most, but not *all*).

My Monterey Pop Festival was spent by day in the press office taking care of more stress than I encountered until Apple was set up to administer the Beatles' desire to save the world. After each show, Joan and I went to a restaurant in the town to get loaded with Harry Dean Stanton and Fred Roos. My patience was miraculous throughout the weekend. I was so full of lysergic fervour – though mainly drug-free during working hours – that I reserved my real compassion for the counter-culturalists and their representatives on the underground press.

With my conviction that better times would only come by supporting the likes of the *Los Angeles Free Press, Open City, IT* or *Oracle*, I disregarded the endless whinings of the Big Guys of the Straight Media. Used to buddy-buddy treatment and assuming privilege over those with less power, Big Writers were often a pain. One night, at dinner I told the *Time* man that, though it might astonish him to hear it, it would come as no surprise to most people at the festival to hear me say that he was a person of no greater importance than the humblest hippie, and that he could stick his head up his arse if he expected special status. I wouldn't say such things today, but it is still true.

Thus June moved into its second half to merge with the high Summer of Love, with verdicts galore and a boom in the sale of everything pop: caftans, records, bells, stick-on moustaches, dolly-bird dresses, granny dresses, hipster undershorts, Indian mottoes, silly shoes, and buttons that said everything from 'Save Water, Bath with a Friend' to 'Make Love, Not War'.

Rolling Stone was launched in the autumn and ran a story asking where the money from Monterey had gone. I had no idea. What I was wondering was where all that goodwill had gone.

In his history of popular music, *All You Need Is Love*, Tony Palmer, in a chapter I researched for the book, states:

❮ Although few realised it then, [Monterey] marked the climax of seventy years of popular music and the beginning of the end. Within a very few years the hopes and aspirations that had goaded this music into immense achievements were dissipated and destroyed.'

Perfect harmony. More in common than separated them.

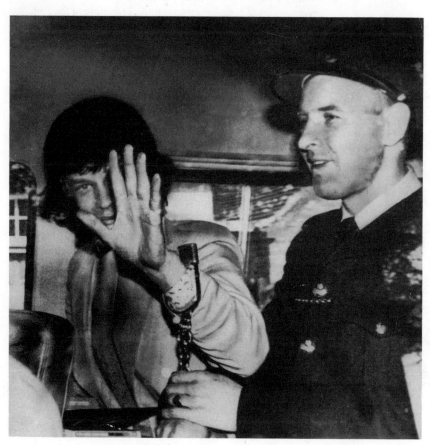

Mick Jagger and escort
providing the artist Richard
Hamilton with the raw
materials for a classic piece
of modern art. Jagger and
Robert Frazer were
handcuffed on drugs
charges. Many
complained. It was in the
public interest, said the
Government.

THREE

TO FATHOM HELL OR SOAR ANGELIC

In August 1964, Bob Dylan was taken to meet the Beatles in Manhattan. It was not a casual arrangement. It was at night, with the curtains closed, in a hotel suite thick with anticipation and smoke.

Having misheard the phrase 'I can't hide' in 'I Want to Hold Your Hand' as 'I get high', Bob Dylan, who did, thought *they* did. But they didn't. So the young poet and his friends, Al Aronowitz and Victor Mamudas, rolled up to the Del Monico Hotel, rolled up a storm and made sure it was a night to remember for the Beatles. Neil Aspinall, Mal Evans and Brian Epstein were there, and it changed their lives, too.

I was in the suite next door, running a very courtly, if tense, holding operation with a lot of extremely nice Greenwich Villagers and suchlike who were eager to get to hang out with the Beatles, these Rough and Tumble Exquisites from over the ocean. At that time I didn't know anything at all about marijuana except what I'd heard in legend and the yellow press: that foreigners gave it in 'reefers' to unsuspecting virgins in drinking-dens in seaports and ruined their lives. Scarcely able to restrain my guests, and knowing that under no circumstances were the experimenting Beatles to be 'invaded', I went next door alone to find out what was going on and try to arrange some wider access later.

In the Beatles' lair I was immediately aware of a very unusual atmosphere. In the middle of it, somehow epitomising it, was the bright-eyed Dylan: very thin, dressed in black, and laughing; a mysterious fragile bird of youth. 'It's as if we're up *there*,' Paul said to me, grabbing my arm and pointing to the ceiling. 'Up there, looking down on us!'

George Harrison, the Quiet One of Beatles Myth, wrote later: 'It was an amazing night and I woke up the next day thinking: "What was that? Something happened last night. I felt really good. That was a hell of a night."'

Now, if they could not hide, the Beatles could and did get high. It was a great day's night.

In 1986, having lost touch with Dylan in the 1970s, I met him again. We talked about that first night.

'That hotel,' Dylan suddenly remarked. 'What was the name of that hotel?'

'Del Monico.'

'That was it!' he said. 'The Del Monico. That was a night!'

Those who see poisoned legacies and suchlike horrors emanating from the sixties may well care to see this meeting as 'where the rot set in'. In fact this seemingly chance encounter had been years in the making.

In 1957, Aronowitz, Alfred G., a reporter on the *New York Post*, had been sent to write something mean: a piece critical of the 'Beat' writer Jack Kerouac. Instead Aronowitz became enthralled by the great author and figurehead, who, alone and with friends, regularly used drugs to change his consciousness. It has been written by Kerouac's biographer, Dennis McNally, that the 'beat aesthetic turned Aronowitz inside out'. In his reporting Aronowitz in turn moved popular awareness right along. His hero and friend, Bob Dylan, many years his junior, was to become the great catalyst.

The formative influence on him of Kerouac and his poet disciple, Allen Ginsberg, is freely admitted by Dylan himself. In *Desolate Angel*, McNally says: 'Though Dylan came to fame as a protégé of Woody Guthrie, he was never a regulation member of the folk crowd ... he would acknowledge that: "It was Ginsberg and Jack Kerouac who inspired me first."'

And then came the Beatles, with the first four letters of their name a riddle for all time. 'Beat' as in rhythm or as in 'beatnik'? Or did it matter any more? At any rate Aronowitz took his friend Bob Dylan to meet the Beatles, and a friendship instigated and pursued through mutually admired recordings was made flesh through marijuana and the shared exploration of deepest inner space.

Today, George Harrison is clear on Dylan's influence on the Beatles, even before they met:

❛ The day Bob Dylan *really* turned us on was the day we heard his album, *The Freewheelin' Bob Dylan*. Right from that moment we recognised some vital energy, a voice crying out somewhere, toiling in the darkness. When we actually met him in '64 it had a certain effect on us, but I think the seed was already sown by the album. ❜

Paul McCartney agrees. 'Dylan was a big hero. We admired him a lot. We'd all liked his early talking blues and he was entering now in the mid-sixties into a very poetic period. We liked him because he was a poet, far out, a friend of Ginsberg, on the same road as Jack Kerouac.'

So, all roads led to the same spot: the search for truth.

That the Beatles were given marijuana when their eyes were open and LSD while they were looking the other way is, perhaps, irrelevant. It was, after all, inevitable that in the royal hunt for the sunny side of the street in the endless sixties summer they would pick up on all the good substances that had been around for so long but didn't come in a glass over the counter of the neighbourhood bar. Heavy drinking would not have been a fitting course of action for the moptops. Paul McCartney remembers:

❛ A lot of young people were knocking booze on the head. You'd go to a party and say: "God, whisky! How can you *do* that stuff, man? It kills you, you know?" So it was becoming very uncool. It was healthier to be involved in the pot scene. It seemed clearer, cleaner, more peaceful. It was pointed out that if you drink too much you can go kill someone quite easily on the road or murder someone in your family, whereas I'd never heard of anyone on pot doing anything like that. The worst the pot overdosers used to do was fall asleep a lot. ❜

The way now was *out*, to wilder shores. It would not be long before people of like mind would discern that the Beatles were up to something.

Some people were very good to get high with. The Byrds and the Beatles together were dynamic. Crosby and McGuinn, raising their consciousness on Mexican marijuana, and the Beatles with access to very good hashish, could put together some dreamy afternoons and nights-into-daze when the Byrds visited England or the Beatles visited Los Angeles. There was a still a need for the utmost stealth, however. 'Is it cool, man?' was a necessary, and wonderfully dated, phrase of the day.

To allow the pungent smoke to disperse, rooftops of buildings in London and outdoor patios in Californian dwellings and studios were favoured places, but there was some pretty fair paranoia none the less. I remember one evening being cornered by a narcotics agent hunting the Byrds for having allegedly left some hashish behind on a flight back from London to Los Angeles. The Beatles themselves – or, rather, George and Paul – were actually with the Byrds in Columbia studios. Fortunately, the agent liked a drink, so to pursue our discussion further I took him to the La Brea Inn where he got surprisingly drunk while I remained astonishingly sober and, I would say, slippery. Yes, of course I had *heard* of hashish: 'But, as you can see, Officer, I'm a gin man, man. That's *my* poison. And you, Officer? Another vodka, perhaps?' 'Derek, if you could see the human wreckage I've seen with drugs.' I couldn't but agree. Terrible!

Bob Dylan, despite his warning not to follow leaders, was fated to be one, and today millions still look to him for wisdom. They are rarely disappointed. His detractors continue to gnash their teeth. Gnash on, folks.

87

Loaded in Hyde Park: mum
with marijuana, daughter
with sherbet at London
'Legalise Pot' rally

Later, at Columbia, I warned the groups. Crosby was very relaxed. 'Hey, man, what's the problem? It's cool. I'll just get up to the house and clean the place up.'

There were a lot of people getting up to houses and cleaning up in those days. More Mexican grass was flushed down lavatories than ever was smoked in the sixties. It was as well it was only $10 a lid.

We should not be naïve nor should we dissemble. We are talking here of drugs, of the drugs of choice of the middle to late sixties. Today Paul McCartney's response to the question 'What was the life that was reflected in the Sgt Pepper album?' is:

❻ Drugs, basically. They got reflected in the music. When you mention drugs these days, heroin and crack and cocaine and all of that serious stuff comes to mind. Remember, drug-taking in 1967 was much more in the musicians' tradition. We'd heard of Ellington and Basie and jazz guys smoking a bit of pot, and now it arrived on our music scene. It started to find its way into everything we did, really. It coloured our perceptions. I think we started to realise there weren't as many frontiers as we'd thought there were. And we realised we could break barriers.'

When Bob Dylan gave pot to the Beatles and they started to feel much taller and broader of mind they were joining a spiritual caravan of awareness that stretched back to the dawn of botanical delight. Cannabis, the basic drug of choice, had a long history before it pitched up in Western lives. The 'pot' of the 1960s was known and used and enjoyed three thousand years before the birth of Christ. The Emperor Shen Nung of China wrote a pharmaceutical textbook in which he showed great understanding of it.

The botanical facts are that what we know as 'pot' comes from a warm-weather plant, Cannabis Sativa, which has a male and a female form. The female flowering tops produce Cannabis Indica which Shen Nung said helped 'female weakness, gout, rheumatism, malaria, beri beri, constipation and absent-mindedness'. Cannabis was known by the ancient Chinese as 'the delight giver'.

It reached India in about 800 BC and was absorbed into religious ritual and philosophy. The Indians called it 'smoother of grief', 'poor man's heaven' and 'the heavenly guide'. All ancients who knew it praised it. But in the early twentieth century, for whatever reason, most of the countries of the West declared it illegal, and so it has remained. In the sixties mere possession could carry a gaol sentence of up to ten years; in some American states as much as thirty. No one could be allowed to know in 1965 and 1966 that those nice boys next door, soon to be awarded the MBE, were smoking dope. Not that anyone would have believed it, with the Beatles so pleasant, their temperament ever more equable and their music getting better and better.

Cannabis is grown wherever people take the trouble to use a warm climate. Tastes in pot are very individual and subjective, but in 1967 it was thought that the best hashish (resin) came from the Muslim, Buddhist and Hindu areas, including Afghanistan and the Lebanon long before their trails were blasted into confusion, and the best marijuana (grass) available generally came from Mexico.

It was made available by local street dealers, often friends or friends of friends. At the end of a long journey it would have changed hands many times, each dealer making just a little profit as well as taking as much as he needed for his own private use. These dealers didn't trade in other substances – *never* hard stuff – with the exception of LSD, also a consciousness-raiser and much loved by musicians and others who like to see the sights. Pot was known by users, and confirmed by doctors, not to be addictive or anti-social. Instead, the user became much more peaceful and agreeable, and the new counter-culture of affluent and aware young people looking for an alternative to alcohol took to cannabis as if it were the greatest *new* thing in town since sex. Old hipsters were much amused when young rock musicians began to smile in strangely familiar ways. Louis Armstrong was one of the many famous jazz musicians who had been smoking dope since early youth. Why else do you think Louis was always smiling – because he said to himself 'What a wonderful world'? He certainly wasn't going to tell the truth to an unready press on *that* subject.

There were, after his death, many great stories, not all of them apocryphal. For instance, once he and his wife were due to attend an audience with the Pope. Obsessed with his bowel movements and grumpy at not having had one that morning, Louis compensated by lighting an enormous reefer in the limousine. Inside the Vatican, he seemed very happy and full of beans. The Pope asked the couple whether they had any children and Louis, with fine abandon, replied that no, they didn't have any yet but 'We havin' a real good time tryin', your Holiness'. The Pope was led away before translation.

Before the years of pot, 'speed' had fuelled unruly youth. It came in tablet form, available from doctors on prescription or from robberies. One's parents took it either to stay awake or as appetite suppressants. A famous British politician in a post-war Tory government had prescribed benzedrine delivered perfectly openly on a folded napkin with a glass of water before his budget speech. The Beatles' drug of choice in Hamburg days was Preludin, a barnstormer of a pill. By the mid-sixties doctors were prescribing amphetamine products in their millions in tablet and capsule and spansule form. Likewise barbiturates: those who got 'blocked' or 'wired' during the day found it difficult to sleep. So it was natural that half-and-half products would arrive on the pharmaceutical scene, combining both 'downer' and 'upper' to present a beautiful balance. The trouble there was that the young, always prone to excess and deprived of sober and rational information in the frenzy of low-life media exploitation of the new 'Pill Craze', used to take them in handfuls. 'Mods' (those pop fans who succeeded Teddy Boys and preceded hippies and, later, punks in the demonology of the popular media) were great users of purple hearts and so, for that matter, was your mother, and so were lots of her friends, and so was I.

These drugs were only illegal if unprescribed for the user. Demand grew so large, however, that there were robberies to obtain them in vast numbers and their price on the black market could be quite high – say, £15 per hundred. The pop groups loved them. You could rave all night for a couple of pounds.

The beatniks, the Beat poets and writers of the United States, east and west coasts, Jack Kerouac, Allen Ginsberg, William S. Burroughs, Michael McClure and Gregory Corso, had been putting drugs of all sorts into their bodies in the fifties and early sixties, some addictive, some inducing psychic dependence, some 'soft' and some psychedelic. This last category was to be the Big Bad One of the sixties. It was the tide in the affairs of our young men and women which, taken at the flood, would lead on to caverns of delight and wonder – and, for some, madness and death.

'Psychedelic' drugs embraced everything from nature's cannabis, peyote and mescaline to the new products of modern chemistry, most notably LSD-25, lysergic acid diethylamide.

Waiting for Ginsberg: members of the audience at the Institute of Contemporary Arts in London where Allen Ginsberg and many others of the counter-culture were made to feel at home

This astonishing drug was first synthesised for use in formal medicine by Dr Albert Hofmann of the Sandoz laboratories in Switzerland in 1938. It was the product of the twenty-fifth variation in a series of experiments involving derivatives of ergot (a fungus found in ears of rye). Hofmann and his colleagues were researching into advances in obstetrics and circulatory stimulants. It wasn't until 1943 when he began to investigate the compound further that Dr Hofmann made the discovery that would change a tributary of the course of history for ever. He absorbed a small dose through his fingertips. It went to his head. He noted many of the results in his diary, among them 'an intense stimulation of the imagination and *an altered state of awareness of the world*'. Dr Hofmann noted that on one 'trip', in the phraseology of a quarter of a century later, he lost all control of time. 'Space and time became more and more disorganised, occasionally I felt I was outside my body. I thought I had died.'

Herbs that could induce similar visions and hallucinations have been used from prehistory. Peyote, used by the indigenous Indians of North America for religious rites, was one. Mescaline, well known to Mexican Indians, was another. The English writer Aldous Huxley, aware of the usefulness of drugs in controlling behaviour from his research for *Brave New World* in the 1930s, had come to see that by contrast hallucinogens could have a liberating effect, relaxing rigidity of mind, conditioned reflexes, class mores, and inherited prejudices. Meeting Dr Humphrey Osmond in the early fifties, Huxley asked the young English psychiatrist to supervise him on a trip with mescaline. The results are elegantly catalogued in *The Doors of Perception*, the travelogue for many late-sixties day and night trippers.

An hour and a half later, I was sitting in my study looking intently at a small glass vase ... at breakfast that morning I had been struck by the lively dissonance of its colours. But that was no longer the point. I was not looking now at an unusual flower arrangement. I was seeing what Adam had seen on the morning of his creation – the miracle, moment by moment, of naked existence.'

Huxley gave his readers the very best version of his experiences to support his delight in exploration. He spoke warmly of the pleasures of contemplation to which mescaline was yet another door. One of Huxley's memorable discoveries (much treasured and quoted by later 'seekers') was the nature of his trousers. He wrote: 'those folds in the trousers – what a labyrinth of endlessly significant complexity! And the texture of the grey flannel – how rich, how deeply, mysteriously sumptuous.'

Huxley and Osmond became friends and collaborated to find a new word for the hallucinogens. Huxley wrote to Osmond:

> 'To make this trivial world sublime
> Take half a gramme of phanerothyme.'

Osmond replied to Huxley in similar form in the epochal couplet:

> 'To fathom hell or soar angelic,
> Just take a pinch of psychedelic.'

Nothing to fear but fear itself: the Free Clinic in the Haight-Ashbury knew how to help people down if they had soared too high, or up if they had fathomed too deeply

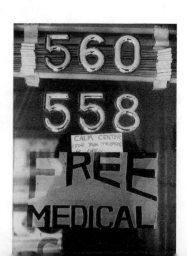

Osmond scored a beautiful bull's eye, and a word entered common usage and abusage. The game had a name. In the years that followed more and more people found that it was fun finding out what lay inside. They took mescaline, psilocybin, peyote, LSD. They were reckless times.

Huxley died in 1963 – on the same day President Kennedy was shot. Osmond lives on in splendid awareness. In 1973 he wrote: 'Let us hope that we will learn to use hallucinogens wisely and well rather than as trivial entertainments.'

In 1967, Paul McCartney, challenged about his use of LSD, remarked: 'It opened my eyes. We only use one-tenth of our brain. Just think what we could all accomplish if we could only tap that hidden part. It would mean a whole new world.'

In *Fifty Years Adrift*, George Harrison said this of LSD:

❛ Once you'd had it, it was important that people you were close to took it too. It showed you backwards and forwards and time stood still. It had nothing to do with getting high. It was devastating because it cut right through the physical body, the mind, the ego. It's shattering because it's as though someone suddenly wipes away all you were taught or brought up to believe as a child and says: "That's not it." You've gone so far, your thoughts have become so lofty and there's no way of getting back.'

Neither Beatle-response to LSD sounds trivial or ill-informed. There were dangers in its unsupervised or indiscriminate use, though.

There is no doubt that there were drug casualties in the Haight. On 17 June the *San Francisco Chronicle* ran a piece on something called the Free Clinic, run by Dr David Smith. It was part of Happening House, which had always been a place of good intent with turned-on academics and good vibes available to anyone who happened by. Dr Smith was director of the alcohol- and drug-abuse screening unit at the city's general hospital and had given up three hours every night to be medical director of the free clinic on Clayton Street. Every kid admitted had used drugs, from methedrine to acid, through DMT, marijuana, barbiturates. There was also an increase in VD in the Haight.

The Mayor was in no mood to equivocate when he visited the district to meet the Haight-Ashbury Neighborhood Council. Asked why he and his colleagues were so negative towards the district, he replied: 'Young hippies need someone to tell them more than simply that their trips are just great and that what they're smoking is great.' He added: 'I'll be very honest with you. I don't like trips and I don't like smoking pot. I've seen a few young kids at San Francisco Hospital with permanent brain damage from trips.'

The stories of 'brain damage' were many and lurid. There is no doubt that some were exaggerated, but equally no doubt that LSD was not the glorious voyage for all that we had been promised in the brochure of our own Utopian imagings. I, however, continued using and had no regrets – but, then, I was thirty-five and had a room with a view. It was not so easy out in the hard world of concrete and clay, and there were many bad trips. The Free Clinic was dealing with thirty patients a day suffering from drug-related illness, and there was considerable strain on the staff.

In 1967, the message from Timothy Leary, a dismissed Harvard lecturer, was 'Turn on, tune in and drop out'. In fact, doing those things unsupervised on LSD – something which Leary definitely did *not* advocate – could lead the young unformed mind into dangerous corridors of perceptual misunderstanding. Where, if a young person had not yet found his place, was he to return when the adventure was over? The San Francisco Diggers, that band of anarchic preachers of '*free*' everything, said in one of their mimeographed broadsheets distributed on Haight-Ashbury: 'Acid could send people spinning on a 360 degree tour through their own senses and rekindle childhood's loss of presence.' Enough here to underline this book's warning against use by unprepared adults and all children.

The musician and poet Donovan says today:

❝ It was a very heavy change, the hallucinatory drugs.... I tend to think that the drugs didn't make me write the way I wrote songs.... I believe that very early, before I had taken acid, I was writing dream-state songs, but they were certainly increased and heightened by the use of acid.'

The Book of Common Prayer declares: 'There was never anything by the wit of man so well devised or so sure established which in continuance of time hath not been corrupted.' And so it was with psychedelic drugs. Huxley and Osmond were agreed that on them you could fathom hell or soar angelic. The CIA came upon LSD in the 1950s, using it as a means of inducing anxiety. They experimented widely, and discovered that it was very easy to break someone who was exposed to highly stressful stimuli while high on the stuff.

The poet Allen Ginsberg, on the advice of author William S. Burroughs, chose to assist in scientific experiments – not conducted by the CIA! – to see what else might be discovered. Ever adventurous, he agreed to take LSD while a stroboscope blinked in synchronisation with his alpha rhythms. In due course, however, he felt he was being absorbed into nothing less than the electrical network grid of the entire nation – and you know that *can't* be good. His soul began to tell him it was

An unsupervised exercise
in mind expansion? Or just
plain getting loaded?

vanishing into the wall-socket and thence into oblivion. This was enough even for a brave poet, and he asked that the light be put out – before *he* was.

Ginsberg continued to experience difficulties on the trip, seeing himself trapped in a spider's web, being hunted by God or by the Devil, but the experienced Beat put it all down to the price of exploration and decided that you could learn from a 'bummer' just as much as from the good trips. And for Ginsberg and his beatnik friends there were to be plenty of those. They were, after all, dedicated to seeking.

In the earlier sixties other bold travellers had been busy seeking their stripped-down selves. The novelist Ken Kesey was an eager test-case for the government-funded investigators into the drug at Stanford University. Kesey was a good American, honest, big, strong, and very anti-bullshit. Having taken a lot of acid from men in white coats while they observed him, he found (observing them) that they didn't know *what* was happening. He did duty in the psychiatric ward of a veterans hospital and with his new 'acid understanding' saw that the people in the ward had more of a handle on the nature of the predicament of life than the people watching over them. It was a true awakening and led to *One Flew over the Cuckoo's Nest*, a novel which gave Kesey enormous credibility with the young.

It also brought him enough money to buy a little spread south of San Francisco at La Honda and there begin a very wild LSD scene, quite the antithesis of the programming of acid trips on the other side of the continent at Millbrook where Dr Timothy Leary and his friend Dr Richard Alpert, now sacked by Harvard for turning their students on to LSD, were having themselves a high old time, strictly in the spirit of scientific inquiry. Both sets of tripsters were doing it in the woods, but Kesey was a wild West Coast wizard, careless of demons, and Leary – although never a physician – was still very much the doctor. In his tidy way, he liked the notion of set and setting; prepare the trip and do it carefully. Kesey was all for doing it anywhere. Why don't we do it in the road?

Or *on* the road. He had an old school bus painted in fabulous colours with all manner of internationalist symbols and the word 'Furthur' (sic), and filled it with the friends who became the Merry Pranksters, key travellers and message-bearers in the first free-form madness of the acid movement, documented by Tom Wolfe in his *The Electric Kool Aid Acid Test*. Kesey, with the true frontier mentality, was all for pushing forward, getting on the road and taking the high ground wherever the challenge seemed worth the trouble. The importance of breaking down rigid forms was never questioned. Like Ginsberg, he was for letting the trip take the traveller where it would. Tripster or Merry Prankster, they must have been quite a worry to their parents.

Kesey's bus was a well-loved symbol of the new freedom in the mid-sixties. With twenty people on board, men and women in fantastic clothes, the old Harvester vehicle gleamed under the first mobile psychedelic designs, everyone adding their own. A sign at the rear read: 'Caution – Weird Load.' Everyone was nicknamed to replace their old identity, as open as the road ahead. Drenched in acid, listening to Bob Dylan or the Beatles, and driven by Neal Cassady, loaded to the edge of his psyche on amphetamines, the same man who had driven Jack Kerouac and been immortalised as Dean Moriarty in *On the Road* – here they were, the Merry Pranksters, looking for fun and fresh fields.

Kesey would tackle anything and anyone. Entrusting his bus to the speeding Neal Cassady was in itself a daily act of daring, and his decision

The 'Trips Festival' at Longshoremen's Hall near Fisherman's Wharf, San Francisco. It was a paradigm of all the Fine Madness of the times. 'A great rout,' wrote Tom Wolfe.

Gerald Scarfe's sculpture
(still extant) for *Time* – a
breakthrough in modern
art

Days of innocence. A
period of calm. Nothing to
say but it's OK. Good
morning

The wall of the Apple shop
in Baker Street, London,
designed by The Fool, a
crazed Dutch design unit
with a lot of class and great
originality. The public
were outraged

Donovan and friends
waiting for the number 53
to Regent's Park

The Grateful Dead at the
Monterey Pop Festival,
June 1967

Members of Jefferson
Airplane, untameable
heroes and heroine of the
era. Like all the good
bands, they had brains and
a sense of irony and fun

'Wavy Gravy' (formerly
Hugh Romney), who
founded the freewheeling
time-travelling 'Hog Farm'
and amazed Americans
everywhere. He still does

Ken Kesey's fabulous bus.
He and his Merry
Pranksters pioneered
inner-space travel and took
the show on the road

Timothy Leary and friend
at Millbrook

to bring the Hell's Angels into his corral at La Honda was another. They were a fine challenge, and once inside his compound, where the trees were hung with speakers blasting out the best of trips music and artefacts to boggle any mind, they took the acid that would change them and became as little children, walking comfortably among intellectuals and very un-Angel types with great calm and aplomb. Hunter S. Thompson, who had introduced them to Kesey, said that dropping acid with the Angels was an adventure: 'They were too ignorant to know what to expect, and too wild to care.'

Allen Ginsberg wrote a poem:

First Party at Ken Kesey's with Hell's Angels

Cool black nights thru redwoods
cars parked outside in shade
behind the gate, stars dim above
the ravine, a fire burning by the side
porch and a few tired souls hunched over
in black leather jackets. In the huge
wooden house, a yellow chandelier
at 3 AM the blast of loudspeakers
hi-fi Rolling Stones Ray Charles Beatles
Jumping Joe Jackson and twenty youths
dancing to the vibration thru floor,
a little weed in the bathroom, girls in scarlet
tights, one muscular smooth skinned man
sweating dancing for hours, beer cans
bent littering the yard, a hanged man
sculpture dangling from a high creek branch,
children sleeping softly in bedroom bunks,
And 4 police cars parked outside the painted
gate, red lights revolving in the leaves.

When LSD was outlawed in October 1966, it seemed a crass act. Acidheads remained absolutely impervious to the law and didn't believe a word the government were saying. If the law 'n' order people had been wrong about 'reefer madness', they could be wrong about LSD.

Allen Ginsberg says now:

❝ People seeing it [LSD] illegalised, having had their own experience of it, mind-manifesting and metaphysical, realised that the government had no business intruding, getting on our backs, and that they were trying to repress an alteration of perception – not merely behaviour but perception itself! – and it became a classical situation that the government was outlawing an elixir that had some real scientific usefulness as well as general democratic usefulness for those who were interested.'

Timothy Leary, without whom ...

It didn't make any sense. There were so few casualties that anyone knew. Some of us, to this day, know none, though there are many myths and horror stories. In April 1967, Ken Kesey pitched up in San Francisco Superior Court and told Judge Joseph Karesh that he had planned to hold an 'acid test graduation ceremony' last Hallowe'en to help young people caught in a 'rat's maze' of LSD visions.

'Acid?' queried the judge.

'I felt that acid, meaning LSD, is a door that can be used to go into another room.' The point, said the bestselling author, was that being stuck in a doorway was dangerous.

The headline on the story was 'Kesey Gives Judge the Word', and the tenor of the reporting, and indeed of the judge's response, was sympathetic. Kesey was arraigned on a marijuana charge, not his first. He was wearing a scarlet vest with a whistle dangling from his neck and was described as the author of *Sometimes a Great Notion*, another successful novel.

He is well and powerful still today, with another book out last year. He still believes in LSD, though 'You don't need it often and you don't need it much.' He abhors cocaine, the eighties drug, and remembers his sixties acid experimentation fondly.

❻ The first drug trips were for most of us shell-shattering ordeals that left us blinking knee deep in the cracked crusts of our pie-in-the-sky personalities. Suddenly people were stripped before one another and behold: we were beautiful. Naked and helpless and sensitive as a snake after skinning but far more human than that shining nightmare that had stood creaking in previous parade rest. We were alive and life was with us.'

98

Searches, seizures, harassments and busts for drugs assumed quite a statistical high in the mid-sixties, and by 1967 some other famous names were appearing in the newspapers. In the counter-culture they were seen as noble martyrs; straight society viewed them as pariahs. Timothy Leary was raided by police officers at Millbrook led into the premises by none other than G. Gordon Liddy, then doing his law-enforcement stint. Leary was sentenced to thirty years' gaol in a small marijuana-possession case, but didn't in the event serve a lot of time. Neither Leary nor Kesey in their strenuous defences, and all-American recourse to all available legal rights, recanted on their belief in LSD/acid as a worthy substance for experiment.

(Incidentally, I found interesting Leary's use of the initials LSD to describe the drug in contrast to the looser, more casual 'acid' favoured by Kesey. The difference between doctor and author perhaps? The euphony of Kesey's Acid Tests would have been quite altered by calling them LSD Tests. In the end, for what it's worth, I'd say 'acid' won out in America and also among British users, while 'LSD' remained the chosen media description and parent-frightener. And still is.)

Neither Leary nor Kesey was at that time charged with LSD offences, though the Psychedelic Twins' activities in that field rendered them vulnerable indeed. The drug was, however, so recently illegal that the police were at first tentative about LSD busts and, anyway, the tablets were so small that marijuana was easier to find and identify. Arrest figures could be bumped up quite nicely with the more obvious and bulky bundles of herbs. Among the counter-culture, please note, use of heroin and cocaine was extremely rare. Marijuana was not only a soft drug but also a soft target. In later years, California was among the first states to decriminalise the possession of cannabis for one's own use.

Ken Kesey and Timothy Leary, these two born (or reborn) leaders of psychedelic drug-taking, were different types; and, though tolerance and acid would burn away much of the dead wood that separated their patches of Magicland, there would always be different 'schools' of attitude to acid. I was ever so slightly cautious, maybe because I was from Hoylake via Hollywood, certainly less Kesey than Leary. By the time I came to fathom hell and soar angelic in 1967, Ken Kesey had become the subject of much hassling for one drug or another and was less conspicuous in Los Angeles consciousness than Dr Leary, and it was only in 1968 when Kesey came to visit Apple that I became aware of his special and spacious sense of self and freedom.

Other groups and individuals were much influenced by Kesey and the Merry Pranksters. The benevolent Wavy Gravy (formerly Hugh Romney, an improvisational performer) had a set-up which became known as the Hog Farm. One of his gang was David Lebrun, today a *very* together film-maker, who saw the Hog Farm begin as a small group comprising some Pranksters and grow to include a whole range of people, some who built geodesic domes, others who put on light shows, played music, all sorts and conditions of young bright people who took the show on the road, with anything from five to forty buses travelling around the country putting on mixed-media happenings.

Lebrun says:

◄ Wavy Gravy discovered in work with autistic children that he could get children who wouldn't talk to or touch each other to talk and make contact using improvisational methods. Operating on the assumption that by the late sixties the whole world was very autistic, very polarised, out of touch but actually wanting to make contact, we used these techniques and went right into middle America.

'The Hog Farm happenings were aimed at an entire community – church, police, students – people who didn't usually talk to each other. Through the day more and more people would arrive at a site, find themselves a task to do and create a very complex organism whereby a complete show was set up by nightfall.

'Acid, Eastern religion, theatre and the Pranksters' example were a strong combination. Camp would be like a circus. There would be washing machines in the woods and speakers in the trees and feedback coming out of the machines; the police would always stop us, but we learned to switch roles so, rather than them just being police and us being hippies, we would change all the parts around. We would start taking movies of them, asking them to take pictures of us playing "Home on the Range" to them on kazoos, or getting out all kinds of toys, and the police would be disarmed. So was middle America. It was *very* powerful.'

The Hog Farm had a technique called the Pile.

❛ Using theatre, we would get this whole group of people to start going through imagination games. They would start thinking they were a forest, that they were a pile, a single organism, a fire in which they were all flames, part of the earth together: Wavy Gravy would be leading them through this on the microphone, and the music would start weaving in and out and people would start making sounds on their own, and through this process, by the end of the evening, a kind of holy feeling would come over everybody that they had merged into something that was beyond the individual.

'No group of people that size had ever participated in happenings like this before, and it was wonderful. Anyone would take part: law students, street people, housewives, physicists. I myself had been a very organised and rather right person before. Now I was part of this family, this group which was a whole organism, and it was an extraordinary experience that I'll have never again and I would never be able to replace. One of the things that was going on then, partly because of all the psychedelic drugs that were around, partly because of what was in the air at the time, was this feeling that extraordinary things were about to happen and it felt as if we were at the centre of things, *making* them happen. It always felt good when we were with the Hog Farm. It was like: "Any moment now the skies are going to burst open and everything will change." The skies did burst open. Then they would close again of course. But it did seem to happen that when we were doing our shows we had our highest experience.'

Reach out ... I'll be there. Togetherness at the Trips Festival.

Wavy Gravy, Lebrun and others still live peaceable creative lives. The Hog Farm lives on in good memories. By 1965 in San Francisco there were many follow-on effects from Kesey's thrust to new frontiers. In the old public halls of San Francisco, the Pranksters, assisted by the city's promoters and musicians and young people, put on what became known as Trips Festivals – acid-soaked affairs with dancing and lights and much fine madness. The Grateful Dead, Big Brother and the Holding Company, the Quicksilver Messenger Service and Jefferson Airplane – themselves fully committed to the new acid freedoms, together with much of their management and friends, neighbours and assistants – became the soundtrack, fully live and very electric, for these long mixed-media events. There was theatre from Kesey and the Pranksters, and from the San Francisco Mime Troupe and their offspring, the Diggers; and, above all, there were the kids themselves, who had become by 1967 the media's hippies (nowadays described in *Webster's Dictionary* as 'young people who reject the mores of established society as by dressing unconventionally or favouring communal living, advocating a non-violent ethic and often using psychedelic drugs or marijuana'). It would have suited Kesey enough to dig himself and his friends – but to have a few hundred or thousand others freaking out, too, was even better.

And by now there was a powerful new figure on the scene, slight of build but gigantic of brain: Augustus Owsley Stanley III, who was some kind of genius. Owsley was to manufacture millions of tabs of specially refined and pure (and eventually thoroughly illegal) acid, first in liquid, then in very professional-looking tablet (tabs) form, with different names and colours to identify the age and strength and nature of each batch. He prided himself on the quality of his acid, charging very little and giving away as much as he sold. He had another passion: the music of the Grateful Dead, who had, in a way, become Kesey's house band.

The Dead's Phil Lesh said: 'We became the Grateful Dead at the Acid Tests. We had great chemistry.' Their biographer, David Gans, says they had a great chemist, too, in Owsley. 'The Bear turned on millions,' said Lesh, and I believe him. He certainly got to the Beatles and to Joan and me. He visited me once at A & M Records, and I introduced him very formally to Herb Alpert, the company's co-owner with Jerry Moss, who was quite impressed and very polite.

In the years 1965–7 it had all come together astonishingly coherently. There were clear catalysts whose hold on spiritual values kept the thing on track. Dylan was one, his music threading through Kesey's trees at La Honda; the Beatles, who had inspired many of the San Francisco musicians to form bands and dress up, were another. Then there were the Beats – Cassady driving the Pranksters' bus – and maybe a special place of honour goes to Allen Ginsberg, who knew everybody and charmed even the Hell's Angels at La Honda and the British police with his finger cymbals. He was everywhere – at the Be-In in San Francisco in January, in England for a Summer Smoke-In, reading *Howl* to people eager for his words.

Jerry Garcia, Sunshine and Mountain Girl, without a care

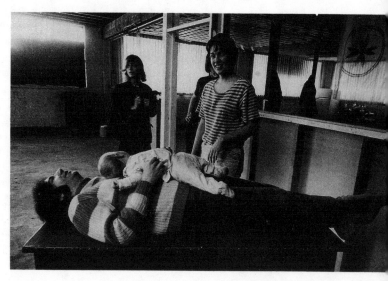

102

Says the Dead's Lesh: 'I liked *Howl* so much I set it to music.' The lead guitarist, Jerry (Captain Trips) Garcia, one of the counter-culture's greatest heroes, gave a memorable description of the sensation of playing a concert against the background of collective acid-taking: 'It wasn't a gig, it was *the* acid test. Anything was OK. Thousands of people, all helplessly stoned, finding themselves in a room full of other people, none of whom were afraid. It was magic, far-out beautiful magic.'

It is astonishing, in retrospect, that the rest of the world didn't know more of what was going on – it was so public and so free. But they didn't. Had the Pranksters operated within the narrower confines of England, there would have been a very swift move to check them.

Messages from the 'Free' had already been passed in code. In the 1966 album *Revolver,* for example, there was a quote from Dr Timothy Leary's version of the Tibetan Book of the Dead: 'Turn off your minds, relax and float down-stream.' And then there were the surreal visions of Strawberry Fields, where even the word 'forever' seemed to hold something otherworldly in the plaintive resonance of Lennon's voice. They'd travelled so much further than just from wanting to hold our hand, or give us all their loving.

But it was not yet the Beatles who were attracting the attention of the British law-enforcement agencies. There persists a view that the police knew that the Beatles smoked marijuana but chose not to move against them. They were too much a part of the cosy fabric of British life, Harold Wilson's secret weapon from Liverpool, his highly exportable Members of the order of the British Empire. No – the police were stalking a less favoured prey.

We were living in Los Angeles, picking up the distant 'vibrations' from Britain, and thanks to David Crosby of the Byrds I had become a dedicated believer in all forms of cannabis, a user and a seeker after whatever new truths might be obtained. In November 1966 I was in England with the Beach Boys where their 'Good Vibrations' was, as it was everywhere, number one. I dropped by a Manchester 'newspaper' pub where a crime reporter, whom I had known previously, commented on my relationship with the pop world and declared: 'The Old Bill are looking to get the Rolling Stones. They know what they're up to.' And he tapped the side of his grog-blossom nose, cackled, and said: 'Mine's a large Scotch while you're at it. You fellows are rolling in loot.'

I found that the marijuana that created such a bond between users also cut one off from some – but by no means all – old relationships. It wasn't anything to do with career structures or changes in environment. It went deeper. It was a matter of . . . vibrations. And in that pub, at that moment, the vibrations were bad. Why should the police be out to *get* the Rolling Stones? What had they *done?*

They had never been liked by parents but, then, neither had Elvis Presley, and nor for that matter had any of the early rock 'n' roll stars in their first incarnation – not even Cliff Richard, or before him Tommy Steele when he made girls scream. But the Stones showed no sign of reformation. They were *so* beyond the pale they refused to 'revolve' at the end of the television show 'Sunday Night at the London Palladium'.

This show, long in the tooth but dear to the hearts of the nation, had featured the Beatles in 1963, and they, like all before and after them, at the end of the programme had stood on the revolving stage with the other performers and waved like good boys to the unseen millions in their homes far beyond the guests in the Palladium audience.

There was much talk in the newspaper reports of 'breaks with tradition' when the Rolling Stones left straight after their set not only at rehearsal but also upon transmission. There was a running row from afternoon until evening, with Andrew Oldham, the Stones' young manager, every bit as 'difficult' as his famously 'evil' charges, arguing with the show's director, one Albert Locke, before trying to obtain a compromise with Mick Jagger, forgiveness from Mr Locke, and understanding from the press. He might as well have asked a tiger to give up meat. It was the classic sixties confrontation; it had everything: a generation gap, a rude gesture at old ways, New Pop rejecting Old Showbiz.

For the newspapers it had the vital bottom line of the Rolling Stones doing all that could possibly be asked of them: being very rude. The same night Mick Jagger observed: 'Anyone would think this show is sacred or something. That revolving stage isn't an altar, it's a drag.' Mr Locke could not have disagreed more. It *was* the high altar of showbusiness, the London Palladium. To Britons, the honour of appearing there far outshone the honour in America of appearing on 'The Ed Sullivan Show' because the Palladium, as a theatre, had status, power, even majesty. Royalty itself was proud to grace its boxes. And Mr Locke declared: 'Every artist that has ever played the Palladium has got on the revolving stage at the end of the show. Who do the Stones think they are?'

The answer was that the Rolling Stones by now *knew* who they were. They had seen themselves from the outside looking in, and having now refused to revolve they brought down the curse of old Music-Hall. The Gods of Variety Theatre refused to smile for much of that year upon Pop's Bad Boys. In the pubs and clubs, millions shook their heads: 'Did you see the Rolling Stones just walked off after the show? They didn't go round and round waving with the others. Terrible, isn't it?'

It must have been the final straw. Six days later a series was launched in the *News of the World*: 'Drugs and Pop Stars. Facts That Will Shock You.' Week one lashed out at Donovan, the gentle 'Flower Child' who

Mick Jagger and Keith
Richards with lethal legal
drugs during the hearing of
charges that they were
involved with illegal
substances

had upset no one. In week two it was the turn of the Rolling Stones –
in the person of Mick Jagger, the Devil's Disciple.

The *News of the World* declared:

> Another pop idol who admits he has sampled LSD and other drugs
> is Mick Jagger of the Rolling Stones.... He told us: "I don't go
> much on it [LSD] now the fans have taken it up. It'll just get a dirty
> name. I remember the first time I took it. It was on our first tour
> with Bo Diddley and Little Richard." '

The journalist continued:

> During the times we were at Blaises Jagger took about six
> benzedrine tablets. 'I just wouldn't keep awake at places like this
> if I didn't have them,' he said.... Later, he showed a companion
> and two girls a small piece of hash (marijuana) [sic] and invited
> them to his flat for "a smoke". '

On the day this article appeared, Mick Jagger went on the Eamonn
Andrews television show and told the audience that he was issuing a
writ for libel against the *News of the World*. It would appear that the *News
of the World* reporter had confused him with Brian Jones. The writ was
served. The following week saw the third episode of the newspaper's
moral crusade. That same night, Sunday, 12 February, tipped off by the
News of the World that there was to be a 'party' at Keith Richards's home,
Redlands, in West Wittering, Sussex, the local police mounted a raid.
The story did not break until the following week when the *News of the
World* published a report, under the headline 'Drug Squad Raid Pop
Star's Party'. The only details divulged in a surprisingly coy account were
'Several stars, at least three of them nationally known names, were present
at the party. It was held at a secluded country house near the South
Coast.' The *Sunday Telegraph* gave more details than the newspaper
threatened with a libel action and named Keith Richards and Mick Jagger,
mentioned drugs, searches, substances, tests, and all the paraphernalia of
what would soon become the standard Pop Star Bust, by avengers from
the police spurred to action by the *News of the World* and other high-
toned defenders of public and private morality.

George Harrison today throws a very interesting light on the story:

> I was at that party, and the funny thing about it was that they said
> in the newspapers later: "Another internationally famous pop star
> and his wife escaped moments before the net closed in." I left there

105

about 7 a.m., so it showed me they were waiting until I had gone because they were still climbing the ladder, working their way up. They didn't want to get to the Fabs yet.'

On 10 May the two Stones and a friend, Robert Frazer (also a friend of the Beatles and the linkman in the *Sgt Pepper* album-cover plans), were sent for trial. Jagger was accused of the unauthorised possession of four tablets containing amphetamine sulphate and methylamphetamine hydrochloride (i.e., 'uppers'). Richards was accused of allowing his house to be used for the purpose of smoking cannabis resin (i.e., people had been getting high at his party). Frazer was accused of possessing heroin and methylamphetamine hydrochloride (i.e., trouble!).

The next weeks were a time of great concern in the Crazy World of Pop. The day before the hearing against Jagger, Richards and Frazer, the police busted Brian Jones for possession of cannabis, and with him two exotically titled friends. All three were well-known and popular figures 'on the scene' and, although there was no opportunity in Britain for public comment on the specific Stones offences (since by then the charges were *sub judice*), there was much talk in private, not only in Britain but also in America where there had been a vigorous increase in police anti-drugs activity, particularly in San Francisco.

The aspect that fazed many in positions of responsibility in both countries was the usual one: ignorance not malice. For years musicians and other artists had been changing their consciousness with substances legal and illegal, but there had been little or no public knowledge of this. Such as there was had been warped by prejudice, informed by anxiety, and any attempt to illuminate was countered by the pushers of confusion

A part of the price of fame when it meets infamy: their publicist, much loved – now late lamented – Les Perrin guides the Devilish Duo through 'well-wishers' during a break in the hearing. Puzzle: find the famous Allen Klein in this picture.

in the popular media. To the aware it was quite clear that the prohibition of drugs would be as unsuccessful and, in the long run, as dangerous as the prohibition of alcohol had been in the 1920s, giving rise to lawbreaking on a massive scale and the accumulation of vast illicit fortunes.

Now and again, some good sense raised its head above the parapet, and in the 'straight press' there were some enlightened editorial decisions. On 2 February 1967 the *San Francisco Chronicle* reported a meeting between Lieutenant Norbert Currie, head of San Francisco's narcotic detail, and a 'group of hippies' to 'find out the attraction of drugs'. Under the headline 'Hippie's Strange Offer to Narcotics Chief', the *Chronicle* reported that a bearded hippie named Anderson, who admitted to having used marijuana over the past ten years, had told the policeman: 'I would be willing to take you home and turn you on. We cannot explain its attraction because it is basically subjective. You have to find out for yourself.'

Approximately two hundred hippies, hippie-watchers, church members and nuns attended the meeting, and the *Chronicle* reported that the event was a success. It brought applause for Lieutenant Currie at the beginning and the end of his hour's appearance. One 'multi-hued hippie' asked him: 'Are you aware that prison is the best schooling a guy can get to become a good crook? What's the good of sending guys to jail for selling marijuana? You can't possibly enforce all the laws in the book. You would have to work a 100 hour week. You have to make a choice. Do you have to be so zealous about going after mind-expanding drugs?'

Peter Cohon, now Peter Coyote, the actor, but then with the San Francisco Mime Troupe and one of the Diggers of the era, claimed that one of the reasons for the upsurge of the use of LSD and marijuana was that a lot of fears about the harmful effect of non-addictive drugs had disappeared.

Lieutenant Currie's reply was described by the *Chronicle* as 'mild'. 'This is what I came to hear,' he said. The newspaper added: 'He made no comment on the offer to turn on.' Sister Bernadette, one of the benevolent spectators, described the get-together as a valuable experience. 'We have to find out how to communicate with these people. I don't say that I agree with what they say, but they are very honest.'

In the months to come, throughout the so-called Summer of Love, the city would experience a plethora of unprecedented challenges to old norms. There would be a Be-In, a Chalk-In, Banana-Ins and Walk-In-Front-Of-The-Traffic-Ins. The Diggers were adept at street theatre; the pamphleteers were mimeographing instructions on how to be free, and how to respond to reaction as soon as anything happened. There was an Attitude that defied known forms. All real drugs so far discovered were by now illegal, so the hippies were ready for the great banana hype. Wrote the *Chronicle* after much early gullibility on both sides of the credibility gap: 'Bananas, the newest psychedelic adventure in Bay Area hippiedom, were being viewed with more amusement than enthusiasm in the Haight-Ashbury district yesterday.'

Nat Friedland of the *Los Angeles Free Press* planned to make $100,000 off bananas by mail order but interviews showed that several hippies had tried the dried scraping of banana skins without anything happening. A trip was impossible to simulate. You couldn't get high if you stayed where you were! Nevertheless, grocers were selling vast quantities of bananas across America. The underground press were very keen. The *Berkeley Barb* had offered a recipe, Donovan's 'Mellow Yellow' was said to have been inspired by the fruit, but the *Chronicle* said there was serious doubt among hippies: '"I think the whole thing is propaganda put out by the United Fruit Company," said one bearded youth.'

There was by now a determination to get loaded at all costs: 1967 was a year of too many drugs, no question about that. STP had arrived – a frightener producing trips of three days' duration, and a substance not only *not* responsive to the LSD antidote, thorazine, used for those few tripsters in trouble, but positively aggravated by it.

After the failure of bananas, extract of wheat sprouts was supposed to be the next best thing in town. But that, too, was a flop. A Haight-Ashbury newsletter supported the substance and said it worked miraculously but there was a discernible cooling off when it was found that an acreage had to be cultivated and even then the stuff had to be fermented between wet blotters, allowing the wheat to grow a mould, and then squeezed through a juice extractor, drop by drop. Better just to buy two dollars' worth of good Owsley.

In England, there was now open debate on the drugs question. The Tory MP Quintin Hogg (now Lord Hailsham and 'Britain's Legal Boss', the Lord Chancellor) called for 'no mercy' in a debate in the House of Commons. The *Daily Mirror* reported: 'Pop singers who say soft drugs are harmless were described as criminals.... Mr Hogg said he hoped the Minister of Health ... was not going to be lured by these pop singers who write to *The Times* asking for a letting up on cannabis.'

Hogg added:

❝ I hope he [the Minister of Health] and the Home Secretary will pursue the attacks on cannabis, hashish or pot or marijuana or whatever with the utmost severity the law allows.... I hope they [the pop singers] will find themselves at the Old Bailey, and, however distinguished their position in the Top Ten may be, that they will be treated as criminals deserve to be treated. '

A reply from the higher reaches of the medical profession was not long

Peter Coyote – once a Digger always a Digger, but now a movie actor as well. A living, breathing advertisement for pushing out boundaries.

in coming. In April, in the course of a long, reasoned two-part study of drug dependence, Dr David Stafford Clark, a senior medical man well known to television viewers, quoted from the World Health Organisation's report on drug addiction and habit and was careful to distinguish between the drugs of addiction, psychic dependence and habituation. Stern words were directed to alcohol and the morphine derivatives, and to barbiturates, amphetamines and cocaine. Of the Cannabis Indica drugs he said:

‹ They produce effects which are socially harmless ... there is no physical dependence, no withdrawal symptoms and little tendency to increase the dose or evidence of tolerance to its effects. Nor is there any evidence of the kind of physiological damage from prolonged usage which inevitably follows with alcohol and even with prolonged intensive cigarette smoking when straightforward tobacco is used. Cannabis Indica, whether smoked or taken by mouth, is less toxic than the politically acceptable alternative of a cigar or a large brandy. But which side of the Old Bailey dock would Mr Hogg be if his strictures were applied with comparable severity to alcohol and tobacco?'

In the second part of his examination, Dr Stafford Clark made a key point, one of eminent fairness: 'It is a harsh fact that whereas some intoxicants are an undiluted curse, none is an unmixed blessing....
Enlightened social responsibility is inseparable from any practical answer. And the only foundation for that is understanding.'

Not all Members of Parliament had shared Quintin Hogg's views during the debate. Mr William Deedes, then a Conservative MP, later a Minister and, until his retirement in 1986, the editor of the conservative *Daily Telegraph*, commented: 'It is being strongly urged that the enforcement of this [Dangerous Drugs] bill is weakened by the inclusion of cannabis and marijuana [sic] on the list. A great many people besides pop singers believe that we would be in a stronger position over heroin if we ceased to put cannabis in the same category.'

There was a trace of fun in the debate when Gwyneth Dunwoody, a Labour MP, told the House she was horrified at the effect upon her of some purple hearts. 'They made me feel completely invincible after quite small doses. I firmly believed I could do whatever I liked.'

Many a Mod must have smiled. But it would not be long before Drinamyl (purple hearts) became very unfashionable, and they at least would leave the scene. Speed in other forms remained. So did marijuana, hashish and LSD. The pop world began to take sides as consumption and paranoia increased. A member of the Troggs was reported as 'quitting' because he was tired of the drug-addict image of being in the pop scene. 'You've only got to have long hair and play in a beat group and everyone assumes you're a junkie. It had reached the stage where people look at the size of your pupils before they talk to you. It has really sickened me.'

An American psychologist, Steve Abrams, a leading advocate of reform of the laws against marijuana, had been looking into the possibility of research into cannabis-smoking since the end of 1966. He approached the police in Britain as an honest broker. He says now: 'The head of the Drugs Squad said that if they arrested Mick Jagger for possession every kid in the country would want to smoke dope.' And yet the raid did take place; and when, in June, Jagger, Richards and Frazer went to the Assizes in Lewes, in the full blaze of press publicity, to the horror of most people Jagger and Frazer were brought to and from the court in handcuffs. They were also detained in gaol during the hearing. When, after sentence, the Home Secretary, Roy Jenkins, was asked to comment on the use of handcuffs – an apparently unnecessary and inhumane act against two very unthreatening men – the distinguished statesman replied: 'It is the primary duty of the governor to ensure that prisoners do not escape. He is given guidance in Prison Standing Orders, a copy of which is in the library of the House, but it is his responsibility to decide whether or not handcuffs should be used. Less may be known about the reaction of a prisoner on his way to trial than about those of a prisoner serving a sentence and Governors must have reasonable discretion.'

At any rate, worse was to come. Mick Jagger was sentenced to three months in gaol and Keith Richards to twelve months. It was scarcely credible. Fans in court were aghast. So was the country at large. News spread abroad. Gaol!

Jagger's defence had been that the pills he had, though not prescribed for him, *would have been prescribed* had he asked his doctor. His doctor confirmed that he would certainly have prescribed something similar. He had told Jagger it was 'all right to use them'. The judge said this was not a defence to the charge.

In the case of Keith Richards, much had been made of the presence at Redlands on the night of the 'bust' of a 'nude girl' wrapped in a rug and of a 'strong sweet smell' said to be cannabis. It was implied that cannabis had lowered the girl's inhibitions. Richards told the prosecution that he thought the girl was in a completely normal state. 'We are not old men. We are not interested in petty morals.'

Mr Michael Havers, now Sir Michael, Attorney-General, on behalf of Jagger and Richards, told the court that on 5 February an article had been published in the *News of the World* which, if untrue, would constitute a grave and disgusting libel. A writ had therefore been issued. Mr Havers

Steve Abrams, an American in London who organised the protest advertisement in *The Times* calling for kindness to pot-smokers. A brave thoughtful man.

went on: 'In the remaining five days this man was subjected to being followed and observed wherever he went or whatever he did. A van or car was constantly outside his flat. And within a week this well-known national newspaper tips off the police to go to West Wittering, not just for anything but for drugs.'

Havers's defence was passionate, but it was not enough to save the defendants. The country turned its full attention upon the two Rolling Stones. Robert Frazer, having pleaded guilty to possession of twenty-four tablets of heroin was subsequently refused leave to appeal and served his six-month sentence. Bail was granted to the Rolling Stones, pending appeal against conviction and sentence.

Everyone had a view on the case. There were numerous articles and letters in the press. In the *Daily Mail* Monica Furlong said:

❝ What one cannot and should not forget is that their wealth and fame has come to them almost entirely because everything in their songs and appearance was a protest against conventional society and its attitudes.... Some forms of protest no doubt are healthy and help to produce a useful tension against the rigid traditions of society. But in others, as I believe in this case, there is the smell of decadence which is to say the absence of any real ideas and real joy.'

In fact the Rolling Stones were enormous fun. They had friends everywhere, quite unrelated to their apparent wealth or undoubted fame. They were also very sweet and aware and open. Paul McCartney remembers Mick backstage at a concert featuring both bands:

❝ We were there putting on our Leichner pancake with a sponge. "What you doin' there?" Mick asked. "Don't you know about that, Mick? This is show business, you know. You look so pale under those lights." It's funny, Mick not knowing about make-up – later he got well into it.'

They were very *young*. 'Let them be,' we said, and we were not alone. On 1 July, William Rees-Mogg, later Sir William, the editor of *The Times*, wrote and published a leading article entitled (after Pope) 'Who Breaks a Butterfly on a Wheel?' Rees-Mogg said that it was surprising that the judge should have decided to sentence Mr Jagger to gaol for a first offence, and 'particularly surprising as the case was about as mild a drug case as can ever have been brought before a court'.

He asked if the sentence would have been the same if the defendant had not been famous, arousing criticism and resentment as a result of his celebrity. He called on sound traditional British values of tolerance and integrity to be shown to someone who might seem to symbolise the new hedonism which challenged sound British values, and concluded: 'It should be the particular quality of British justice to ensure that Mr Jagger is treated exactly the same as anyone else, no better and no worse. There must remain a suspicion in this case that Mr Jagger received a more severe sentence than would have been thought proper for any purely anonymous young man.'

The leading article, more than a thousand words long, was a model of decency and mature generosity of spirit. Portia-like, it drew on the British sense of fair play: the quality of mercy, Rees-Mogg argued, should not be strained.

On the front page of the same issue, *The Times* reported that four hundred young people had massed around Eros at Piccadilly Circus in London at 2 a.m. to protest against the prison sentences. There were four arrests. Leaflets were circulated asking the police, the Sunday newspapers and magistrates to calm down. 'The laws will change,' said the leaflets, 'and we will win. Why not get things in perspective? We are not a threat to government or to law and order. We just don't like to see our people hurt.'

Joe Boyd of UFO and Pink Floyd remembers other protests that took the form of a march down to the *News of the World* offices. 'We went to Fleet Street and picketed and tried to block some of the vans coming out with copies of the *News of the World*, and then everybody trooped back to UFO and there was a triumphant set by a group called Tomorrow featuring Steve Howe on guitar.' The folk at UFO would pay dearly for that protest against the *News of the World*, as we shall see in Chapter 5.

Steve Abrams remembers marches taking place every night for a week. 'It was pointed out that nobody had demonstrated in Fleet Street since before the First World War, when there was a time when newspaper editors had to be escorted to their carriages by the police. Nobody had cared enough to demonstrate in Fleet Street and nobody has cared since.'

There was much support from public figures for the two Stones. John Osborne, the playwright, found it 'alarming that the *News of the World* should pass on random tip-offs from informers about what may or may not be going on in somebody's private house'. Viscount Lambton said it was 'only the extreme seriousness of the *News of the World* tip off that prevented the *News of the World* suddenly appearing as the custodians of public morals as being something positively comic'. He concluded: 'God help this country if the police have to take their cue from the *News of the World*.'

The *News of the World*, in a letter to *The Times* from its then editor, Stafford Somerfield, spoke of its plain duty to assist the police. 'Let me make it clear,' Somerfield urged, 'the *News of the World* believe that

TIMES PAST · THE TIMES · FUTURE

PRINTING HOUSE SQUARE, LONDON, E.C.4. TELEPHONE: 01-236 2000

WHO BREAKS A BUTTERFLY ON A WHEEL?

MR. JAGGER has been sentenced to imprisonment for three months. He is appealing against conviction and sentence, and has been granted bail until the hearing of the appeal later in the year. In the meantime, the sentence of imprisonment is bound to be widely discussed by the public. And the circumstances are sufficiently unusual to warrant such discussion in the public interest.

MR. JAGGER was charged with being in possession of four tablets containing amphetamine sulphate and methyl amphetamine hydrochloride; these tablets had been bought, perfectly legally, in Italy, and brought back to this country. They are not a highly dangerous drug, or in proper dosage a dangerous drug at all. They are of the benzedrine type and the Italian manufacturers recommend them both as a stimulant and as a remedy for travel sickness.

In Britain it is an offence to possess these drugs without a doctor's prescription. MR. JAGGER's doctor says that he knew and had authorized their use, but he did not give a prescription for them as indeed they had already been purchased. His evidence was not challenged. This was therefore an offence of a technical character, which before this case drew the point to public attention any honest man might have been liable to commit. If after his visit to the POPE the ARCHIE shop of CANTERBURY had bought proprietary airsickness pills on ROME airport, and imported the unused tablets into Britain on his return, he would have risked committing precisely the same offence. No one who has ever travelled and bought proprietary drugs abroad can be sure that he has not broken the law.

JUDGE BLOCK directed the jury that the approval of a doctor was not a defence in law to the charge of possessing drugs without a prescription, and the jury convicted. MR. JAGGER was not charged with complicity in any other drug offence that occurred in the same house.

They were separate cases, and no evidence was produced to suggest that he knew that MR. FRASER had heroin tablets or that the vanishing MR. SNEIDERMANN had cannabis resin. It is indeed no offence to be in the same building or the same company as people possessing or even using drugs, nor could it reasonably be made an offence. The drugs which MR. JAGGER had in his possession must therefore be treated on their own, as a separate issue from the other drugs that other people may have had in their possession at the same time. It may be difficult for lay opinion to make this distinction clearly, but obviously justice cannot be done if one man is to be punished for a purely contingent association with someone else's offence.

We have, therefore, a conviction against MR. JAGGER purely on the ground that he possessed four Italian pep pills, quite legally bought but not legally imported without a prescription. Four is not a large number. This is not the quantity which a pusher of drugs would have on him, nor even the quantity one would expect in an addict. In any case MR. JAGGER's career is obviously one that does involve great personal strain and exhaustion; his doctor says that he approved the occasional use of these drugs, and it seems likely that similar drugs would have been prescribed if there was a need for them. Millions of similar drugs are prescribed in Britain every year, and for a variety of conditions.

One has to ask, therefore, how it is that this technical offence, divorced as it must be from other people's offences, was thought to deserve the penalty of imprisonment. In the courts at large it is most uncommon for imprisonment to be imposed on first offenders where the drugs are not major drugs of addiction and there is no question of drug traffic. The normal penalty is probation, and the purpose of probation is to encourage the offender to develop his career and to avoid the drug risks in the future. It is surprising therefore

that JUDGE BLOCK should have decided to sentence MR. JAGGER to imprisonment, and particularly surprising as MR. JAGGER's is about as mild a drug case as can ever have been brought before the Courts.

It would be wrong to speculate on the JUDGE's reasons, which we do not know. It is, however, possible to consider the public reaction. There are many people who take a primitive view of the matter, what one might call a pre-legal view of the matter. They consider that MR. JAGGER has "got what was coming to to him". They resent the anarchic quality of the Rolling Stones' performances, dislike their songs, dislike their influence on teenagers and broadly suspect them of decadence, a word used by MISS MONICA FURLONG in the Daily Mail.

As a sociological concern this may be reasonable enough, and at an emotional level it is very understandable, but it has nothing at all to do with the case. One has to ask a different question: has MR. JAGGER received the same treatment as he would have received if he had not been a famous figure, with all the criticism and resentment his celebrity has aroused ? If a promising undergraduate had come back from a summer visit to Italy with four pep pills in his pocket would it have been thought right to ruin his career by sending him to prison for three months ? Would it also have been thought necessary to display him handcuffed to the public ?

There are cases in which a single figure becomes the focus for public concern about some aspect of public morality. The Stephen Ward case, with its dubious evidence and questionable verdict, was one of them, and that verdict killed STEPHEN WARD. There are elements of the same emotions in the reactions to this case. If we are going to make any case a symbol of the conflict between the sound traditional values of Britain and the new hedonism, then we must be sure that the sound traditional values include those of tolerance and equity. It should be the particular quality of British justice to ensure that MR. JAGGER is treated exactly the same as anyone else, no better and no worse. There must remain a suspicion in this case that MR. JAGGER received a more severe sentence than would have been thought proper for any purely anonymous young man.

...ARY

...monwealth, a posi-
...r kingdoms and

Those were other times and this was another *Times*. All the words shown here were from the editor, William Rees-Mogg, quoting Alexander Pope in support of a fair deal for the Rolling Stones. 'I think you defend freedom in the unpopular areas,' he says today.

thousands of parents are rightly concerned about it. We believe that the police have a difficult task in keeping this disturbing situation under control. We shall continue to help them in any way we can.' He had, in his own newspaper, absolutely denied that he had anyone follow Mick Jagger after the issuing of the libel writ. All the *News of the World* had done was its duty.

The views of *The Times* leader were, however, percolating through the thinking, chattering classes. Britain did not consider itself an intolerant society. Indeed, the weighty cautious commentator Kenneth Harris had published a very optimistic and liberal book, *About Britain*, extracts from which had appeared in *The Times*. He stated: 'They [the British] have developed a curiously protective attitude to "great characters" which enables extraordinary heretics and rebels not merely to survive but in time to be approved of.'

Having described the British as 'conventional and to an extent hypocritical', Harris went on to say that in a fast-changing society it could be dangerous to generalise. On the subject of youth he was generous indeed: 'Young people are searching for values and for sincere human relationships, individual and social, as never before and their destructiveness is directed only at the falsities and hypocrisies of the older generation.'

The editor obviously agreed. Today, looking back on the leader (written when he was an elderly sobersides of thirty-eight) Sir William remembers:

❬ The quotation from Pope, "Who breaks a butterfly upon a wheel?" reflected this extraordinary feeling of the contrast between the slim figure of Mick Jagger and the full weight of the law – for doing what? For having a couple of pills from his friend's doctor which would have required a prescription if he'd got them in Britain. It was obviously a ridiculous basis for any kind of criminal charge to be brought, and it was this sense that he was being prosecuted because he was famous, because he represented aggressive responses to our existing culture, that made me feel very strongly that our existing culture was letting itself down.'

Sir William's recollection is that in general the reaction to the leader on Jagger was favourable. People recognised that he hadn't been reasonably treated in court, and that everybody, however famous or however unknown, was entitled to justice from the courts.

Not everybody agreed, however. Not even the young. Two weeks later the *Daily Mail* stated that an opinion poll showed that more than half of the young people in Britain between the ages of twenty-one and twenty-four thought the sentence on Mick Jagger *was not severe enough*. Nearly 30 per cent thought it fair. Only 12 per cent of young people thought it too severe.

The *Sunday Express*, my old newspaper, seized upon these poll findings to exclaim: 'What a lesson for those who mistake the chatter at a few avant garde parties for the voice of youth. The vast majority of young people want nothing to do with drugs. They look upon them, rightly, as only for the sick in mind.'

Battle was about to be well and truly joined. On Monday, 24 July, a full-page advertisement was published in *The Times* calling for the legalisation of marijuana. A bold panel five inches square was centred over a page of dense text, detailing opinion, specialised information, definitions, quotations and, most fascinating of all, a list of sixty-four signatories to a bold petition.

The specially bordered panel read: 'The law against marijuana is

w against
uana is
ral in
iple and
rkable in
tice

hich can be violated without doing
injury are laughed at. Nay, so far
om doing anything to control the
passions of man that, on the contrary,
and incite men's thoughts toward
objects; for we always strive toward
bidden and desire the things we are
d to have. And men of leisure are
ient in the ingenuity needed to enable
utwit laws framed to regulate things
not be entirely forbidden. . . . He who
termine everything by law will foment
her than lessen it."—Spinoza

annabis sativa, known as 'Marihuana' or 'Hashish',
under the Dangerous Drugs Act (1965). The maximum
smoking cannabis is ten years' imprisonment and a fine
of informed medical opinion supports the view that cannabis is
harmful of pleasure-giving drugs, and is, in particular, far
than alcohol. Cannabis is non-addictive, and prosecutions
behaviour under its influence are unknown.

se of cannabis is increasing, and the rate of increase is
. Cannabis smoking is widespread in the universities,
tom has been taken up by writers, teachers, doctors, business-
cians, scientists, and priests. Such persons do not fit the
of the unemployed criminal dope fiend. Smoking the herb
a traditional part of the social and religious life of hundreds
nds of immigrants to Britain.
ading article in *The Lancet* (9 November, 1963) has suggested
' worth considering . . . giving cannabis the same status
al by legalizing its import and consumption . . . Besides the
and attraction of reducing, for once, the number of crimes
ember of our society can commit, and of allowing the wider
f something that can give pleasure, a greater revenue would
come to the State from taxation than from fines. . . . Addi-
ains might be the reduction of inter-racial tension, as well as
tween generations.'
main justification for the prohibition of cannabis has been the
tion that its use leads to heroin addiction. This contention does
m to be supported by any documented evidence, and has been
s to be refuted by several authoritative studies. It is almost certainly
s to state that the risk to cannabis smokers of becoming heroin
s is far less than the risk to drinkers of becoming alcoholics.
cannabis is usually taken by normal persons for the purpose of
acing sensory experience. Heroin is taken almost exclusively
ak and disturbed individuals for the purpose of withdrawing from
. By prohibiting cannabis Parliament has created a black market
e heroin could occasionally be offered to persons who would not
rwise have had access to it. Potential addicts, having found can-
as to be a poor escape route, may doubtless been tempted to try
in ; and it is probable that their experience of the harmlessness and
addictive quality of cannabis has led them to underestimate the
gers of heroin. It is the prohibition of cannabis, and not cannabis
lf, which may contribute to heroin addiction.
The present system of controls has strongly discouraged the
of cannabis preparations in medicine. It is arguable that claims
hich were formerly made for the effectiveness of cannabis in psychiatric
tment might now bear re-examination in the light of modern views
drug therapy; and a case could also be made out for further investi-
ation of the antibiotic properties of cannabidiolic acid, one of the
constituents of the herb. The possibility of alleviating suffering
used because the medical use of cannabis preparations should not be dis-
through the medical use of cannabis preparations should not be dismissed because of prejudice concerning the social effects of ' drugs '.
The Government ought to welcome and encourage research into
all aspects of cannabis smoking, but according to the law as it stands
no one is permitted to smoke cannabis under any circumstances, and
exceptions cannot be made for scientific and medical research. It
is a scandal that doctors who are entitled to prescribe heroin, cocaine,
amphetamines and barbiturates risk being sent to prison for personally
investigating a drug which is known to be less damaging than alcohol
or even tobacco.
A recent leader in *The Times* called attention to the great danger
of the " deliberate sensationalism " which underlies the present campaign against ' drugs ' and cautioned that : ' Past cases have show
what can happen when press, police and public all join in a manhun

at a moment of nati
of cannabis smokers
increasing proportio
the crime at issue is

The prohibition
has demoralized pe
arbitrarily classifie
unjust law. Unco
and loss of livelih
contempt in the s
to suffer in prison
stopped on the str
Council for Civ
drugs have appe
Chief Constable
bours and childr
to civil liberties
been unable to

Abuse of
serious nation
as the prohib
the resources
dangerous dr
potential bre
ism. Simila
of both alco
criminal co
lose sight o

MEDIC

" Th
and no i
between
never be
members
and law
within
directly

Dr. J.
Gillesen

wise i
and
direc
with
of ca
myt

Dr.
Tim

The full-page *Times*
advertisement. The laws
haven't changed. The
debate rages on. Cannabis
'offenders' are, however,
more leniently treated.
Gaol was 'normal' in 1967.

immoral in principle and unworkable in practice.' On the left side of the
page was a petition to the Home Secretary calling for five points to be
taken up: (1) research into all aspects of cannabis use; (2) permission for
cannabis to be smoked legally in private; (3) its removal from the
dangerous-drugs lists so that it would be controlled rather than
prohibited; (4) a change in the law making possession of marijuana a
misdemeanour, punishable by a fine, rather than a criminal offence
punishable by gaol; and (5) the commuting of all sentences for those in
gaol for cannabis offences.

Among those who signed it were more than a dozen doctors, two
Members of Parliament, a raft of poets, artists, authors and playwrights –
including Graham Greene and John Piper of the Quintin Hogg 'class', a
generation previously thought to be unanimous in its disapproval. Most
interesting of all to the popular media were the names of John Lennon,
Paul McCartney, George Harrison and Ringo Starr of the Beatles, all
declaring their MBEs. Right alongside was the name of their manager,
the usually discreet Brian Epstein. It was obviously High Time to Come
Out.

Actually, word was out on the Beatles a month earlier. In the weekend
of the Monterey Pop Festival news quickly spread among thousands of
young people listening to the music in the festival grounds that Paul
McCartney of the Beatles was on the record in another sense. He had
stated in *Life* magazine that he had used LSD 'more than once, that it
had brought him closer to God, and that it made it very difficult for him
to tell a lie'. It seemed to all of us that Monterey was a thoroughly
appropriate time and place for one of the Beatles to come clean. It had
been obvious in all but print that they were expanding their minds. Now
it was out, what next?

In London's *Daily Mirror* on Monday, 19 June, the first publication
date after the *Life* magazine article could be assessed, Paul was quoted
as saying: 'I don't regret that I've spoken out. I hope my fans will
understand.'

The *Mirror* reported: '[He] followed up his shock confession that he
had taken the hallucination [sic] drug LSD by saying that it was possible
that he might take it again. But Paul, 25, yesterday said that his four
experiences with LSD had such a deep effect that at the moment he does
not feel the need for more.' The *Mirror* went on: 'At the studio I asked
Paul if any other Beatles had taken LSD. "I can't speak for the others,"
said Paul.'

There was then a statement from the Home Office that it was not an
offence to say one had taken it but that possession was illegal. Medical
'evidence' was offered in the *Mirror* that the drug could 'lead to insanity
and may harm unborn children'.

115

In its comment column the *Mirror* headlined their opinion: 'Beatle Paul, MBE, LSD and BF.' They suggested, 'The millionaire Beatle should see a psychiatrist,' and said that by talking so enthusiastically about LSD he was encouraging his fans to break the law. They concluded: 'Isn't he encouraging them to try the drug themselves? Most teenagers fortunately will have more sense than to mess about with dangerous drugs. Most teenagers will continue to regard LSD as a menace.'

When Independent Television News interviewed McCartney he was asked whether he should have kept quiet about it. He replied that he had been asked a question, had told the truth, though he would not have said anything if he had not been asked. 'I'm not trying to spread the word about this. The man from the newspaper is the man from the mass media. *I'll* keep it a personal thing if *he* does, too, you know. If he keeps it quiet, I will. It's his responsibility for spreading it, not mine.'

He told the interviewer: 'I mean that you are spreading this now *at this moment*. This is going into all the homes in Britain, and I'd rather it didn't. You're asking me the question, you want me to be honest, I'll be honest. But it's you who have got the responsibility not to spread this now.'

The interview was duly broadcast that night on the ITV network in England. The decision to spread the word *was* made by ITN.

The Beatles' manager, Brian Epstein, was quick to join Paul in admitting that he, too, had taken LSD. In an interview in August he explained why.

> **Paul rang me to say he had told the press he had taken LSD. I was very worried. I came up to London knowing I was going to be asked to comment on Paul's decision. I finally decided that I would admit I had taken LSD as well. There were several reasons for this. One was certainly to make things easier for Paul. People don't particularly enjoy being lone wolves. And I didn't feel like being dishonest and covering up, especially as I believe that a lot of good has come from hallucinatory drugs.'**

Brian Epstein said he had taken it five times, didn't know whether he would take it again, and had never had a hangover from it and indeed had come to know himself better and was now less bad-tempered because of it. It had lessened his ego. We, his friends, applauded him.

John and George then joined Paul and Brian in conceding publicly that they, too, had used LSD. It had 'taken them into some interesting places'. No, they didn't know whether they would go on taking it.

Paul, the public-relations man, had proved that he was quite as up front as the more obviously abrasive John, who had been in so much

116

trouble in 1966 with his 'more popular than Jesus' aside.

Now Billy Graham told the press he would pray for Paul. 'My heart goes out to him,' said Dr Graham. 'He has reached the top of his profession and now he is searching for the true purpose of life. But he will not find it through taking LSD. There is only one way and that is through real Christian experience.'

So, over the next furiously interesting six months of 1967, several strands were emerging in the fabric of Drugs versus the Rest. There was clearly a serious generation gap. The young were not altogether united in their view of drugs, but they were substantially the people who were using illegal drugs. The 'old' (with the exception of the brave explorers Leary and Kesey and Allen Ginsberg and suchlike media-styled 'high priests') were against. But the *Times* leader, appealing for natural justice, was quite well supported by older folk, so there *were* subtleties.

Another strand was the emergence of an overt philosophy of 'love and peace'. In San Francisco, indeed, a Summer of Love had been proclaimed by the committee representing Haight-Ashbury. So far as could be ascertained by July, when the *Times* petition had appeared, peace and love had quite a good name. Monterey had passed without an arrest. The LSD- and marijuana-taking Beatles had produced a brilliant long-playing record, bringing popular music to a plateau previously thought unattainable, irritating those critics who thought they should have learned to read and write music first.

The American magazine *Newsweek* asked for realism and tolerance, and in the *Times* petition here were all these worthies arguing that marijuana should be treated at worst like a parking offence, at best like a glass of beer.

The moving force behind the petition was the American psychologist Steve Abrams. He says today:

❝ I went with my friend Miles to see Paul to discuss my plans for the advertisement. Miles [of the Indica bookshop and the *International Times*] had the freedom to come and go with Paul. Paul was easy to talk to, like someone you've known for a long time. His position was perfectly responsible. He knew the power of the Beatles, the power of their making or not making endorsements. Though they didn't particularly want the publicity, he was willing to guarantee the cost of the advertisement. In the end it proved impossible to keep his financial involvement a secret. '

The Times insisted that it required verification from all signatories to the advertisement. Graham Greene is supposed to have walked two miles to the post office to send a cable to the editor confirming his signature.

Steve Abrams says *The Times* requested payment on the eve of publication and he obtained a personal cheque for £1,800 signed by a Beatles assistant. 'I was subsequently told by someone that it was credited to the Beatles advertising account and in fact the four Beatles and Brian Epstein would have paid equal shares.'

Sir William Rees-Mogg, recalling his decision, as editor, to publish the advertisement, says that it was less well received than his leader on the Stones.

❛ We *were* much more criticised over our decision to run the advertisement which called for the legalisation of marijuana – it wasn't a view with which I agreed, incidentally – but I felt it was a matter which ought to be argued out and that we shouldn't deprive people of the opportunity to make their case if they wished to. I decided to run it because as an editor I had a commitment to freedom of debate. I'm quite convinced that, even if you very strongly disapprove of a view, as an editor you actually have a duty to allow free debate to take place. I was against the decriminalisation

Allen Ginsberg was told, pleasantly enough, that he couldn't play music without a licence in Hyde Park. The occasion was a 'Legalise Pot' rally. The police were pelted with flowers and told 'We love you'. Without his portable instrument, Ginsberg continued chanting.

of cannabis. I thought it was undesirable and in fact it's never happened.'

Sir William, later deputy chairman of the BBC and chairman of the Arts Council of Great Britain, remembers that there were those who said that freedom of debate was not applicable in this case and that much harm would follow from the advertisement. 'It seems to me', he argues now, 'that saying that is like saying you shouldn't allow people to hold an unpopular opinion. *But I think you defend freedom in the unpopular areas*' (my italics).

'The Legalise Pot rally in Hyde Park got a very good press,' Steve Abrams remembers. 'I think it got two pages of publicity in every national newspaper. There were thousands of people there. The only paper which behaved badly was the *Daily Sketch* [a now defunct tabloid]. They found a junkie and paid him to inject himself and took a photograph and put it in the *Sketch*.'

There was a further debate in the House of Commons. For the government, Alice Bacon, Minister of State at the Home Office, said she was horrified by the way some pop idols encouraged drug-taking. 'It is time to make it clear that drug-taking is ill-advised, if not dangerous to personality and health.' Miss Bacon had read some 'offensive views' while sitting reading a magazine under the drier at her hairdresser's. She said that the only person 'with any sense' quoted in the article seemed to be the little pop singer Lulu. She had said: 'Love is far older than pot and goes right back to Jesus. I am a believer.' The magazine quoted from was *Queen*; Paul's 'admission' and Epstein's pleas for understanding were the offending passages.

The newspaper headlined it 'Lulu vs Epstein'. The Beatles manager said later: 'Alice Bacon's outlook is prejudiced, narrow and singularly ill-informed. There is now a more definite division of opinion about the smoking of pot which is not only thought to be not criminal by pop stars but by other responsible persons.'

At the end of July, seven days after the publication of the *Times* advertisement, and three days after the Commons debate on drugs, the two Rolling Stones, Mick Jagger and Keith Richards, were brought before the Lord Chief Justice's court for the hearing of their appeals. In the case of Richards the conviction itself was quashed, and the lead guitarist left the court 'without a stain on his character'. Lord Chief Justice Parker, discussing the question of the 'nude girl' and whether her lack of inhibition might have been caused by cannabis, observed: 'Nobody could possibly say that she *had* been smoking cannabis resin because she was gravely unconcerned.'

In the case of Mick Jagger and his pills, the doctor's evidence that they were all right by him was now considered strong mitigation, and so, although Jagger remained convicted of actually possessing the pills, the sentence was quashed and he was conditionally discharged.

Both men were free to go home or wherever they chose. The hearing had started at 10.20 a.m. and was over by lunchtime. It was the case of the year. Much of the nation cheered. Justice had been seen to be done to the Rolling Stones. Robert Frazer served his six-month sentence. August loomed ahead in the Summer of Love. Now what?

Mick Jagger appeared to show the way on the evening of his discharge from the threat of gaol. Taken by car and helicopter to a secret rendezvous, he appeared on Granada Television's 'World in Action' in some interesting company. Sitting with William Rees-Mogg, Lord Stow Hill (formerly Sir Frank Soskice, a Labour Home Secretary), Father Corbishley, the Jesuit, and the Bishop of Woolwich, Dr John Robinson, Mick Jagger talked calmly of personal liberty.

Rees-Mogg has a clear memory of the occasion:

❝ It was very pleasant. We were sitting in a garden, I remember. Mick Jagger arrived by helicopter. I was fascinated by the way all his arguments turned on those classic propositions that people ought to be absolutely free and that there ought to be as little government as possible. As he put forward these views which were so much against the grain of the currently fashionable left-wing ideology, I suddenly realised that Mick Jagger was in essence a right-wing libertarian. Straight John Stuart Mill!'

Stephen Jessel in *The Times* commented that massive publicity had turned Jagger into a latter-day Nero. In any poll for the best-hated men in Britain taken among people over forty, Jagger would be near the top. Equally, a poll among young people would reflect the special respect and admiration in which *they* held him.

❝ He is so unlike the cartoon stereotype as to be almost unrecognisable in reality. He is a slighter figure than you expect and thin to the point of skinniness. He is quieter and has much more grace of manner than one would have expected. He is articulate, and the philosophy he outlines is obviously the product of sustained consideration. Two attitudes are fundamental to [it], the belief that people have a right to absolute tolerance and the belief that life is a constant process of redefining the frontiers of experience.'

That redefinition led Jagger to tell Jessel: 'I was very cynical; we were all cynical people. We just grew up a bit and learnt a bit and thought a

Mick Jagger prepares for filming by 'World in Action' team after being freed on drugs charges. William Rees-Mogg noted his grace of manner.

bit and talked a bit and became less cynical.'

So now it was made clear to the British public – and to the rest of the world reachable through the pop culture – that the Stones and the Beatles, once seemingly so different, were now strong and united in the vanguard of the exploration of Things Beyond the aims of simple pop, commonly assumed to be the accumulation of wealth, loutishness and the unthinking taking of drugs just for the hell of it.

For instance, the Beatles, particularly George Harrison, and Brian Jones of the Stones were now interested in the music of the East. Roll over Chuck Berry, tell Buddy Holly the news. And where influential Western musicians led, Western audiences followed like lambs. The orchids that had been thrown out over the audience at Ravi Shankar's Sunday-afternoon Monterey concert had fallen among mere pop fans, yet when the great Brahmin sitar-player had asked that there should be no smoking there was an immediate response from the audience of 8,000. The joints went out together with the straight cigarettes, and the only smell was of incense and flowers. As can be seen in the festival films, the reaction to Ravi Shankar's music was overwhelming. The audience that had raved over Janis Joplin and the plethora of great blues bands, over Otis Redding, and Simon and Garfunkel the previous day, and the breadth of pure pop music available in that great summer from Frank Zappa to acid rock to the Byrds, were totally astonished by this virtuoso performance, from a far-off land of which most Americans knew nothing at all.

George Harrison now decided to come to Los Angeles to help his new friend open a sitar school. There was also to be a concert at the Hollywood Bowl. I and a very pregnant Joan were invited over to George and Pattie's house on Blue Jay Way, and got lost in the fog. George wrote a song, eventually released on the *Magical Mystery Tour* tracks, while he was waiting. Writing in his book *Twilight of the Gods*, Wilfred Mellers says of 'the friends who lost their way in the fog': 'The fade out leaves us feeling there's not much hope of the lost young joining him.'

Well, maybe George meant that as well. . . . It was, anyway, one of those magical mystical months. Fresh out of the music, love and flowers of the festival offices, still waiting for our fifth child to be born, I was full of optimism. I persuaded George and Pattie, Neil Aspinall, Magic Alex of Apple fame and Pattie's sister Jennie to come to Haight-Ashbury. We flew to San Francisco by private Lear jet, very fast, very sixties and rather frightening.

Paul had, as we've seen, been there earlier in the year. He recalls the visit today with happy memories but with a note of caution which may not only be hindsight.

❛ I liked it. I like Americans anyway and it was a good scene so it was generally a lot of fun. I remember going to Haight-Ashbury where the Grateful Dead lived and going round to see them because we had mutual friends. I called on lots of people. There was Grace Slick, getting out of a sleeping-bag. It was like that – just mates. ❜

'We're off to see the Wizard....' George and Ringo hurry for the train to north Wales to hear Maharishi, a man they still like.

Paul went to San Francisco in April, and remembers thinking: 'I can't see this lasting because the media are going to get here and pretty soon it will turn into Rip Off Street.'

By the time George and Pattie arrived there in August, it was too late to see San Francisco at its best. Looking back on the visit now, George remembers that he had expected to see:

❛ All healthy wonderful enlightened people making nice little things like I'd seen in India – little carvings and stuff. When we got there it was just horror. It was like the Bowery – all the drunks and down-and-outs and these little spotty schoolkids who'd dropped out. When we walked down that street people were saying "Hey, man, how about having this?" and "Hey, man, how about that?" And it was just "Hey, man" for about an hour by all these horrible people. I thought: I don't like these people relating to me as if I am a leader. ❜

In *Fifty Years Adrift* he concedes that he was on acid during the walk through Haight-Ashbury.

‹ We were all buzzing like mad. We just wanted to escape from this scene in Haight-Ashbury which was like the manifestation of a Hieronymus Bosch painting getting bigger and bigger. Fish with heads, faces like vacuum cleaners coming out of shop doorways, just like the horrors. We managed to get back to the car before our heads exploded.'

Later, leaving San Francisco in a Lear jet, there was a stall-scare in mid-air.

‹ I was sitting behind the pilot. The plane dropped and all the buttons along the top of the dashboard lit up red, saying UNSAFE UNSAFE UNSAFE. Alex was chanting "Hare Krishna, Hare Krishna", and I was saying, "Om – Christ! – om," and then suddenly the plane was OK again ... that's when I stopped taking acid and tried to make up for all those hideous people that we'd seen in Haight-Ashbury who'd somehow tripped themselves through us, misunderstanding.'

It did seem as if George had missed the best of San Francisco's Summer of Love. As we shall see, the good people of that neighbourhood, now overpopulated, underfunded, misunderstood and media'd out, would themselves take steps to explode the myth and start again. The late summer/early autumn of 1967 was a time of change, of renewal. The year was full of turning-points.

Back in Los Angeles, George and party met up with Ravi. We all went to the Hollywood Bowl packed to the mountain-tops with sober incense-burning fans of all ages. I went to a special concert given one evening in a beautiful little garden by the maestro and his tabla-playing friend Alla Rakha, no less of a leader in his field, and as a reward for having been so sober and respectful during the music I was afterwards offered much strong liquor, which I loved in those days. Such broad-mindedness, I thought, in the company of many wise teetotallers. Om. Christ. Bottoms up!

George and Pattie returned to England with Neil, Alex and Jennie. Dominic Taylor was born in Hollywood Community Hospital on 13 August. The Beatles were thinking about their Magical Mystery Tour. *Sgt Pepper* had sold millions. Everyone we knew was having a wonderful time. The record companies were starting to appoint house hippies to their staff. A & M Records co-opted me and put me on a big white wicker throne. I was fully psychedelic in thought, word and beads. Joan and I stocked up with candles and pretty dresses for the autumn. What now could possibly go wrong?

123

On 27 August the *Daily Express*, my old friends, published a report under the headlines 'Thinking Is IN! Beatles Entranced by a Holy Man's Words'.

❝ Beatles John Lennon, Paul McCartney and George Harrison discovered last night that the secret of real happiness is all in the mind. For more than an hour they sat cross-legged in a semi-trance listening to an old man from the East expound his theories. Earlier the Beatles had sat with 1,500 other people for more than two hours at a Think-In, a lecture on transcendental meditation – given by the Maharishi Mahesh Yogi, leader of a Kashmir cult.

'His theory is that a dormant inner power, discovered by deep meditation, can be used to ease the strains of life. At the end everyone sat in meditation for five minutes. The Beatles had their special audience.

'The 56-year-old Maharishi told them: "You have created a magic air through your names. You have now got to use that magic influence on the generation who look up to you. You have a big responsibility." The Beatles, all twiddling red flowers, nodded agreement.'

The report was published on a Friday. Later that day, all four Beatles and their partners, together with Mick Jagger and Marianne Faithfull, went to Euston to catch a train to Bangor in north Wales. John's wife, Cynthia, missed the train but made the papers, who, always quick to spot someone in distress, caught her crying: 'Beatle Wife Misses Train!' She followed by car, and all of that weekend, at a teachers' training college, the leaders of Western youth sat at the feet of the holy man and heard strange things.

In the words of the *Daily Express*: 'Maharishi Mahesh Yogi said later that: "When the Beatles heard my lecture they saw the possibility of creating a better world of peace and harmony through meditation. I believe they will come out with a blowing trumpet of transcendental meditation." '

Mick Jagger found it 'intriguing'. John said he 'hoped to learn more'. I wondered what it would do to the LSD movement. I loved LSD and pot by now. An answer came quickly. John told a newspaper: 'We don't regret taking drugs but we realise that if we'd met Maharishi before we had taken LSD, we would not have needed to take it.'

The Maharishi said: 'It is very important to me because they are Beatles. They can do a great deal for the whole humanity and particularly the youth which they lead. I can bring them up as very practical philosophers of their age ... all four of them. They live life together.' And flowers were handed round and everyone held carnations. It did look pretty good to

In Bangor listening to
Maharishi. *Left to right:*
Jennie Boyd, Mick Jagger,
Marianne Faithfull, Pattie
Harrison.

me. Then that weekend, of all weekends, Brian Epstein was found dead.

It was front-page news around the world. Brian was thirty-two. The cause of death – a mystery at first – was later found to be accidental poisoning: a mixture of alcohol and prescribed barbiturates. The man who in 1967 had found humility, tranquillity, ego loss and music, love and flowers all at once, and who had so enjoyed the Summer of Love, had died alone and unable to reach any friends. Press and public were greatly saddened. The Beatles were shattered. But theirs was not a secular response. Now they had Maharishi, and their comments to the press were as symbolic of 1967 as anything else that was said that year.

Ringo said:

❝ It was lucky, in a funny way, that we got the news when we were in Bangor with Maharishi. We asked him what to do and he told us we mustn't let it get us down. If we got really brought down Brian would know this because he would be able to feel *our* feelings in his spiritual state and depression is no good for anybody. If we try to spread happiness, then Brian will be happy too because although he is dead, his spirit is still here. ❞

John said:

❝ These talks on transcendental meditation have helped us to stand up to it so much better ... it's up to us now to sort out the way we and Brian wanted things to go. He might be dead physically but that's a negative way of thinking. He helped to give us the strength to do what we did and the same urge is still alive. He was due to come to Bangor to join us in the meditations. It's a drag he didn't make it.'

There was no doubt now that the Beatles had gone beyond drugs, beyond those 'kicks' which had so horrified the MPs Hogg and Bacon. Soon *Disc and Music Echo* was reporting a boom in meditation. Pete Townshend was saying:

❛ It goes a lot deeper than working, living and dying. A couple of years ago I didn't believe in this life after death bit, or God. Now I do. If we don't reach a state of understanding of how we can escape the world situation, we'll just fade away. The only real escape is meditation.... You don't have to be intelligent or have experienced LSD, been turned on or freaked out – you just have to have faith in something big.'

The times they *were* a-changing, though detractors remained. 'Come off it, hippies, who are you trying to kid?' wrote Manfred Mann, but Alan Price replied in *Disc and Music Echo* in October:

❛ Flower power knockers might be tempted to knock the latest hippie trend of transcendental meditation, but I'm not going to join them. After being present while John and George were interviewed on the David Frost show in front of millions about their views on transcendental meditation, I still know nothing about it but I am convinced it may be the answer for some people.'

126

Among the public, the discussion ranged across the whole gamut of opinion, with the popular press making much sport with the Maharishi, soon to become known as The Giggling Guru.

Then George Harrison nailed his new colours to the mast:

❛ A hippie is somebody who is aware. You're hip if you know what's going on. But if you're really hip you don't get involved with LSD and things like that. You see the potential that it has and the good it can do but you also see that you don't really need it. I needed it the first time I had it. It was a good thing but it showed me that LSD isn't really the answer to everything. It can help you go from A to B but when you get to B you can see C and you see that to get really high you have to do it straight. There are special ways of getting high without drugs – with yoga, meditation, and all those things. So this was the disappointing thing about LSD. In this physical world we live in there's always duality – good and bad, black and white, yes and no. Whatever there is, there's always the opposite. There's always something equal and something opposite to everything and this is why you can't say LSD is good or bad because it's good AND bad. It's both of them and neither of them all together.'

The Quiet One was right out on a limb now, talking spiritually to the readers of *Melody Maker* in the autumn of the year that had begun with the question: 'What are the Beatles up to?' When even a photograph of them with beards could take up a whole page in a newspaper with elaborate wide-eyed captionings describing each nuance of facial hair. They had been up to a lot of things – LSD and marijuana for sure, and now, of all things, *Religion*. It looked as if drugs were out.

Mal Evans, the Beatles'
friend and road manager,
says 'Au revoir' to
Maharishi after attending
the latter's birthday-party

Eric Burdon, newly truly
psychedelic, was active as
singer and 'messenger' on
the international music,
love and flowers network.
Here he carries the Word
to the floral British at a
London event.

FOUR

GOODBYE TO THE TEXAS WAR DIET

The Beatles' move to spirituality astonished the whole world. George Harrison today sees the problem Joe Public had when the moptops from Liverpool started to talk about things spiritual. 'They thought we'd gone crackers. Yet, as with anything, when you *don't know* it's one thing: when you *do know*, it's another. And all it is is crossing over from one side of the street to another.'

Paul McCartney, last of the Beatles to take LSD, first to say he had, moved easily on to meditation.

‹ **All we'd been doing was trying to find out things, just for our own curiosity. First, we'd come down from Liverpool, found what London was about, how it worked. Then we'd gone to America, found out about that. And when we came upon Indian philosophy, and meditation started to come into our lives, it wasn't really different to what was happening earlier. It was just finding out.'**

Allen Ginsberg sees the progress of the Beatles from heart-throbs to disciples of the Maharishi as a 'paradigm for the whole era', symptomatic of the total culture change the sixties ushered in. Drugs were the door, the crucial catalyst. The Indian influence which was to pervade the era was first felt via the use of pot or cannabis, which has traditional religious associations in India. The use of what Ginsberg terms 'the divine herbs and grasses' was later applied, by extension, to the new psychedelics by Timothy Leary in his version of the Tibetan Book of the Dead.

It seemed that not only the substances but also the spirit in which they were taken had infiltrated into Western consciousness. Or perhaps it was no longer a case of East and West, more of one world – in the words of Gary Snyder, 'a fresh planet'.

Snyder and Ginsberg had been to India, Snyder more than once. Ginsberg sees India's contribution to the changing face of the sixties not

129

only in the introduction of new religious thinking but also in the increasingly widespread adoption of vegetarianism:

‹ the switch away from the heavy meat-eating Texas War Diet (aggressive meat filled with the adrenalin of frightened animals); the change in music heralded by such as Ravi Shankar and Ali Akbar Khan; and the change in clothes – the notion of free clothes, loose clothes that allowed sexual freedom of the genitals, widespread use of paisley and flower patterns. Paisley is the sperm symbol, simultaneously erotic, spiritual and ecological. A whole new style of dress came out of that.'

The Indian connection, so crucial to George Harrison's spiritual development, wasn't taking place in a vacuum. It was everywhere. And there was everywhere a sense of impatient yearning for something beyond ourselves and what was known. 'Only through the development of an inner peace in the individual and the pure manifestation of that reflection can we ever hope to attain the kind of peace in this world for which we yearn,' Prince Charles said in a speech delivered in Canada in 1986. Afterwards he was treated to much rubbishing in the British tabloids. He was nineteen in 1967, an impressionable age in an influential era. Is it too fanciful to see a legacy of the 1960s in these words?

George Harrison remembers:

‹ One of the things after LSD was this sudden desire within me to find out about the science of God consciousness, the science of realisation. I was born with my mother a Catholic and my father not. I was taken to church, but the only thing I ever saw in a church that had any significance for me were the Stations of the Cross – the paintings round the walls of this person being spat on, scourged, forced to drag a heavy wooden cross. Apart from that there was nothing I could see. I was not interested in what people call religion. In fact even now I don't relate to the word "religion".'

Of Maharishi he says today:

‹ He had a big impact on me because I was getting into meditation, and what you have to do with that is lose all your thoughts, get rid of trivia, and there is a technique to doing that. Just as I was thinking, Where am I going to get this mantra from? Maharishi suddenly appeared in London. He'd actually been coming for about ten years and nobody had paid much attention to him in the media until we got involved, but he's still great and he's still training millions of people and having a great effect.'

Allen Cohen of the *San Francisco Oracle* greatly deplores the quick-change aspect of what he terms 'the East Indian guru effect'. 'The interest in Eastern culture came because we were exploring states of consciousness and basically the Eastern religions in their purest form also did this, in a more direct way than Western religions.' But, he points out, the Indian child is born into a rigid culture and undergoes certain rites of passage before even attempting to surrender his ego. Allen Cohen saw the teenagers of 1960s America going straight from adolescence into the search for a guru to turn them on to life's mysteries. 'That makes sense in the East but not in the West,' he argued.

And yet the *Oracle* itself was born in a dream. Cohen recalls: 'I woke up in the morning and remembered seeing in a dream a newspaper with rainbows on it read all over the world. And I went out into the streets and started to tell people and they said: "Wow, what a great idea. Let's do it." And ideas were magical at the time. We always had the sense we could bring them directly into reality.'

This prevailing notion of 'let's do it' was endorsed in a separate conversation I held with musician Al Kooper when he said: 'In 1967 it felt like every day when you woke up you could really do something that day, either in a small way or in a big way. It wasn't just like "Oh, I've got to have breakfast now, or shower...". It was as if you could really *do* something, and it was a great feeling, a wonderful feeling.'

Allen Cohen's dream of a rainbow-coloured newspaper was achieved by mixing inks in a new way in the printing 'fountain', using wooden bars to split them into separate channels as they flowed towards the roller. At the roller the inks met and mingled so the finished sheets shimmered with the flash and dazzle and strobe of an acid-rush. All of this colour was applied to some pretty exotic designs: Eastern, American Indian, Victorian, Baroque, or just simply impossible to categorise. Such designs were, after all, realised dreams. They were New. They were Underground. Their difference was as much a part of the game as the difficulty the uninitiated or 'straight' person would experience reading the *Oracle*.

The term 'underground press' had irresistible appeal for those genuinely outside society, or wishing to be. The busting of the *International Times* of London (see Chapter 5) enhanced the impetus to go deeper underground. Raised on books and films which featured brave resistance fighters battling against the heavy metal of repressive forces – Nazis, Secret Police or sci fi robots – the idea of being underground was natural for the young in heart in the late sixties. Hardly anyone got paid for work in the underground press. I, for instance, would work more happily, unpaid, for LA's *Open City* than for any paper before or since.

Editorial freedom was total, and the writing consequently could be very sloppy, the views right out *there* and wild. It was a case of 'Come

It's that man again. Allen Ginsberg takes care of bliss business. His friend the respected and much travelled poet Gary Snyder is on the left.

131

A street hawker from within the counter-culture sells the *Oracle* and companion underground newspaper in the Haight

and get me, Copper'. Everyone was a 'contributing editor' with their name on the masthead – a practice that appears to persist to this day on *Rolling Stone*, itself born in November 1967. The prevailing mood of benevolent anarchy certainly isn't around in any magazine or newspaper I know which is published today.

Allen Cohen sees in the old *Oracle* and its brothers and sisters the upsurge of a tremendous creative movement:

❛ The artists and the poets and the writers who are well known now had their beginnings in the underground press movement. The political education, the merger of art and poetry and politics and journalism, was very creative. There were probably a couple of thousand underground papers in the country – that and rock and roll were the two genuinely creative aspects of the time. '

The underground newspapers had a wonderful user-friendliness and a devotion to their causes that had to do with their springing from the street. They really were what newspapers are supposed to be about. They were the truth.

When not looking to the East for inspiration, the counter-culture turned locally to the American Indian, with his peyote and his verifiably hideous treatment at the hands of Them, the plunderers of the Old West. An issue of the *Oracle* in June 1967, says Charles Perry, in his history of the Haight, featured a design incorporating a mountain and an op-art pattern of purple rays on a flow-colour background of turquoise shading into violet to form the face of a folk-hero, Chief Joseph of the Nez Percé, looming over the mountain.

Perry reports the issue being printed with *Oracle* workers squirting the rollers at random with coloured inks from ketchup-dispensers, giving each copy a unique colour scheme. The whole run was scented with Jasmine Mist perfume.

But figurehead Indians like Chief Joseph's descendants in the West, or of the East like Ravi Shankar, were not going to allow themselves to be co-opted by the counter-culture without making an attempt to set the record straight. Ravi Shankar was quick to state his position as being outside the counter-culture and firmly on the side of study, rigorous application to ancient form and custom combined with a search for perfection and real purity. He hated seeing dope-smokers at his concerts. On behalf of the American Indians, Rupert Costo, President of the American Indian Historical Society, wrote angrily to the *San Francisco Chronicle*: 'The way of the hippie is completely at variance to that of the Indian. It is disgusting. It is demeaning. It is the way of the bum.... We are for real. We believe in work and love and innovation. We are far from being square. But we despise fraud and hypocrisy. The hippies exemplify both.'

That *hurt*. It hurts even today. However, chiefs over from the other side of North America, visiting the San Francisco Indian Center, told the *Chronicle* they were 'flattered at the young people's interest but a little sceptical. These people are confused. They're looking for something spiritual so they find the Indians, and they read up on us. But they just read. They don't *know* the Indians personally.'

Rolling Thunder, chief of the Shoshone Tribal Council in Carlin, Nevada, met some hippies in Golden Gate Park on 21 September 1967, the autumn equinox. 'Many of my people are still hardened when it comes to hippies,' he said, but he hoped that the equinox meeting and other contacts could lead to what he termed 'a mutual enrichment of hippie and Indian life. The hippies want to know all about our old way of life, that rich sense of sharing we once had and that belief in the Great Spirit.' The Chief said that this aspiration was something that young Indians, now concerned with fast cars and a fast American life, could benefit from equally.

It was clear that Rolling Thunder and his son Buffalo Horse, aged eighteen, were perfectly willing to teach the Haight-Ashbury tribe all they knew, but was it, by the autumn of 1967, too late? By the end of the year a movement away from the counter-cultural city centres had become apparent. Time was to show that despite the dissemination of the hippie tribe the attachment to things Indian was neither insincere nor transient, though it might have begun in the spirit of innocence pejoratively described as naiveté. The spirit endured, and much was saved.

Peter Coyote, who took his name from an animal of the wild, understood and respected the Indian view.

◖ One thing that is important to remember is that I'm not an Indian, I never wanted to be an Indian and I *can't* be an Indian. Gary Snyder said a very interesting thing about Zen practice, however. "Enlightenment is a Pan-species phenomenon." All people and all cultures have encountered it. The Hopi is under no obligation to reach me, because I am not a Hopi. But Zen Buddhism as a world religion *is* under the obligation to take me in and teach me. That's why I am a Zen Buddhist. When we began to leave the cities after the '67 era was when we began to realise that we were relatively ignorant of whole processes under the asphalt. The *only* indigenous

John, Paul, and Jane Asher returning to London after a trip to Greece undertaken with a view to buying an island. The original caption read: 'Flower power it seems has really taken root.'

people were the Indians. They were the only people who knew how to live here and you had to have congress with them.'

This view was sincerely held in the Haight where there was a great interest in, and awareness of, American Indian history and culture. A popular hero of this century as well as of his own – the nineteenth – was Chief Joseph of the Nez Percé, he of the *Oracle* cover, whose military genius earned him the nickname 'The Indian Napoleon' – a misnomer since he was a civil chief, and both principled and merciful. He made light of his military skills with the dictum: 'The Great Spirit puts it in the heart and head of a man to know how to defend himself.'

The hippies could dig that, and quite reasonably asked for understanding from Indians of their sincere desire to hang on to such basic truths from old Americans long dead and therefore safely beyond the reach of the concrete and steel and crass commercialism of the new America. They *did* read up on the Indians and when possible visited them and always welcomed them in their midst. Although it was not so comfortable for American Indians to reciprocate, because their rituals were more structured and precious, some non-Indians were permitted membership of the Indian Church.

In his angry letter to the *Chronicle*, Rupert Costo of the American Indian Historical Society had been quick to say of the hippies: 'I don't believe my people admitted these hippies to a native American church peyote meeting.' Only a few people were admitted, but that could not prevent the hippies from emulating the meetings. They found their own mescaline and made their own LSD and did it their way.

One famous Haight poster depicted a long-haired American Indian wearing a tall hat, a cigarette hanging from his lips. Chet Helms designed the poster, and its caption – 'May the Baby Jesus Shut Your Mouth and Open Your Mind' – became the motto of the Family Dog. The choice of an Indian theme for the design was felt to be much more appropriate to the era than anything derived from the late twentieth century. Just as the British turned nostalgically to 'granny clothes', so the Americans returned to a nobler pre-industrial era. The harsher realities of Victorian or American Indian life were subsumed in the popular vision of an idealised past.

So it was hope and Hopis, youth and Yogis, hippies and pioneers carrying no more than they could eat that represented the best of the studied attempts to get close to a new reality. Helen Perry, psychiatrist and chronicler of San Francisco's Human Be-In, wrote that in many ways the aim of what she terms the 'harmless people' was but an echo of the Indian tribes who turned to the Ghost Dance religion in their despair over the violence of the white man, believing there must be a time when the whole Indian race could come to a state of freedom from death, disease and misery by discarding all things warlike and practising peace, honesty and goodwill.

And not just the Indians. Perhaps one day we could *all* be happy. George Harrison, as firm today as twenty years ago in his belief in the Better Way, says that in writing the song 'Baby You're a Rich Man' John and Paul had a didactic aim.

❛ For a while we thought we were having some influence, and the idea was to show that we, by being rich and famous and having all these experiences, had realised that there was a greater thing to be got out of life – and what's the point of having that on your own? You want all your friends and everybody else to do it, too.'

And not necessarily by first becoming rich and famous. George Harrison explains:

❛ Sri Yukteswar, one of the Yogis shown on the *Sgt Pepper* album cover, says he came to realise that no barrier existed between man and God except in man's spiritual unadventurousness, so what I'm thankful for is that the Beatles enabled me to be adventurous. It saved me from some other mundane kind of life. But, having said that, I think whatever I'd done there would have been a way through it. All you have to do is have a desire to know something or do something. A desire or a thought is very strong. It's like a seed, and the more you think about it, the more you water that seed, the better it grows – and so in a way I don't think enlightenment was a matter of luck. To the four of us, and all those other millions of people it came to, it would have happened anyway because that's the way it was scripted.'

George Harrison was untutored in divinity or theology or any of the formal routes in Western spiritual activity. He says it was listening to Ravi Shankar's music that first introduced him to a higher consciousness: 'Although the music was so complex and there was no reason why I should understand it, I felt it made absolute sense. It made more sense to me than anything I've heard since.' After tracking down Ravi and taking lessons for three years he felt he had a deeper understanding not only of the music but also of himself. It was clear to him that no one in the West, however lovingly and earnestly, could pick up the sitar and catch up with a master so he did not pursue the quest for virtuosity. Something else had emerged.

❛ Indian music is tied into the spiritual life, so there's no way you can

The Grateful Dead at home in San Francisco. They lived in beautiful harmony in a Victorian house at 71 Ashbury. The Dead House was their headquarters and a beacon to the movement of which they were, in Gene Anthony's words, 'the centre band'.

get seriously involved with a classical study of Indian music without finding out what's behind it. And behind anything that has any depth you'll find the Yogis of the Himalayas.

'One of the first things I read in this period was a book by Swami Vivekananda, who was one of the first of the Indian Swamis to come to the West in the 1800s. He said: "Each soul is potentially divine. The goal is to manifest that divinity." He said also: "Do this through Yoga meditation and through work and various things and become free." Vivekananda said if there's a God we must see him and if there's a soul we must perceive it otherwise it's better not to believe. It's better to be an outspoken atheist than a hypocrite.

'I got involved through Vivekananda and, as they say, "Knock and the door will be opened". My trips to India were just knocking on every door I could find that was something to do with learning about Indian music, or learning about the soul, and I'm pleased to say I found out a lot.'

George became friends with one of the travelling Swamis who came to Haight-Ashbury in January 1967. He was Swami A. C. Bhaktivedanta who, at the age of seventy-one, opened a temple on Frederick Street. His arrival was hailed with much warmth by his friend, Allen Ginsberg, who said that the leader was 'very conservative ... to his faith what a hard sell Baptist is to Christianity'. Ginsberg knew that the holy man – later to become a friend of George Harrison and a 'lodger' at John Lennon's house in Ascot, England – would not tolerate marijuana, LSD or alcohol. He was also a vegetarian, and opposed to sexual improprieties, sloth, tea and coffee. Whatever most of the Haight were into, the Swami was against it.

Chet Helms of the Avalon saw a unity between his family background of evangelism and LSD. He says now:

❝ I suppose by nature I'm a zealot and so I attempted to apply what I knew and the skills that I had acquired to the circumstances of the dances. The manifestation of that for me was the ballroom, which in some sense was my church. The people who came to it were my congregation and I was the minister. They were the people I cared about and that I ministered to in many respects ... because when people would freak out it was not unusual for the police actually to drive someone to my front door and say: "We don't know how to deal with this person, can you?" ❞

He could.

❝ The bottom line with psychedelics is that by definition they're hypnotics. When people are under their influence they're very suggestible and so the key to it was not to see them as victims or people who needed help but to go to them and say: "I need help. Will you help me? You're a strong person. Come this way, help me." And there were very few people I couldn't bring out in that manner. ❞

He applied the same gentle persuasion to drunken sailors – trying to bring them into the body of the 'church' of what was happening. It was spiritual and it worked.

Perceiving the link between psychedelics or cannabis and spiritual realisation was a small step for the initiated but a giant leap of the imagination for the press and police. Drug busts continued. 'I thought they'd all found God,' said Joe Public. Well, yes and no. Brian Jones, as peaceable a wild man as you could wish to join on a trip, was none the less sentenced to nine months' gaol for possession of cannabis. Bailed to appeal, he was later relieved to have the sentence set aside, but it was nasty while it lasted.

In October 1967 the Grateful Dead's place on Ashbury Street, San Francisco, was raided. State narcotics agents and San Francisco police walked into the thirteen-room house and picked up an alleged five kilograms of marijuana, which even then was quite some stash. They arrested the group's organist and Bob Weir, the rhythm guitarist, plus the managers (and senior wranglers in counter-culturalism), Rock Scully and Danny Rifkin, and equipment manager, Bob Matthews, and six girls. The *San Francisco Chronicle* led on the story, went into enormous detail, and at the same time was kind and relaxed enough to review the band's career as leading exponents of the 'San Francisco sound'. The report concluded: 'The name of the group, informed sources commented ironically, comes from an Egyptian prayer: "We grateful dead praise you, Osiris."' Religion again! There was no case against the Grateful Dead; the raid had been unlawful. Free again, they played on.

San Francisco's contribution to the sound of 1967 has been described in Chapter 2. Its special contribution to visual art was in breaking into new ground labelled by the media 'psychedelic design', which was really freedom from that old enemy 'rigid forms'. Stanley 'Mouse' Miller, one of the great poster artists who helped publicise the heydays and 'hey, man' nights of the Avalon, Fillmore and other ballrooms, stands firm today in pointing to the graphic sterility that had preceded his work and that of his peers.

❛ Everything had been totally vacant of any interesting visuals. Graphics was usually just words, typeset words, with the idea that you would have to be able to read it within three seconds and get the message and that was it. There was nothing that you could get *involved* in at all. Any kind of involvement was taboo.'

Definite later-sixties Los Angeles design. This from *World Countdown*, a cheerfully apolitical underground newspaper owned and edited by a gigantic red-haired Englishman named Charles Royal, who gave away far more copies than he sold.

His reaction to what he saw as that grey world, together with that of his friend Alton Kelley, was to design something that would stop people and make them look again. 'The harder it was to read,' says Kelley, 'the better it worked out. The more outrageous and the more flashy the image, it seemed the better the dance actually was.'

Mouse remembers: 'We would drive round the neighbourhood and we would see our posters up in store windows and there would be a crowd of people around them, looking at them and trying to figure out what they said.'

Kelley and Mouse utilised images from the past, things that had been almost forgotten, and transformed them into posters that somehow encapsulated the mood of 1967. It might be an American Indian or a hotrod or the bearded man off the Zig Zag cigarette-paper packet. 'We just figured out there weren't any rules,' Kelley says today. 'I mean, it's art and there aren't any rules in art.'

Love had a lot to do with it, says Mouse. 'We really liked what we did, and we didn't get paid very much at all – seventy-five dollars a poster. We split it, and it just about paid our studio rent, and so they *had* to be works of love because there wasn't much profit in the thing.'

As for the much talked about effect of psychedelics on the era's visual output, Kelley says:

❛ They didn't really *do* anything. We were already doing this work and then the word "psychedelic" was put on it. The drugs just showed you there was another way of looking at things, but it didn't have any actual influence. I wouldn't even think about trying to do a poster under the influence of acid. '

Victor Moscoso, another poster artist of the day, was trained in art school and then had to jettison much of what he had learned there.

◄ I saw what those other guys were doing, and I was impressed. It really bothered me that I wasn't doing that, so I got down and caught up with them as fast as I could. We were all competing for the same poster, don't forget. There was only one poster for the Avalon every week. So everyone was trying, coming in with their own pitch. But there was always space, too, space on the beach, even if it was competitive.'

A car on Haight Street. It took real mad courage to drive one even then. Janis Joplin had a beautiful Paisley car, last sighted by the author in Bearsville, New York.

Poster art in sixties San Francisco is recognised as quite as good as and as important as the work of Lautrec and his peers in their milieu. The San Francisco artists had a similarly good time, and in the great years between 1966 and 1971 about 550 posters were designed. Each had to be better than the last. The work was delightful and painstaking. 'Made difficult to read for fun rather than for perversity,' as Jack McDonough has said in his generous book, *San Francisco Rock*.

Just as much as a four-hour set by the Grateful Dead, or the sight of a lovely girl with long long hair, wistful eyes, bare feet and a flower, as much as the tinkle of bells, or the bonfire smell of good marijuana burning in the breeze by the Panhandle, a poster from the ballrooms of romance tells us today why for some it *was* heaven to be alive in 1967.

By the time the sun was at its height in 1967 there was almost total freedom of expression in visual, musical and verbal terms. Looking back, of course, we can see some fabulously daft products of the new freedom, particularly in terms of clothes, and some wondrously dated inanimate objects. (Gonks?)

The idea of painting vehicles came to Britain in 1967. John Lennon's Rolls-Royce, unveiled in May, was a famous example of colourful outrage. It was immediately labelled 'psychedelic', but the designs were more Romany than anything else. The press went into a horror-crouch. 'Cross between a psychedelic nightmare and an autumn garden on wheels,' said the *Express*. 'A shrieking yellow,' shouted the *Mirror*. With its scrolls, zodiac signs, flowers, real beauty in paint for £1,000 on top of £6,000 for a Phantom V, it seemed a snip to John. The car now changes hands at hugely inflated prices: two million Canadian dollars at the last transaction.

In September 1967 the Suffolk police busted a student for failing to notify the authorities that his fourteen-year-old Ford Anglia had changed colour from black to multicoloured flowers. 'I'm not a hippie,' pleaded the student. 'I just did it to hide the rust.' He was fined a pound. The car had a yellow boot, green bumpers, orange headlamps, red wings, and it was dressed all over in flower patterns. *Not a hippie?*

Even a joyful anarchist like George Melly was baffled by some of the

141

attitudinal and sartorial excesses of the time. In his book *Revolt into Style* he recalls:

‘ Just about the time "Strawberry Fields" was released my wife and I went to dinner with a friend of ours whose whole life is devoted to sensation. The actual dinner party was staid enough although the conversation tended to roam over some pretty recherché sexual territory involving rubber, sado-masochism and baths full of machine oil, but while we were sipping our brandy the doorbell rang. In came a *Comus*-like rout of exotic creatures – the first time I'd laid eyes on the beautiful people, as it happens, although I'd known several of them in the days when they'd worn ordinary if fashionable suits and floral ties. There was a girl in the shortest mini I'd ever seen who lit up a joint and blew smoke into our mouths. There were other girls hung with as-then esoteric beads and bells and there were several young men in kaftans or matador pants and floral shirts or shepherd's smocks. ’

In fact, throughout the ages, affluent youth has enjoyed dressing in fancy clothes. It is axiomatic that the adventurous young with slim bodies and a desire to attract sexually will seek to adorn themselves in finery. Until recent times, however, even in the comparatively wealthy West, the mass of young people did not have the money fully to indulge this taste. Up to the Second World War the working-class Briton would wait all week to put on smart ‘weekend clothes’, if he had any, while that same weekend his upper-class contemporary was dressing down for ‘roughing it’ in the country. By the mid-fifties, however, influenced by Elvis bravado, swaggering peacock men were sighted in every High Street, and pretty girls of all classes were breaking free of mother's cast-offs and narrow fashion perspectives.

The beauty of late-sixties dressing was that any clothes would do so long as they were dreamlike. They could be – and often were, in London – Victorian military finery with an emphasis on scarlet and gold, or your aunty's feather boa and ball gown. Anything went. In San Francisco or London or Los Angeles nothing seemed more natural than dressing in an escalating variety of pretty clothes, although caftans were not nearly so popular as people today suppose. We wore fabulous braided, beribboned, rick-racked, gilded, star-spangled, belled and beaded blouses, shirts and tunics over flared hipster trousers or long flowing skirts, with moccasins or laced-up reverse calf boots.

At the height of my own clothes-madness I was wearing three scarves at once and silvered bells front and back over a velvet tunic from somewhere around the time of King Arthur (Hollywood's concept of) together with no less than fifteen ropes of cheap beads, some self-threaded and bought from dazzling 'head-shops' in Haight-Ashbury, Sunset Strip or the Monterey Peninsula.

As I have previously written in *As Time Goes By*, Jerry Moss of A & M Records took me to lunch in the autumn of 1967 and asked me if he could pose a 'difficult' personal question. 'Sure,' I said. He was my boss and, besides, what had I to hide? 'Are you sane, man?' he asked. I said I hoped I was but that I might not be the best man to ask. He said he had been driving home west on Sunset and worrying about my clothing, wondering whether I hadn't 'gone too far'. I said I hoped not, and that was more or less that, but I haven't forgotten it, as you can see. I told him the bells were so people could hear me coming and prepare a welcome. Ha!

Little hippie shops or, in the fashionable parlance of the time, boutiques were sprouting like magic mushrooms in west Los Angeles, Westwood, Brentwood and Beverly Hills. Clothes prices were keen, and there was a huge variety of accessories: beads you could thread yourselves, feathers for arranging in headbands or on belts, and bells galore. Joan sewed bells into her own clothing and into mine. We could always hear each other approaching. Up there in Laurel Canyon everyone except Frank Zappa

Here comes the best man in what the 1967 newspaper caption called "a kimono-style dressing gown". The young women are guests Carolyn Jones and Debbie Hughes, pretty as a picture. The wedding was of Sandra Pickup and Pierfranco Pudda.

143

was doing it. (Frank's trip was music and strobes and he was, anyway, quite freaky enough without taking LSD and wearing bells. The Frank Zappa dances were the first 'freakouts' we attended, drugless, in 1966.)

When we decided to slip home to England for a winter holiday at the end of 1967, we flew first to New York with our five children, stayed overnight at the Americana (now the Sheraton Center and none the better for it), and then embarked in the Cunard liner *Franconia* bound for Liverpool. We had passed from a benign Californian autumn into a damp and rather mean New York winter, so we had already changed into clothing more modest than our height-of-acid Hollywood finery. Even so, after reaching our stateroom in the ship I said to Joan that I had picked up more than a hint of disapproval from other passengers. 'I don't think we're in fantasy land any more,' I said, and went off timidly in the plainest of sweaters and corduroys to have a drastic haircut and my moustache trimmed. Looking like an elfin Ronald Colman I changed into a navy reefer jacket buttoned up to the top, and Joan slipped on a Jaeger coat. We walked on the promenade deck at dusk, ashamed and full of regret at our denial of the subculture.

An English officer paused beside us, detaining a brother officer. 'Excuse me, sir, ' he said, 'are you a flower man?' Startled, I said that yes, I probably was. How could he tell? He pointed to a two-and-a-half-inch-diameter orange, green and yellow brooch, baked like a biscuit by a hippie pedlar from San Francisco, one of half a dozen I'd bought in the souks at the Monterey Pop Festival bazaar. Whatever it was we had been doing and thinking that year, it showed!

Even when we thought we were safe in the anonymity of formal evening dress, strangers came over to our table and, unsolicited, offered a rendezvous for a joint. On the final night of the voyage, I went below deck where I took just 250 micrograms of acid and saw wondrous visions in the flames of the ship's engine room.

Clothes as symbol were so important that when we arrived in England we decided to dress up a bit, and what the hell? In London it was fairly

Mick and Marianne at a party in Ireland. The date was August, the event a very snobbish affair at a time when snobbery was in decline. Needless to say that the beautiful couple were the best dressed.

easy, even in winter, but provincial England never did relax conventions to anything like the extent of San Francisco or Los Angeles. Our reception in Liverpool was even frostier than the weather.

London's visual spirit was given expression by Nigel Waymouth, today a fine artist, in 1967 not long out of college and ripe for adventure. He used to go to the Portobello Road with his girlfriend to buy old clothes. He had discovered LSD in 1964 and when his favourite secondhand-clothes shop in the Portobello Road closed he and his friend decided to take it over and, in the spirit of the new acid ethos, call it 'Granny Takes a Trip'. It combined the sale of goods which were the best from the past – immaculate Edwardian frock-coats, long lace-covered silk tea-dresses, fluttering feather fans – with a certain way of wearing them which was utterly sixties and can never be repeated. Above all, the shop was about Doing It and Having Fun.

Nigel Waymouth says today: 'We did have a lot of fun. People asked me if I'd ever considered opening a string of shops. I said that was quite out of the question, against everything we stood for – being relaxed, casual and uncommercial. We went bust, of course.'

In partnership with Michael English, Waymouth also sold posters, trading under the name 'Hapshash and the Coloured Coat'. In the shop they listened to a lot of music. Coming from a love of jazz to newer music, via a meeting with Duke Ellington who said he *loved* rock 'n' roll, Nigel Waymouth and his friends were representative of a strand of British life where intelligence, the appreciation of music and art, the use of acid, and the flowering of real creative energy all came together at the most opportune of times.

Waymouth is hopeful of a resurgence of the spirit of that age: 'There was money and optimism and a sense of freedom which may return – not like that, but it will come around again. The humanist lives on.'

The stars in London really shone in public by day or night, in or out of trouble. At the time of Mick Jagger and Keith Richards's arrest and hearing, their clothes were a colourful distraction from the outcome of the case. *The Times* reported: 'Mr Jagger, dressed in purple trousers and a richly embroidered shirt, talked to reporters and posed for photographs.' Later he had changed into 'mauve satin trousers and a cream smock edged with maroon and green around the neck and cuffs'.

On another day, Mr Jagger, 'pale, and trembling slightly, wore tight trousers and a yellow flounced shirt with a large green tie. On his trouser belt was a button badge, "Mick is Sex".' Keith Richards on bail was described in the *Express* as wearing 'a Regency-style suit and silk choker, contrasting with the blue jeans he wore in Wormwood Scrubs'.

The night their acquittal was celebrated, a group of about fifteen hippies wearing beads and bells went to Westminster Abbey. According to the *Mirror*: 'Flower Person Caroline Coon, 20, an art student, laid a bunch of flowers in gratitude in the Cloisters. ... Middle-aged Mrs Eva Taylor of Brixton said, "They're up the pole, all of them."'

Who cared? At the *Sgt Pepper* launch in May, the scribblers were kept manically busy describing the Famous Four's new line in threads. Norrie Drummond in the *New Musical Express*:

> Apart from his green frilly shirt John was wearing maroon trousers and round his waist was a sporran. "Why the sporran?" I enquired. "As there are no pockets in these trousers it comes in handy for holding my cigarettes or front door keys." George was wearing dark trousers and a maroon velvet jacket. Their flamboyant clothes made even Jimmy Saville look startled.'

Jack Hutton of the *Melody Maker* covered the same event:

> Lennon won the sartorial stakes with a green flower-patterned shirt, red cord trousers, yellow socks, and what looked like cord shoes. His ensemble was completed by a sporran. With his bushy sideboards and National Health specs he resembled an animated Victorian watchmaker. Paul McCartney, sans moustache, wore a loosely tied scarf over a shirt, a striped double-breasted jacket, and looked like someone out of a Scott Fitzgerald novel.'

In August the Beatles slipped over to Greece, ignorant of the Colonels' nasty habits, and the *Mirror* noted: 'Flower Power fashion has really taken root. And on no less a person than John Lennon. John favoured a jacket covered with huge open flowers. In the centre of one flower was a button reading, "Exciting New Offer". Paul wasn't to be outdone. He sported an embroidered waistcoat over a flowery pattern shirt.'

When Eric Burdon got married, the *Daily Mirror* reported on 8 September: 'The bridegroom wore a sheepskin jacket over an oriental silk tunic and his bride arrived in gold sari and sandals.'

Likewise Sandra Pickup, a jazz-club waitress, marrying Pierfranco Pudda, a language student, earned from the *Mirror* a page-high picture, three columns wide: 'It was, as they say, a beautiful scene with practically everyone wearing exotic clothes and flowers in their hair.' (This was 9 August, with 'Flower Power' about to peak.) 'Sandra, 18, wore a green and purple sari with roses and cyclamen in her hair. Her Italian groom was clad in a black Indian-style suit and a fashionable droopy moustache. The best man appeared in a kimono-type dressing gown.'

On the same page someone called 'Beatle George Harrison' was described as being 'at a friendly freakout in Hippieland itself'. I was with

Brian Jones, Rolling Stone, at Heathrow after being turned over by Her Majesty's Customs. A nicer young man you couldn't wish to know in the pop world – and a very, very good musician, too.

him. We, too, had 'hippy-style' droopy moustaches, and he was wearing heart-shaped glasses, scarves, and beads. Pattie and Jennie Boyd, flower children beyond all imaginings, were there. We had hoped to remain anonymous. Some hope when a Sandra Pickup couldn't get married in Kensington Registry Office without making the front page of the *Mirror*!

The previous day Pattie had featured in a whole-page article by the *Mirror* fashion editor, Felicity Green. Headlined 'Where Did Pattie Get That Gear?' the copy began: 'The hippie cult, like it or loathe it, is here. Compared with its baubles, bangles, beads and bells, the Quant type mini-skirts pale into Establishment respectability. Where does it all come from?'

She divulged her secret fashion source off Montagu Square, the workshop of the design company The Fool, where 'the founder members of the hippie haute couture hang out. Two girls, a man and a business manager co-habit here among the paraphernalia of psychedelia, turning out those snappy little hippy numbers for boys and girls that are being so enthusiastically received by the Pop elite.'

The designers were two Dutch girls, Marijke Koger and Joskje Leeger, both aged twenty-three. Helping them were Marijke's husband, Simon, and their friend, Barry Finch. All had been involved with Brian Epstein's Saville Theatre. Between them they were responsible for some great designs in 1967, including a piano for John, a wall for the Apple shop in Baker Street (later condemned as being too gaudy and ordered to be repainted plain white in the post-psychedelic backlash) and a fireplace for George and Pattie's bungalow in Esher. The Fool were, in anyone's terms, *very far out*.

Felicity Green described three of them. Simon had 'longer hair than either of the girls, wearing a pendant, a purple velvet tunic, pale yellow peep-toe sandals, and some extremely form-fitting pants in pink and lime satin stripes, bias cut'.

Joskje was wearing 'blue-printed, silk braid-bound pyjamas, a blouse in three multi-coloured unrelated prints, snakeskin thong sandals up to her knees, a jewelled breastplate, and a bandeau and beads in her freak out hairdo so recently acclaimed by Paris'.

Marijke was comparatively tamely dressed in 'pigtails, purple thong sandals, beads, a string of hippie bells and a multi-coloured minifrock in the psychedelic manner'.

Their front door was 'electric blue with yellow stars'.

Those *were* the days. The aim of the group – and I remember it well – was 'to make clothes so beautiful that people would not be able to bear not wearing them'.

Today, Simon Posthuma is back in Amsterdam, and no longer married to Marijke, whom he describes as a brilliant commercial artist. They married in 1964, got high together, saw a barge called *The Beatles* on the

Rhine and thought it a sign. They took off to Athens, then Morocco, lived for a time with Bedouins in the Sahara, and thence to Madrid and Ibiza with sponsorship from 'Frederik' (whose partnership with 'Nina' was much treasured in pop's last pre-Beatle fling), and after designing a poster for Bob Dylan they fell in with Donovan, who liked them, and then with Barry Finch, who said he knew the Beatles. Then things really got off the ground.

◄ John walked into our place and saw our stuff – furniture and posters as well as clothes – and he said: "This is where I want to live."

'We did the total look. We tried to give people the total philosophy. We made people beautiful. We made men feminine – no, *not* feminine but like Louis XIV, the Sun King. We put colour into the wardrobe, into the mind and into the consciousness. Men became cavaliers. We dressed them in drug colours. In our clothes you were telling the world you turned on, had taken LSD. And of course everyone was interested. We changed what had been a drab world. The girls we dressed not sexily but like angels from Botticelli. We lived our dreams.'

Joskje and Barry Finch also live in Amsterdam, the parents of five children. They are still as happy as can be.

The fashion press in England had taken on board 'psychedelic fashion', uncomfortably but not ungenerously, by May 1967. Though the attitude to drugs never really relaxed, there was a curiously ambivalent attitude to the clothes that so obviously mirrored a wearer's openness to new sensation. In May, Jill Evans reported in the *Mirror*: 'Most people would not want to know about young men walking down Knightsbridge in their yellow and purple underwear.' Under a four-column picture seven inches high, showing a young couple embracing while a cop looks away, the story proceeds:

◄ But male model Maldwyn was merely drawing attention to a new fashion yesterday ... psychedelic underwear. "I use the word", said designer Michael Rainey, "because psychedelic is doing what you want to do. And these undersets are for when you want to take your clothes off." Purists may say that psychedelic actually means hallucination-inducing, but who is to say that the fashion is not aptly named?'

In July the *Daily Express* had the fashion artist Robb walk down King's Road with his sketchbook. Six columns wide, his drawing showed nine young people above the caption:

⟨ Is Robb exaggerating? Not a bit of it. Any fine Saturday you can see the full psychedelic fancy dress parade – everything the "delics" have thought up or even found in the old junk shops. And, of course, the current craze, bare feel with everything. The most startling stunt just in is psychedelic make-up. A flower pattern is painted or stencilled in pale pastel shades on the forehead and cheeks. The effect is strange, not really horrific if properly done, but the mind boggles at what could happen. '

There follows a list of the clothes Robb observed: striped pyjamas, frilled lace cravats, chiffon scarves, silk brocade jackets, laced sandals and so many other things that later became *so* funny ... and yet they were certainly pretty.

Even a pretty refrigerator made it into the *Daily Mirror*. One with the label 'pop art model' boasted a picture door in orange, purple, green and yellow.

Vivid descriptions of clothing and furniture swiftly became *de rigueur* in any piece of journalism. The *New Musical Express*, for instance, visited Paul in 1967 and found him 'dressed in a green floral patterned shirt and green slacks, sitting cross-legged in a large green velvet armchair. Mike McGear, Paul's brother, was just leaving with several kaftans over his arm.'

Paul McCartney remembers that for the 'All You Need Is Love' session at EMI studios in Abbey Road he wore a shirt he had painted himself. 'I stayed up all night the night before. I didn't mean to but I was drawing on a shirt. I had these pen things that you used to draw with and the ink didn't wash out. I stayed up all night doing it, and the shirt was nicked the next day. Who has it, I don't know. One of these days Sotheby's will tell.'

People in the 'youth culture' everywhere were starting to grow hair and moustaches by the end of 1967. The Beatles were certainly influential in this area, but I remember Chris Hillman of the Byrds saying that it was the Beats who had first impressed him with their long hair, way back in the late fifties.

Talking today, Chet Helms remembers being very conscious of this new visual stimulus as a mode of self-expression.

⟨ Hairstyles had a lot to do with personal identification. They allowed you before 1967 to set yourself apart from the status quo, or else a body of people who did not subscribe to the status quo could identify themselves *to each other* in this way. We've experienced enough in the last twenty years to realise now that whether one has long or short hair is not ultimately the question. '

A collector's delight. This has it all, as one would hope from the Apple Shop in its exotic first phase at the end of 1967. More was stolen and given away than ever was sold.

149

Then, however, it was different.

'People hadn't worn *colour*, by and large, until that time. People didn't wear their hair long, didn't wear facial hair, they didn't wear jewellery – at least in terms of ethnic jewellery and that sort of thing. In the sixties there was a very important move towards tribalism, a point of cohesion for all of these people who were costuming themselves and wearing beads and colour. I remember the very first dances I went to where everyone came in costume: cowboys and Indians in America, gypsies in Europe. We would wear a river-boat gambler's coat or Western gear or a Victorian frock-coat. We had this romantic *alter ego*. We'd all be in costume and we'd look around us at all these people and say: "Well, we're crazy, and we know we're outside the law, outside the status quo, but there's too many of us to put in one gaol. They can't haul us all away.'

George Harrison saw the later Beatles' appearance from the mid-sixties onwards as a statement of dissent.

'We felt obviously that Vietnam was wrong – I think any war is wrong, for that matter – and in some of our lyrics we expressed those feelings and tried to *be* the counter-culture, to try and wake up as many people as we could to the fact that you don't have to fight. You can call a halt to war and you can have a laugh and dress up silly and that's what that period was all about: get your hair long, and grow a moustache, and paint your house psychedelic, and write songs. It was all part of our retaliation against the evil that was taking place and still is taking place.'

(Though perceived by many as trail-blazers in the fashion field, the Beatles were, surprisingly, slower than some of their imitators to adopt new hairstyles and clothes. In 1965, in Virginia City, Nevada, an artistic cat named George Hunter put together a group called the Charlatans. Attracted by the Beatles in their *Hard Day's Night* mode, the Charlatans grew their hair very fast and very long and got into very weird clothes that made the Beatles look like Gene Pitney – which, indeed, in 1965 they almost did. The Red Dog saloon, in Virginia City, Nevada, home of the Charlatans, has an honoured place in counter-cultural history – as has George Hunter. Virginia City was to the San Francisco Scene what Hamburg was to Liverpool.)

When moustaches arrived on famous faces, the *Mirror*'s Christopher Ward remarked:

By the end of 1967 the ubiquity of the moustache was complete in the music business. Here the executive staff of A & M Records in Hollywood pose for a time-capsule. Note the author posing as House Hippie on the right.

◖ This shaggy rash is spreading over the face of Britain. On the face of it, you're nobody in England these days if you haven't got half an inch of nicotine-stained hair hanging from your stiff upper lip.... There's Sean Connery, Terence Stamp, Brian Epstein, Pete Townshend, Keith Richards.... Maybe you're wondering why this ugly rash has suddenly spread across the face of Britain.... The easy and correct answer is that drooping Mexican-style moustaches have suddenly become "in". They're in because George Harrison grew one while learning to play the sitar in India ... Jean-Paul Belmondo grew one and Ursula Andress liked him still more with it ... and as if that weren't enough all the Beatles have now grown moustaches. When I heard that I just had to have one too.'

And he went on to describe buying one ready-made for what was then thirty shillings: today £1.50. Does this seem a lot of fuss about a few moustaches? It was, of course, but that is how it was then. A lot of fuss about everything.

The first 'modern moustache' was worn by a friend of mine, Danny Hutton, in 1965 in Hollywood. Danny wanted to be a successful recording artist, and his record company said they would help him – but only if he shaved off his moustache. I proposed to publicise the dilemma via an article in a fan magazine, written by another friend, Janey Milstead: 'Danny's Hairy Problem'. It was written in the form of a challenge to the readers: 'Shall he or shall he not? YOU must decide whether Danny shaves off this freaky thing.' Well, the readers clipped out and sent off their coupons, and on balance decided that he should remove the offending object and then he would be nice and smooth like all those neat English bands. He could always grow his hair long. The hottest act in the world, they reasoned, was the Beatles and *they* didn't have moustaches.

But Danny Hutton held out, kept his moustache, and in early 1966, to keep him company, I grew one. It was most unusual. Only very old-fashioned and rather *pre-war* men had them – Errol Flynn's peers, David Niven, Douglas Fairbanks, Jun., and chaps like that. Danny and I held on, quite proud of ourselves and very noticeable. In August 1966 the Beatles came to Los Angeles and thought they'd never seen anything so interesting since Jurgen Vollmer combed his hair forward in Hamburg in 1961 in the precursor to the Beatles fringe. So they grew moustaches, too. Now of course, you can see them on every other policeman and lawyer from Maine to Maui.

Fashion in San Francisco, startled into one or other form of modishness by the Beats or the Beatles, saw to its chagrin in February 1967 a distinctly blasé reception accorded to the Haight's first fashion show at the Blushing Peony. Writing in the *San Francisco Chronicle*, Joan Chatfield Taylor reported:

❛ The Haight-Ashbury's first fashion show was a shock to me not because it was so way out and hippie and avant garde but because it was so conservative and establishmentarian.

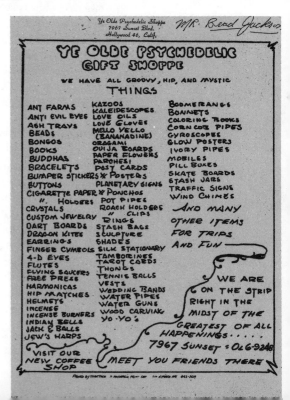

One Hollywood idea of a Good Time. The contents, however, indicate a width and depth of stock that suggest many Good Vibes and everything the local dope-dealer could desire. The author's personal favourites today would be 'hip matches'. And let's be fair – anything that lists items from ant farms to wind chimes is really trying. Note the eclecticism of Fonda and Shankar.

'There were the usual artifacts of every so called hippie event – the far out invitations, the light show, the flowers and the rock 'n' roll – but the atmosphere was no more relaxed and spontaneous than the ritualistic opening of a couture collection at Dior in Paris.... The most successful [designs] were usually the simplest – the swinging tent dresses in huge Paisleys and swirling abstract prints.'

By March 1967 the *Washington Post* was reporting that 'Psychedelia had gone mainstream'. In a long article, Leroy F. Aarons noted that there was no denying the symbols, sights, sounds and ambience of the 'so-called drug culture' were being rapidly appropriated by the taste-making establishment – the publicists and press agents, the advertising agencies and fashion designers 'who mold the tastes of New York and by extension the nation'.

◀ With this development comes a second phenomenon: the emergence of a new breed of youth promoters, young enterprising ideas people who are plugged into the under-25 scene and are thus in a position to sell their services to an older generation anxious to exploit the multi-billion dollar youth market.'

Such people, commonplace today, made news then. The article talks in arch terms of 'visionary artists whose work is LSD-based'. The New York Coliseum was to be 'turned over to the first International Psychedelic Exposition, a showcase of art, crafts, medical and legal information, and a psychedelic market-place featuring such goods as a handmade waterpipe for smoking marijuana or hashish. The exposition is the idea of Murray Levy, 24, an artist who sees almost unlimited commercial possibilities in the psychedelic movement.'

It was explained that the cultural trappings of the 'drug cult' were becoming part of the fabric of everyday life. Peter Max made an early appearance in the article, described as a

153

◀ one-man idea factory producing glassware, wallpaper, fabrics, tiles, running a yoga school and serving as an industry consultant on the youth market ... Max, an LSD alumnus, says that psychedelic art is "the new innovatory carryover of pop and mod, but sort of refined". His own designs are kaleidoscopic, making use of the Eastern mandala form (a circle encompassing a field of sinuous convoluted objects; an image used an an object of meditation by Buddhist monks and adopted as a symbol by the LSD cult) and organic flower forms in modified art nouveau style.'

There was enormous fun to be had from guessing who among the unreachably famous had 'turned on' or 'dropped acid' and all of that. 'JFK got high' was often heard among the hissings of dopers, in between the sharp intakes of breath as the joint was inhaled, accompanied by a little fresh air to help the smoke 'hit' the bloodstream more quickly. I even heard someone say, 'Selwyn Lloyd was turned on by ——,' naming one of the young movers who were such a part of the sixties, bright young things who were somewhat on the make, but not anti the counter-culture and altogether nicer as a 'gang' than Eighties Thrusters and Big Bangers. Selwyn Lloyd or JFK – who knew? It was a cheerful concept, and we were convinced that if these people did indeed smoke marijuana or had LSD they would be all the better for it and would certainly, in their innermosts, be anti-war. What dreams!

However, there were some interestingly wrong assumptions about some of the most obviously artistic and energetic members of the counter-culture, or those who sympathised with, financed or supported it. A lot of people didn't 'take drugs' at all, or came to them either 'after work' or after the height of the madness – say, in 1968 or 1969. By his own account, Joe Boyd, moving comfortably among the swirls and paisleys and tripped-out hepcats of UFO, didn't take LSD until after that was all over. Peter Blake, whose *Sgt Pepper* cover, folded out, stood up and surrounded by candles made many an altarpiece for an acid trip from the second half of 1967 until the turn of the decade, has never taken any drugs at all.

The essence of 'belonging' was in fact in 'being'. That was why the Beatles sang 'Baby you're a rich man too'. We could all come into the land of the truly living if we were open and free. There was now available a different way of seeing that need have nothing to do with drug-taking.

The changed consciousness of the sixties resulted from an observer's response to the stimuli all around him. There was now every sort of chance to tune in to the new freedoms: in long hair and moustaches; in the wearing of nostalgic or ethnic clothes, brightly coloured, hectically

William S. Burroughs, 'Bill' to his friends. Still alive and very well despite a ruggedly 'different' life, Burroughs was a Figure to stop the counter-cultural traffic in the sixties.

154

patterned, or of fragrant oils (patchouli was *the* fragrance of the era); and – as we've seen – by the adoption of Eastern religions. In the affluence and expansiveness of the age, anyone could join anything, and it was quite beyond me why everyone I knew didn't take LSD. Then they would have been on the inside, having so much *fun*, instead of on the outside, grizzling.

Society does need order; thankfully not everyone took LSD. One who didn't was Jim Haynes – a leading cheerer-up of the era. He was involved in so many innovations in the alternative arts, including the primary stages of *IT*, the newspaper, and UFO, the club. An American with a fondness for Europe, Jim had a theatrical background. In Edinburgh in the early sixties he opened a bookshop and theatre, the Traverse. Haynes was all for letting *everything* hang out and he rapidly became everybody's friend. He was a comfortable reassuring figure, utterly fearless and very inventive. He was, like everyone else, a Beatles fan and had an accurate notion of the special stimulus they brought to the 'underground' where, despite their wealth, they were totally accepted and very much at home.

‹ They were fans of the newspaper, the *International Times*, and of what I was trying to do in the Arts Lab, and really supporters of the whole international underground. This feeling that they were with us was a great source of encouragement and strength. One felt that they were going to spread the word, and it was a good feeling.'

Haynes's Arts Laboratory was one link in a chain of Good Things spread across Europe. Never, as I say, a member of the 'drug' subculture, Haynes today confirms that *his* addictions were to chocolate and women. He functioned to bring people together, which was Pure Sixties and very successful.

‹ Let a million flowers bloom has always been my philosophy. First the bookshop in Edinburgh, and the Traverse Theatre, still today a place that brings people together. Then the Arts Lab in London which became very quickly the headquarters of the underground in the sixties. That and UFO, where the dances were held, were the places people could meet. At the Arts Lab my policy was never to say no. When anyone approached me to do something, I said yes automatically. We just had to see where we could fit it in.

'I remember two dancers arriving from Buenos Aires, wanting to work. The theatre was booked until one in the morning so we put them on then. I said: "Let's see if we can get an audience." We got musicians together for them, and then about 12.30 a.m. the audience drew up in taxis from all over London and the recital ran for a long

time from one in the morning. Where now could you see dance at
1 a.m.?

'We also used space *not* in the Lab in Drury Lane. One of our
outstanding productions was called *Tea with Miss Gentry*. People
would arrive to go to a theatre performance, buy a theatre ticket,
and then we would lead them down Drury Lane and up some
rickety stairs where they would have tea with this incredible woman
and talk to her, and she would talk to them. I think she had once
designed hats for theatrical productions. People came from Holland,
Germany, Spain, France.... We paid for the tea, and Miss Gentry
served it.... She would ask where they were from and talk to them
and it was an outstanding production.'

Haynes and his friends Miles of the Indica bookshop and John Hopkins
of the *International Times* were bookish people. The written word was
still as important as the Visual or the Aural. There was no video (though
there were a few machines in the homes of the wealthy and adventurous,
used only for home taping), and people spent a great deal of time just
talking to each other if talking was their 'bag'. There was a counter-
argument that 'words don't make it, man', which was one of the themes
of dope-smoking, but, for all that, poets were doing well and had an
honoured place on the scene, and of course the underground press was
thriving, nurturing good reporting as well as pretty designs and
surprising photographs.

There were still heroes of the word like Burroughs and Ginsberg, and
Adrian Mitchell and Alexander Trocchi. Jeff Nuttall was a great man of
many words who knew all these others and we have his 1968 book, *Bomb
Culture*, to prove it. He makes it clear that he began the book in autumn
1967 and finished it in autumn 1968, when he wrote in the preface: 'In
that period young people under various pretexts made war on their
elders and their elders made war on them. The war continues.' I love the
book and recommend it to anyone wanting a fabulous ride through the
Upheaval of which 1967 was part.

Other 1967 books of lasting honour and fame are Marshall McLuhan's
The Medium Is the Massage, published in a long narrow format of great
originality. This sort of stuff is commonplace now, but then it was
startlingly new. The layout of the book, its impact in terms of typography,
photographs and design, was to me refreshing and exciting. McLuhan
had his detractors, and has gathered more since his death, but he had a
great original mind and, being in his prime in the explosive sixties, had
been able to bring his unique observation to bear on a world that began
for him just after the death of Edward VII, encompassed two world wars
and then saw satellite television and moon landings. His was the

concept and the phrase 'The Global Village', and today Timothy Leary credits McLuhan with the phrase popularly accredited to him – 'Turn on, tune in and drop out' – which apparently arose during a conversation the two of them had in the earlier sixties.

R. D. (Ronnie) Laing, psychoanalyst, psychiatrist and author, still thrives today, a sagacious and cheerful man whose study of schizophrenia, *The Divided Self*, is respected at the highest levels. His 1967 book, *The Politics of Experience and the Birth of Paradise*, has enormous merit. The most cheering aspect of it for me is that in it Laing shows that there is a means of dealing with life. It is invidious to quote any one passage as being typical, but I will do so anyway.

❛ **True sanity entails in one way or another the dissolution of the normal ego, that false self competently adjusted to our alienated social reality: the emergence of the "inner" archetypal mediators of divine power and through this death, a rebirth and the eventual re-establishment of a new kind of ego functioning, the ego now being the servant of the divine, no longer its betrayer.** ❜

Adrian Mitchell, poet, radical, brilliant performer at readings, and brave dissenter in the sixties, has emerged as a prolific playwright today. Still fired by good causes, a consistent thorn in the side of the illiberal in our society.

The sixties saw, at last, an unembarrassed twentieth-century 'street' poetry primarily made available by Trocchi and Mitchell and by the 'Mersey' (or 'Liverpool') poets: Roger McGough, Brian Patten and Adrian Henri (the last also a painter). The Mersey Poets, though pre-dating 1967 by some years, had made their audience come to terms with a merry naturalness unknown in poetry in this century. In the late sixties they were anthologised, and have received sustained literary and public attention since.

The most famous poets from Liverpool were, of course, John Lennon and Paul McCartney. 'Penny Lane' is a naïve poetic masterpiece, and Allen Ginsberg says that he put the lyrics to 'A Day in the Life' into his anthology of twentieth-century verse because it had clear imagery, a strong use of vernacular (the first time anyone used 'Oh Boy!' in a poem).

Indeed, the whole of *Sgt Pepper* is chockful of poetry. John said later that 'Within You Without You' was his favourite 'George' song, and the message was simple and true: when we had seen beyond ourselves we might find peace of mind.

Poetry was everywhere in 1967, at readings in places as far apart as the Roundhouse or the Fillmore ballroom. Words were a powerful force, and if dope made some folk inarticulate – and it did – it led others to babble twice as fast and fluently as in their 'grounded' condition.

British television went over to colour on the BBC's second channel in

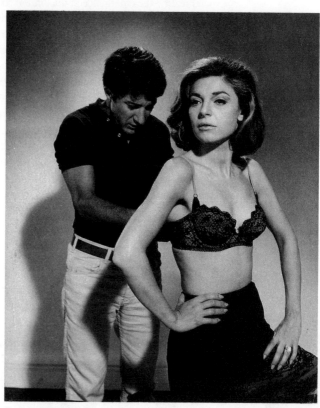

Dustin Hoffman and Ann
Bancroft in a scene from
the film that surely needs
no caption.

1967, and for all seekers the greatest show of the year was 'The Prisoner', the thirteen-parter created by George Markstein and starring the great Patrick McGoohan who also produced it. 'The Prisoner' was a wonderfully baffling, cleverly filmed, totally menacing allegory set in the north Wales architectural showplace of Portmeirion, itself (though rather earlier) very *sixties*, impersonating as closely as possible an Italian village with only the encroachment of damp Welsh weather to give the lie to the illusion. The Prisoner, with his weekly cry in the opening sequence, 'I am not a number – I am a free man!' was perfectly on target for the times. The Beatles met McGoohan by arrangement with a view to doing something together. It never actually happened, but that was often the case.

American television in 1967 was full of colour, and some nice shows were in their prime: 'Bewitched', 'I Dream of Jeannie' and 'The Man from UNCLE' among them. This last launched Robert Vaughn and David McCallum as superstars and sex symbols (particularly McCallum, riding the tide of British in-ness), but there were other shows we should note: 'Gilligan's Island' (described by Andrew J. Edelstein in his iconoclastic breezy book, *The Pop Sixties*, as 'a show that captured perfectly the zeitgeist' – that word again – 'of mid-60s lunacy'); 'I Spy', with Bill Cosby and Robert Culp (a programme of great style, featuring for the first time on television a black actor in a non-comedy part); and 'Get Smart', the show created by Buck Henry and Mel Brooks and starring Don Adams. It launched what became one of the cringe-phrases of the age: 'Would you believe...?' You couldn't go an hour without hearing someone say it in Los Angeles.

The American show that really spoke of the new age of Free was, however, the 'Smothers Brothers Comedy Hour', and this was launched in February 1967. It immediately attracted a young, anti-war, long-haired following. It was bright, up to the minute, and it tried to be brave but it was frequently censored by CBS, who in these fraught times did deserve some credit for standing by the show at all. The censorship now looks extraordinary. Would you believe they banned Pete Seeger from singing a stanza from the anti-war song 'Waist Deep in the Big Muddy'?

The year also saw the arrival of films for the New Year. *The Graduate*, an Oscar nominee beaten to the statuette by *In the Heat of the Night*, was the first film to touch the spot with the Beatles student generation. It starred Dustin Hoffman, bang on time, and the more mature of his two co-stars, Anne Bancroft, though one generation older and hardly counter-culture, seemed off-screen to be one of us. Mike Nichols's direction was right on, and the notion of having Simon and Garfunkel provide the songs was not only an inspiration but also seminal. Rock musicians were totally new to mainstream film soundtracks.

That the hit 'Mrs Robinson' was, incredibly, beaten to a film music Oscar by 'Talk to the Animals' from another 1967 film, the sadly flawed *Doctor Dolittle*, underlines perfectly the time-lag in *understanding* from which the Hollywood establishment has always suffered.

The Beatles had won nothing for the songs in either *A Hard Day's Night* or *Help!* and would have to wait until the seventies for an Oscar (for *Let It Be*).

Movie exploitation of the era was inevitable. *The Trip* was written by Jack Nicholson and starred Peter Fonda, Dennis Hopper, Susan Strasberg and Bruce Dern. This was a Roger Corman enterprise for American International Pictures, who had marketed the Beach Party films. Today Peter Fonda remembers:

❝ Jack wrote an incredibly fine script. After I read it, I burst into tears. I felt privileged to be acting in what I thought would be the first American art film, but I wasn't able to stretch my imagination by going to the editing-room. It turned out to be more of a flashing-light situation. Still I was pleased with the musicians – rock people – I hired. ❞

The film of course involved three of the actors who would make magic of *Easy Rider*.

One of the most keenly awaited films in counter-cultural circles across the world was *How I Won the War*, directed by Richard Lester of *A Hard Day's Night* and *Help!* fame, and featuring, in a generally excellent cast, that unrivalled counter-culturalist, John Lennon. In the event, though seriously made, brightly acted and very anti-war, the film was perhaps something of a disappointment. It was the lead story in the very first edition of *Rolling Stone* in the autumn of 1967 (and was it not the film John saw in 'A Day in the Life'?) but, for all that, he was not afterwards encouraging to anyone who asked him if he wanted to make another film.

Hollywood had blockbusters that year: *Bonnie and Clyde* ensnared and ensured a following (ageing now but still not old) for Warren Beatty and Faye Dunaway. Though a period piece, and violent in a love-and-peace time, the film was somehow just right for the under-thirties audience. *Guess Who's Coming to Dinner* – a *concerned* movie – was another success, and there were, too, *The Dirty Dozen* and the Oscar-winning *In the Heat of the Night* (Rod Steiger got Best Actor for that, and Katherine Hepburn got hers for *Guess Who's Coming to Dinner*). David Hemmings, one of the pin-ups of the year for his display of cool in the 1966 *Blow-Up*, came through the glitzy splendour of the sets and costumes of *Camelot* (alongside hellraiser Richard Harris) as a man to watch.

Poster art in San Francisco

A gentle symbol of the era.
How innocuous it seems
now, with the West
choking on deadly white
powders and drowning in
liquor

A classic poster of the day –
one of many hundreds to
speak volumes about the
counter-culture. This one
was by Alton Kelly
(Mouse–Kelly Studios)

The Fool ham it up for the camera, with Graham Bond (right)

Psychedelic bread at a London railway station. Even then this was not an everyday event – it was baked for an IT Happening

Nigel Waymouth (*centre*)
and fellow-artists. Nigel
opened the shop 'Granny
Takes a Trip', designed
many colourful things and
events, and is now a *fine
artist*.

Pattie and George Harrison
and the author in the
Haight-Ashbury. The scarf
on the right was bought in
Carmel. It is pure silk and
still in service. But where
now is that shirt?

Some of the Merry
Pranksters just hangin' out

A Happening in Piccadilly,
London. John Hopkins and
Suzy Creemcheese were
there. So were Granada
Television's cameras, and
the press and the police in
the end.

A human mandala –
something you won't be
seeing much of from now
on

Young Abbie Hoffman goes bananas burning money

A booth in the bazaar at the Monterey Pop Festival. A wise investor would have bought the lot, but that wasn't where we was at then, man

Harris, a great madman of the period, had part of the set of *Camelot* installed in his house in London. I have a misty recollection of visiting it that Christmas of 1967, shortly after smoking opium, and feeling that the world was indeed a very interesting place and, for one brief shining moment, might just *be* Camelot.

A scene from *How I Won the War* with (*left to right*) Roy Kinnear, Ronald Lacey and John Lennon. Ron and John became friends during the filming, with a shared sense of irony and fun.

This decoration is included
to celebrate the Diggers
and in honour of the late
Emmett Grogan (with
scarf cap and V-sign), who
became my friend.
Granada-interviewed Peter
Berg is second right.

162

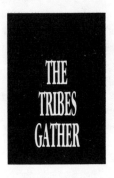

FIVE

THE TRIBES GATHER

The fifties and early sixties were a period of consolidation, a time of unabashed materialistic response to the shortages and privations of world war. The American crewcut, a tonsorial aberration of surpassing ugliness, was symptomatic of the serious *butchness* of the post-war years.

Allen Cohen, founding editor of the San Francisco underground newspaper, the *Oracle*, sees the seeds of the late-sixties counter-culture in this period:

‘ The women went back to their homes, the soldiers came back from the war, the baby boom began, the economy recovered because there was such a release of pent-up consumer demand. The Marshall Aid plan was devised to protect Europe from socialism and to protect a market for United States goods in a Europe that had been devastated. There was, consequently, a prolonged consumer boom of tremendous size, and out of that affluence, reacting against it, came the Beats, followed by the wider cult of the juvenile: "rebels without a cause". Kerouac’s novels, Ginsberg’s *Howl*, expressing the emptiness of the consumer society, were followed by the interaction of spontaneity and jazz with the movement, and then came rock ’n’ roll, and LSD and marijuana. Mix it all together and you get hippies.’

163

Abbie Hoffman, hippie, yippie, radical street fighter, agrees.

‘ The whole of the sixties wouldn’t have happened without the fifties. It might seem a cliché but social change is dictated by cycles and contradictions. At the height of the American Empire we had all the bombs, all the cops in the world – and it was all *ours* – the Cadillacs, the two-car garages, the split-level ranch houses. And at that particular moment, seeing the lifestyle of the status-seekers, the upward mobility of what today are called yuppies – style-conscious, anxious, desperate always to be ahead of fashion – well, enough people looked at that and said: "This is boring. This is spiritually unrewarding. There must be something else." So slowly people started to question authority, to be outraged about racism, to question other things.'

Hoffman says, having taken LSD and marijuana, people read in the media that they were bad for you and couldn't accept that. That was *not* their personal experience. Then they read about the Vietnam war and began to think that possibly they were being lied to about that as well. People could compare what they were experiencing, what they were feeling, seeing, hoping for, with what they were being told. Where their vision of reality conflicted with that which the Establishment offered was the flashpoint of revolution. The numbers of dissenters grew. Maybe they never became a majority, even among the young, but there were enough of them to force changes. And right there, in those changes, were the Beatles.

Suddenly and shockingly, early in 1967, one of the Beatles, Paul McCartney, started to talk politics. Unheard of! On Granada Television in England he said of himself cheerfully:

❝ Oh, people think: "He's cracked now, he's nuts." Once they see you say something about Vietnam they think: "Ah, *that's* what he is – a Vietnam crank. That solves it." I really wish people who look with anger at the weirdos, at the happenings and psychedelic freakouts, would instead of looking with anger look with nothing. If they could be unbiased about it, they'd realise that what these people are talking about is something they'd really like for themselves: personal freedom.'

164

The politicisation of rock 'n' roll performers, so familiar today, was very slow to emerge. I remember being surprised to hear the Beatles boo Los Angeles police restraining a fan at Dodger Stadium in 1966 – it seemed out of character, a Symbolic Statement more Stones than Beatles. As for domestic politics, I never heard them mentioned except in *ad hominem* terms, subjectively, as they related to personal taxation and suchlike.

Abbie Hoffman

The Lennon with the Power to the People salute of 1969 and later was quite unknown in 1967. In fact, I remember my delight and surprise not long before the release of *Sgt Pepper* at hearing him praise a British television play based on Robert Tressell's book, *The Ragged Trousered Philanthropists*. It so impressed him with its skilful interweaving of debate,

Allen Ginsberg. And on the right Gary Snyder blows the conch-shell to celebrate the opening of the Human Be-In in Golden Gate Park on 19 January 1967. We should have them everywhere this year before it's too late. Come out!

plot and characterisation that he watched a recording of it over and over again on his 'new fangled machine'.

The Ragged Trousered Philanthropists is a celebrated narrative of the British left which attacks the deceit, corruption and naïvety among bosses and workers in the jerrybuilding trade, arising out of Tressell's own experience before the First World War. Nothing less 'Beatle' than this book could have been imagined before the awakenings of 1967. After that, all John's thinking-roads led to 'Working-Class Hero' and other songs of social concern that became such a hallmark of his last decade, though I don't think he ever voted in an election subsequent to 1967, and had never voted in any of the preceding years.

Brian Epstein, it's worth noting, had always been a socialist and made a point of voting Labour. I never met another rock 'n' roll manager who took such a position. They were all too keen on their personal fortunes to find attractive the high taxation inevitable under a Labour government.

McCartney's television interview didn't reach America but, later that year, the Beatles' latest album did. 'Hearing *Sgt Pepper*, smoking reefers and planning the revolution in my friend's loft, we were just overwhelmed by their vision,' Abbie Hoffman remembers.

165

❛ It summed up so much of what we were saying politically, culturally, artistically, expressing our inner feelings and our view of the world in a way that was so revolutionary. It was Beethoven coming to the supermarket! It allowed someone like myself to see the vehicle, the style, the modality in which we could put across counter-culture politics – anti-war, anti-racist, anti-bomb – and the rest is history.'

By the spring of 1967, the leaders of the counter-culture believed they were thinking along the same lines on almost everything but that there was a real need for positive action, channelled change. It wasn't enough just to tear down old forms and barriers. There were too many wandering tribes wondering about each other: the politicos, the poets, the musicians – rock, folk, jazz and avant-garde – the hippies, the hedonists, the mystics, the artists, the traders. They had a shared humanity but different goals. The politicos wanted to do something about the Vietnam War. The artists

wanted to paint. The musicians wanted to play, and the poets ... well, the poets always came nearest to seeing what was really needed. In the words of Peter Coyote, formerly a member of the San Francisco Mime Troupe, the poets were 'the public face of the public mind'. All people, the poets and visionaries of San Francisco mused, should just be together. Be *in* it together.

Allen Ginsberg says today: 'Nineteen sixty-seven was a remarkable year for young people because solitary individuals' consciousness seemed finally to come together in the Human Be-In in San Francisco. There was no hyper-rational purpose, it was a community project.'

In other words, there need be no Us and Them. Given the will, we could all *be in* this together. That was the why, the wherefore and the how of the Be-In.

Allen Cohen explains:

> The roots of the Be-In developed when an artist friend, Michael Bowen, and I were sitting on Haight Street and we watched a whole group of hippies running down the street waving signs because their commune had been busted – this was in the midst of our elation with the transcendental experiences we were having with LSD.

'They looked angry and vicious and violent as they circled the police station. We thought there had to be a better way to contend with the establishment without stooping to their level. So about two months after that, when the California legislature was going to make LSD illegal [6 October 1966 – 666, the Rising of the Beast in the Book of Revelation], we decided to have a celebration instead of a demonstration, and we called up the bands that were beginning to flourish in the Haight, and we got the permits, and we held the first outdoor rock concert, in Golden Gate Park in the Panhandle. We brought mushrooms and flowers to the Mayor's office. We got national publicity, and about 2,000 people came out to join us. We saw the vitality of the event and the interest of the press and we knew we had captured the symbolic centre of our movement. So we started to think how to make another event, even larger and more momentous.'

The Beat poet Gary Snyder was a progenitor of the subsequent Be-In, with Allen Ginsberg. 'The event was Snyder's and the Haight-Ashbury group's,' says Ginsberg.

The Human Be-In was one of the great spontaneous honest-to-God collective celebrations of the late twentieth century. The aim: to be. That was all. That was enough. Twenty thousand people came and saw and got zonked. There was no strife, no litter.

◀ Part of it was spirituality; part was ten years after the Beat generation San Francisco poetic renaissance – which was the ground for it to grow – and because we were the fathers of that scene [Gary Snyder was] invited to be the master of ceremonies and [others of us to be] the speakers, and to open and close it. Timothy Leary was invited as one of the wordmen – people had time allotted to them on a fair basis – and Jerry Rubin was there as a politico. Suzuki Roshi was meditating throughout on stage. And of course there were the great bands, the musicians.'

167

The Be-In just caught on. An idea whose time had come (a cliché now, it wasn't then), it couldn't possibly have ignited so many, many bright sparks among the organisers, seized the imagination and curiosity of so many, many thousands of wellwishers, if it hadn't been right on the pulse of the counter-culture. Among those who chose to be outside the mainstream, news of it spread like a wonderful rush of open secrets. It brought together people who had no common commitment other than to a celebration of how good it was to be alive together, in the park, on that day, at that moment in history.

There was no fierce inducement, no status symbolism, no crass business interest directing it – though the Diggers, the Super Hippies, originally members of a San Francisco mime troupe and subsequently shepherds

and marshals of their less politicised *confrères*, as helpful as could be in all practical ways, were highly sceptical about the motivating forces behind the event. Even today, Peter Coyote, an ex-Digger, will say without malice: 'It was a merchandising campaign by the Haight-Ashbury merchants. They wanted to create a national consciousness of Haight-Ashbury.'

To which the merry psychedelic trader Ron Thelin will cheerfully reply: 'Bullshit, absolute bullshit. It was a beautiful event. And the beautiful came.'

There were thousands of initiates into the counter-culture as a result of the Be-In. For some days before the event, scheduled to take place on 14 January, the build-up was overwhelming. 'Welcome' signs appeared everywhere – on boards, in windows, in the underground press – and the people invited were told that if they felt sympathetic to the project they should wear a flower, bring a musical instrument, wear bells.

Helen Perry, who wrote a warm and scholarly book entitled *The Human Be-In*, remembers obeying the injunction: 'Two days before the event, I went into a shop on Haight Street and purchased a silver chain with a bell at each end – from India, the young woman in the shop told me approvingly – and I had a sensation of having taken some monumental step.' I well know how she felt. It happened to me and to Joan later that year. In those days Helen Perry was a middle-aged social scientist studying the Haight, yet she became a seriously committed supporter of what young people represented. 'Acculturated' is her word for her new condition. And ours.

More than 20,000 people attended the Be-In. Charles Perry, a Berkeley hippie, said the scene was mind-boggling.

ᶜ **A seemingly endless sea of people, tens of thousands. And all were present for a purpose too important for words, though a steady stream of words issued from the speakers' platform at the east end of the field. The Diggers had set up tables to pass out thousands of turkey sandwiches, made from several dozen turkeys donated by Owsley Stanley. Owsley had also donated a lot of his latest LSD, White Lightning, and people were walking around in the crowd handing out these tiny white tablets, the most professional-looking and also the strongest LSD tablets yet.'**

Helen Perry remembers a human stream of communicants, men, women, children, babies, dogs. The dogs didn't fight, the babies didn't cry. The Hell's Angels became child-minders, and while the bands played the poets read aloud and the chanters paid no heed to the hubbub. All was sweetness, and the light over the field was clear and clean; it was a perfect San Francisco day, midwinter and yet warm. Children walked around nude. There were banners as at some medieval event. Had there been no visible outgrowth from that first gathering of the tribes, no Monterey festival, no Easter cosmic how's-your-father, no LA Love-Ins, no attempt to levitate the Pentagon, it would still have been a seminal event. As it happened, it began a massive expansion of consciousness and redeemed the year.

Helen Perry writes:

‹ In the midst of the afternoon, out of a clear noiseless sky, a man attached to a billowy parachute that looked like a huge cloud drifted down from the sky above. No-one announced it but the message seemed to go soundlessly throughout the huge crowd ... no airplane was heard, there was no sign of where he came from, and we all treated it as a latter-day miracle.'

There was wine, incense, food and pot.

‹ But none of these was necessary as I can testify ... afterwards, walking towards the car, we did not have much to say ... most of the people looked tired and droopy but our eyes met in a secret delight. We had in common the sound of a different drummer.'

Allen Ginsberg led the clean-up, chanting a kitchen mantra, and there was no litter. It all worked. In the *San Francisco Chronicle*, under the headline 'They Came, Saw, Stared', there was a not ungenerous report on the 'bizarre union of love and activism celebrated on the Polo Field ... marking the first annual feast of the incongruous. All the high priests of both movements turned out in their costumes to be stared at. It was

A Digger handing out free food. The Digger ethic was Free. Free everything. It could work and often did. Today's shibboleth, 'There's no such thing as a free lunch', would have been burned in the market-place in 1967 and the ashes mailed to the Governor's mansion. Of course there's such a thing as a free lunch; the monetarists have them every day – on expense accounts, handing over bits of plastic to pretend they are paying.

169

Hanging out in the Haight: young people in happy times

said to involve the far-out Berkeley political activists and the further-out love-hippies of the Haight-Ashbury district. Mostly it was a staring match, all eyeballs. Many of those staring were dogs.' The *Chronicle* noted the clothes, tiaras, sequins and silver lamé. 'No nudes were noticed,' they said. The entertainment included Lenore Kandel, whose *Love Book* was a favourite in the *Chronicle* reportage of the era. The bands named by the *Chronicle* were the Quicksilver Messenger Service and Jefferson Airplane, but the actual assemblage had included the Grateful Dead (acid's house band), Big Brother and the Holding Company, the Loading Zone, and the Sir Douglas Quintet. (Nationally this last band was the best known, having had a big hit single, 'She's About a Mover'.)

The local newspaper coverage was as exact as could be expected and, as I say, not aggressive. It was, for an unnamed reporter meeting the counter-culture *en masse*, not an easy assignment. For a start he had to describe a former Harvard professor holding a daffodil. 'Dr Timothy Leary, the apostle of LSD, was decked out in white for the occasion. He had a lei of flowers and beads around his neck.' The newsreel cameras also picked up on Leary and his imagery for the television masses outside Golden Gate Park. 'Leary made a speech', continues the newspaper report, 'in which he advised his listeners to "Turn on, tune in and drop out". Turn on to the scene, tune into what's happening, and drop out – of high school, college, grad school, junior executive, senior executive, and follow me, the hard way.'

Leary, not forgetting his colleagues Richard Alpert and Ralph Metzner, was considered quite a martyr. Many of us admired him for the calmness with which he had seen an academic career cut short by what to us was clearly 'The Enemy', the straight world, unable to see the benefits that would flow from the personal discovery of personal inner space. Jerry Rubin, too, was some hero as a political activist. Just bailed out of gaol in Berkeley, he and Leary were two of the tribal 'leaders' so successfully brought together.

On stage, Robert Baker parodied 'The Night before Christmas' with

Santa arriving with marijuana and acid. Chet Helms and his friends danced. The police watched from a distance and made no arrests. City officials wondered how such an event could happen so happily with no more a theme than just 'being'. Was this a first time? Maybe in California, but there were those romantics who pointed to an event far away in Palestine nearly two thousand years earlier, when the multitudes had heard great wisdom, received free food 'out of nowhere', and left without a struggle, feeling, as Helen Perry had said, 'their eyes meeting in a secret delight'. It was as if, now, anything was possible in or near Golden Gate Park. If this was winter, what would spring and summer be like? Hopes were high, and so was the multitude. Very.

There wasn't one arrest at the Be-In but, alas, later that night, with crowds in the Haight prolonging the togetherness, the police waded in. There were arrests for 'refusal to disperse'.

The *Chronicle* reported the events in the Haight as 'a day of merriment and a night of arrests'. Peter Krugg of Haight-Ashbury Independent Proprietors (the HIP project involving thirty 'new wave' stores) said the police had discriminated against the Be-In crowd. 'The crowd were given no chance to disperse.' Police action was termed 'deplorable', but a police spokesman said the cops would not even deny harassment. 'We are not going to get into a debating society.'

The merchants called a meeting to discuss the arrests, described as 'the latest in a long line of problems between hippies and police'. Allen Cohen said that 'the older established groups and the new traders would, combined, draw respect from the whole community'. The Reverend Thomas Dietrich, pastor of Howard Presbyterian Church, said: 'The police role is the biggest problem.'

Battle was joined. The hippies had now decided they had real rights in the street, and insisting on unwritten rights had led to trouble long before people had even heard of hippies. There had indeed been a recent affair some 900 miles south, in Los Angeles, from which salutary lessons might have been learned.

In 1965 the Byrds had begun to attract a few very strange-looking young people to Ciro's, the old and famous club on Sunset Strip in Hollywood where they regularly played. Ciro's had been a fashionable watering-place since middle-period Hollywood when Errol Flynn and other absurdly glamorous and godlike film stars wined and dined and danced and fought there, night after night. In the early sixties the club fell from grace, and it was easy for Jim Dickson and his partner, Eddie Tickner, to get the young, fairly untried Byrds a booking there.

Byrds' 'dancers' swiftly followed: fragile young early 'flower children' in long dresses, with curious glasses hiding dreamy eyes. They moved in vapour-trail patterns to the soaring, twelve-string-led folk-rock rhythms and melodies of the trail-blazing Beatles' favourites. In due course the Lovin' Spoonful arrived from New York, and then the Mamas and the Papas and Buffalo Springfield, and the Turtles, and the Leaves, and the Grassroots, and the whole shebang of nature boys and girls. It was Hollywood A Go Go on the Strip, from the Whiskey to the newly opened Trip, taking in Gazzari's and Pandora's Box and other little hangouts. It had become a wonderful place to be at weekends.

Young people came to see and be seen, to wonder and be wondered at. They were not yet hippies. Los Angeles was not San Francisco, more a vast conurbation dedicated to the great god Automobile, but nevertheless by 1966 the kids *had* taken to the streets – to be met by instant and savage repression.

Jim Dickson, an old fan of the Beats and a contemporary of James Coburn and James Dean, Marlon Brando and Dennis Hopper in latter-day Hollywood, the man who saw what the Byrds could mean, recalls what became known as 'The Sunset Strip Riots':

❮ Kids came up to the Strip in the hopes of seeing the Beatles or the Stones or the Byrds or whoever might be up here. They'd let their hair grow over the summer in 1966 and by winter they were all wearing long hair and bellbottoms and some were barefoot. The police mishandled the situation. Their decision to stop the kids had much more to do with real-estate values than with what the kids were doing. The kids had populated the Strip, made it a high-density youth area, and apparently there were people who wanted them off because they were destroying plans to make the Strip a high-rise financial district. The kids were described as "political", which they weren't; at the time they were just up for the music and the fun. The politicians were angry and hostile to them, and the police just beat them up to get rid of them.'

172

I had been working with Dickson for nearly two years. We shared offices and, to some extent, views. He had been brought up with tough local police as a routine presence in his life, but even *he* was shocked by developments on the Strip. 'The police came in platoons and charged into the crowd and beat people up indiscriminately. The Strip had been my hangout for years, and it made me mad that I couldn't get along it without passing through police lines.' Joan and I, law-abiding immigrants from provincial England, already quite intimidated by gun-toting lawmen, were just amazed. Like a recurring nightmare, each weekend night the street outside our office exploded into violence and vicious repression. It made no sense. Dickson was very American, very Republican, but he felt something had to be done.

❮ I felt I had an obligation to try and publicise what was going on. The kids hadn't done anything evil enough to bring out big crowds of police, whole platoons with billy clubs and helmets just beating people up. They arrested some 300 people one night and it never made the papers – there was nothing in the *Los Angeles Times* – and I thought this was very sinister. I found out later that in fact the figure of 300 people represented the biggest mass-arrest in California since they rounded up the Japanese after Pearl Harbor. '

A couple discussing Allen Ginsberg's 'kitchen mantra' after the Be-In

Dickson now had a duty, and I was happy to be at his side. We formed a citizens' group, Community Action for Facts and Freedom (CAFF), and monitored the demonstrations, advising everyone to obey whatever law there was. The *Los Angeles Free Press* gave us valuable publicity by running a banner headline across their front page on the 2 December 1966 edition: 'Big Money Now Backing LA Youth.'

❮ A powerful group of concerned and resourceful adults has formed to stand with the young people demonstrating for equal treatment on the Sunset Strip. The rallying point has shifted to a conference room in the plush 9000 Sunset Building, and to the Beverly Hills mansion of Woolworth heir Lance Reventlow, and to the dressing room of "Gilligan's Island" star Bob Denver. '

There followed a list of our committee, including Sonny and Cher, Beach Boy and Buffalo Springfield management, Elmer Valentine, owner of the Trip and Whiskey A Go Go clubs.

The cause proved immensely popular in the Los Angeles version of the counter-culture, which was not so much 'big money' as 'LA', an abstraction which usually involves someone having a few million stashed away. (It's one of those things that makes Los Angeles so fascinating and so awful.) CAFF had some really nice people working with it, including Jill St John, Sal Mineo, Peter Fonda, Dennis Hopper, David Anderle, Michael Vosse, and some you never heard of. There was a concert 'in aid of funds' – but really to show our pulling power – featuring Peter, Paul and Mary, the Byrds, Buffalo Springfield and the Doors. Alan Pariser produced it, and I was the MC. It was a great counter-cultural event and *very* annoying to the authorities because it was in a 'regular' venue, extremely well organised and successful.

Dickson was tireless in that period. He handed his duties as co-manager of the Byrds to his partner, Eddie Tickner, and worked only for CAFF. He picks up the story at the end of 1966:

‘ Stephen Stills wrote a protest song as a result of playing music at a club that the police had closed. We discovered that on Christmas and New Year's Eve and other national holidays you didn't need a permit to perform, so we brought the musicians down there – Stephen Stills, a couple of the Byrds and a couple of Buffalo Springfield – and as a result Stephen wrote his song "For What It's Worth". The officials thought the "trouble" was dying down just as that record was going up the charts and it became a hit single, an anthem and a link. It gave everybody the energy to go on with the demonstrations, to go on trying to press their point. In the end the police backed off, the city officials backed off, the Strip did not become high-rise, and the proposed Beverly Hills freeway was not built. ’

174

Ron Thelin and Lenore Kandel at the Human Be-In. These two embodied the Haight at its most cheerfully creative.

A few years earlier, in San Francisco, the protesters of the Haight had derailed similar high-rise and freeway plans in their neighbourhood and saved the Panhandle, which was to be the setting for so many seminal events in the late sixties.

There wasn't then, in Los Angeles, much evidence of political activism, and certainly none among the young on Sunset Strip. Little was heard about the war from the Los Angeles groups. Their feelings about Vietnam only surfaced later. The repression of the Los Angeles young was prompted purely by financial interests, enacted by biased lawmen, and then interpreted by commentators as a movement against 'the change in attitudes'. In fact the only significant change of attitude to be seen among the Sunset Strip demonstrators concerned the optimum length of a man's hair. Dickson says: 'Long hair looked better on a boy, and the girls started not wanting to go out with short-haired boys. So the boys grew their hair, and it started to worry the adults.'

The trouble that was perceived as radical change was really just Boy Meets Girl and Grows His Hair. Nothing more complicated. Not on Sunset Strip anyway.

Al Kooper remembers the impact on his life of long hair. He says today:

❛ Growing my hair meant that I looked better than I had looked before. Long hair saved a lot of people – I'm one of them. And it was also a way of keeping up with the Joneses. There were of course pros and cons. While I looked better in my opinion, it caused me a lot of trouble because, being with Bob Dylan, we went out and toured the country and no one had really seen this hair for real except on the coasts in California and New York. So when we went to certain places it was probably the equivalent of the road warriors pulling into town.

'We used to get shot at, thrown out of restaurants, refused entry into hotels, hissed at at airports – the works. It put a chip on my shoulder for a good many years. My position was "Hey, I'm the same as you only my hair is long". Probably if you were white the closest thing in this country to sharing the Negro experience was to have long hair and travel. You were treated similarly to a Negro except, of course, *you* could cut your hair.'

By 1967 the music and the hair and the street action were indivisible. One man who had been abreast of music, though not part of it, was Peter Fonda, the young actor from a famous family.

❛ I was pretty well rebelling against everything my family stood for.

With actors and the like I stayed pretty much to myself, but I did hang out with musicians. There was some feeling of accomplishment, if you couldn't practise your own art, in being around other artists. There weren't as many movies to make as there were songs that I could sing, so I used to hang out with musicians and sometimes clap hands or "doo wop" in the background or contribute whatever I could. It was enjoyable for me, and it kept me out of trouble.'

His friendship with the Byrds and Dickson drew him to Sunset Strip.

◀ The young people on the Strip felt disenfranchised. One weekend I went down with my camera to photograph it because I felt it was a very specific phenomenon. It was speaking about something which was noticeable and overt: Change. I went down there with David Crosby and Brandon de Wilde and, though we weren't really interested in whether we got past the police into the different clubs or not (we could go to recording studios and have just as much fun or to somebody's living-room to "jam"), those young people who were out there in the streets were the people who bought our records or went to our movies. I thought it was a movement that deserved to be looked at a little more closely and of course I got caught right up in it. I was the first person they arrested. My hands were manacled behind my back, and I was trying to protect my cameras as they were beating me with sticks.'

At the time Joan and I were marching with Bob Denver, then a very well-known actor on television and consequently a man with pull in Hollywood. His partner, Jeannie, had been spat on by the sheriff's deputy, and we were already fired with much anger when we saw Fonda's arrest. He was carted off in a bus. Bob Denver made a telephone call to Fonda's press agent (such is Hollywood) from the Villa Frascati, a restaurant where Denver's dining friends were astonished to see him supporting 'kids'. His agent, in Fonda's words, 'fast-talked the sheriff's department into letting me out ... for obviously I had not been "loitering". The sheriff gave me a long lecture about "not being around with these types". But I *was* these types. I wasn't a hippie, but I was certainly a disenfranchised person.'

Fonda was released that night, and he used the evening of his release first to let the kids know their rights, and next to tell the media what was going on. 'It wasn't fair to be either shut out of a club or shut out of society.' He still believes that now and says that his own children, now grown up, tell him things have changed little. The fight goes on.

The street scene in London never did get out of hand. Maybe it was

Peter Fonda – one who
dared to sing out of tune

something to do with the weather. Maybe the British are just not good at Happenings. But there were good concerts, love-ins and Technicolor dreams that year, indoors and out, and the UFO Club, run by Joe Boyd and John Hopkins, was splendid. Both university graduates, Boyd (Harvard) and 'Hoppy' (Cambridge) had individual strengths and played key parts in the London underground. Boyd was very musical and controlled, an excellent producer. Hoppy was politically sensitive, a photographer who put cameras aside just to *Be* that year. He had founded the Free School – to disseminate alternative education – which gave way to the *International Times* (of which, more later), and the UFO Club was the dance metaphor for both. Go as you please. Do your own thing. *Be!*

Chris Welch told his readers in *Melody Maker* about UFO:

❛ Today in London the Bell People already have their own headquarters, and UFO (it stands for Unidentified Flying Object or Underground Freak Out) is believed to be Britain's first psychedelic club. Happy young people waving sticks of incense danced Greek-like dances, waving frond-like hands with bells jingling, neck scarves fluttering and strange hats abounding.

'There were pretty slides casting beams of light over the jolly throng who stood or squatted in communion, digging the light show or listening to Love [the group] being relayed at sensible non-discothèque volume. There were frequent announcements warning patrons to be cool and that the fuzz [police] might pay a call. In fact two young constables did pop in and seemed wholly satisfied that all was well, and of course all *was* well. The light shows were "wild", the music "weird", but – all was well....'

Joe Boyd said at the time that he had started UFO with Hoppy in September 1966 'basically as a home for groups who were doing experimental things in pop, for the mixing of media – light shows, theatrical happenings, and avant-garde films from New York'. In UFO, an accepted headquarters for the counter-culture, these could be shown and performed before a sympathetic audience. The club was the recreation room of the underground, Pink Floyd its house band. By June 1967 the club was already oversubscribed, and membership had to be closed. Besides Pink Floyd, the bands which played there were all of the counter-culture: Soft Machine, the Bonzo Dog Doo Dah Band, Procol Harum, and the Crazy World of Arthur Brown, among others. 'All the nutters,' Paul McCartney remembers fondly. If you had the right vibes, you could play UFO. It was a friendly place and very *laissez-faire*. Boyd told *Melody Maker*:

‘ No attempt is made to make people fit into the format and this
attracts the further out kids of London. If they want to lie on the
floor they can, or if they want to jump on stage they can, as long as
this doesn't interfere with the group, of course.’

An ally of Boyd and Hoppy, Dave Howson, told *Melody Maker*: 'The
whole essence is peaceful and the message is love. I wish people would
understand and not get at us. It will come but it will take time.'

In its heyday UFO was a wonderful hangout, with a richly mixed
clientele. Paul McCartney remembers it with real affection. Its 'stars' –
actually the house band – Pink Floyd, who had cut their teeth in the Free
School with Hoppy, moving on from Hornsey College of Art where they
had got involved with light and sound experimentation, had developed
a show which linked long, mainly improvised electronic breaks with
slides and oils and moving pictures when such work was very new – well
ahead of the game.

‘ UFO was a "studenty" place, so we had no problems getting around.
It didn't matter if you were famous because students didn't want
to let on they knew you anyway. They wanted to be cool. "Hey,
we're talking about Marx over here, man." I was living in London
at the time so my house was kind of the centre. People would say:
"Let's go and see Paul, he's bound to be in, or if he isn't he'll be
down at such and such a club." It was a very small scene really.

'I think that what people forget about the Beatles is that student
attitude.... We were into films, strange music – Indian,
Stockhausen, electronic. One of the things we used to say was that
we didn't start things, we were just the most high-key participants,

the ones people saw. So in this melting-pot we all had our place, just as in the old days we could have been in, say, a Viennese coffee-shop, exchanging ideas.'

Mention of clubs like UFO in the London of 1967 brings misty eyes to Larry Smith, drummer of the celebrated Bonzo Dog Doo Dah Band, which came to national attention in 1967. They were one of the Beatles' favourite bands, the cabaret at the party to celebrate *Magical Mystery Tour*, prodigiously funny surrealists, tirelessly creative musicians, and still – long after splitting into several other ventures – a famous cult band. Larry Smith recalls:

❛ Ah, yes, I remember it well. We fell into this Irish dance-hall, tripping over hundreds of heavenly bodies that had appeared and were scattered across the ballroom floor ... it was tripping stuff. And all around and about and above, sliding blobs of coloured shapes like a bad attack of acne, floated peacefully across the faces of those wondrously vacant expressions. It was *very* ava-gardy.'

In June 1967, Chris Welch of *Melody Maker*, one of the most original writers on music in the sixties and seventies, and in his own right an accomplished jazzman, concluded firmly:

❛ A new group of young people are emerging in London today who denounce violence; who prefer to create or participate rather than to destroy or mock; who want a collective society rather than a destructive gang; love rather than hate. In the past, Teddy Boys, mods and rockers, were all cults based on violence. They were in turn encouraged by the newspapers and films and at the same time violently condemned. But nobody had shown any alternative.
'We can expect a deluge of drivel about the new people any day now from the Sunday papers, with demands to "stamp out this evil in our midst".'

179

And it was to pre-empt the cliché'd inevitabilities of the tabloid mentality that Welch came up with his own phrase, 'The Bell People'. It never caught on, but it did have a nice ring to it.
There was a supra-human lack of aggravation in UFO and similar clubs – the Middle Earth and other hangouts – owing partly to an almost total absence of alcohol (none was sold or allowed on the premises, and few people arrived with any already inside them), partly to the ingestion of marijuana (mostly off but sometimes on the premises), but perhaps most of all to the prevailing attitude of the times.

Boyd still remembers the tremendously joyful feeling of the early days of UFO:

❝ It was visited first by people who were fairly productive in the counter-culture – who had, say, a stall on Portobello Road or who were graphic artists – and then there was a second wave of what the press might call "hippies", and then there was a third wave of tourists and pop fans, who wanted to see the Pink Floyd because they were now immensely popular.

'UFO went through a series of evolutions, each one getting wider and wider, and always with external trappings of velvet clothes, long hair, incense, paisley patterns, all the clichés you hear about. But there were a lot of people who just came as they were, who didn't wear that sort of thing at all.'

In July the *News of the World* struck out against UFO, with extraordinary warnings against the 'hidden dangers' it represented, waxing extremely long-winded and arch about the reasons for the orderly patience and obedience of the queues that formed every weekend outside the club for the concerts and dancing to be held there. In fact there was no tension because a splendid time was guaranteed for all, from the music, lights and, in Boyd's words, 'a feeling of family or neighbourhood'. UFO was for people who knew each other, not in a cliquey way but finding in each other a sense of mutual warmth and understanding. They dressed alike, enjoyed the same kind of music, had the same interests and the same feelings. The club had, Boyd recalls, a tremendously joyful atmosphere in the early days.

The *News of the World*, in a series of features with 'Shock Probe' headlines, talked of the club-going 'hardcore flower children, sheeplike in devotion to those with loudest voices, with passionate beliefs'. There were lists of 'types' – pacifists, draft-dodgers, work-shy dropouts. 'Your flower child', the paper warned, has 'opted out of all society's accepted patterns. He never drinks alcohol and never eats meat.' And then the killer: 'The most fanatical members of the cult eat only macrobiotic food, things like rice especially imported from China, spiced with special herbs and chutneys from health food shops.'

The article droned on in that escalating, list-making way of similar case-building exercises. The Beatles were sideswiped ever so slightly for signing the Legalise Pot petition, and for providing the year's anthem, 'All You Need Is Love'. (As we have seen, they were still as yet protected property. The time for their 'We Name These Evil Men' treatment was yet to come.) Then there was sex. 'The flower children believe in Free Love, sex for sex's sake with whoever takes their fancy.' As opposed to doing it with someone you *didn't* like?

The paper then named UFO as the hotbed of this pernicious cult and ran pictures of people dancing, 'many with flower motifs ... oblivious faces ... frenzied music ... weirdly dressed men and women jerking to the full volume ... men dancing with men, girls dancing with girls. One girl danced on her own all night.' There was talk of freaking out, couples lying on the floor, people in sequins, loose robes, men in make-up, one in a mink coat.

John Boyd remembers the knocking articles coming thick and fast. Then Joe Gannon, the cheerful Irishman who had let UFO use his ballroom, was visited by the previously indifferent police, who now told him: 'It's over.' Says Boyd:

> The fascinating thing about Mr Gannon's relationship with the police was that he could keep them away under any other circumstances – there'd been all sorts of provocations before then with people taking their clothes off in the dance-hall, drug busts in the queues, etc., etc. – but the *News of the World* articles were too much. The policemen all read the *News of the World*. It provoked a reaction, and that was that. I don't think there was any real commitment behind the newspaper's campaign. The *News of the World* felt that it could sell a lot of papers by focusing national attention on the behaviour of hippies, and the next day Mr Gannon was told by a detective: "You can't let those people have the club or we'll raid it. You'll be on the line."'

Not many days before the San Francisco Be-In, Chet Helms of the Family Dog came to London to see UFO and find out what was happening in the European counter-culture. His visit was monitored by Nick Jones of *Melody Maker*, a young writer generous and committed to the alternative society now establishing itself behind the scenes, and to the underground. Chet Helms told Jones:

> Two very important factors emerged in the evolution of the young in the US; they have altered the whole life structure. First, God died

The Living Theatre auditioning for 'Stars on Sunday' at the Roundhouse. A prize of £10,000 for anyone who finds a similar gathering today.

in 1966. By that I mean that religion no longer holds any water. Secondly, half of America's population is under 25. This has resulted in a generation that has become confident of its youth and its ability to outlive the older generation. Out of this confidence has stemmed the formation of a new institution of social intimacy.'

Recalling that visit today, Chet Helms says that he wanted to hook up with London in 1967:

❝ Because I wanted to make a connection with another powerful world centre of ideas and thought. So, in London, I was going to look for a place and open a club. After three or four days I realised, "This is lunacy. I'm not going to run a business from 8,000 miles away," so then I relaxed and had a good time and met a lot of characters. Hoppy and Miles of IT [*International Times*] showed me around. I was taken to UFO and I saw Pink Floyd in their original incarnation, when I don't think anyone in the band could play a break. At that time it was pretty well all feedback and lights.'

Later that month, in the thick of winter, London was visited by another member of the American counter-culture, Suzy Creamcheese, a lovely nineteen-year-old, beloved of the alternative society and styled by the *Daily Mirror* 'Leader of American Happenings'. She made her public début with Hoppy in Piccadilly Circus, holding a sign saying 'Pot Is Fun' and

Evangelism and fun: Suzy Creamcheese and friends demonstrate in Piccadilly. The police arrived, but there was no unpleasantness.

Chet Helms, the Texan
dreamer who ran the
Avalon in San Francisco,
one of the great ballrooms
of the counter-culture

'Legalise Pot' (the latter with the middle 'l' missing, as the ever pedantic *Mirror* caption-writer pointed out). There were a few journalists standing by, and a Granada television crew. A number of passers-by showed only fleeting interest – the weather, as ever, prompting them to move on quickly – and then, after some fruit had been passed out to onlookers, and two girls had been bound to lamp-posts with toilet paper, the London bobbies, whistling the policemen's song from *The Pirates of Penzance* under their breath, happened by. 'Right, that's enough', and, as the *Mirror* said, 'the Happening was over'.

The great Hoppy later married Suzy Creamcheese. Because he was so much a symbol of the free and joyful essence of the London underground, he was an easy target for the police. He was busted for allowing dope to be smoked in his flat. He was gaoled for nine months on 1 June 1967, the same day as the release of the *Sgt Pepper* album. No summer of love for Hoppy.

The attractive and brilliant young Australian Richard Neville arrived in London at the end of 1966 with the reputation of 'Rebel Aussie Whizz Kid', having been sentenced to six months for publishing 'an obscene magazine' – *OZ*. The sentence was quashed on appeal and Neville, in the more open mood of London, much fêted. The British *OZ* was launched in 1967 and became a great and famous Fun 'n' Freedom magazine of the *later* sixties. The year 1967 for Richard was his British beginning – a happy one, but he was later to end up in the British courts facing a very repressive judge.

The *International Times* had had its share of strife already. Barry Miles, usually known simply by his surname, had more or less begun the thing as an extension, or indeed part, of Indica, a bookshop and gallery he started in a room off Piccadilly in 1966 with his friend John Dunbar. Both were twenty-three. Miles said in 1967:

❛ **The paper and Indica are related in that I'm a director of both. The aims of the shop and the paper are more or less the same. The bookshop is the centre, the collecting point of information *and* the disposing point of information. It's the communication centre of the underground.** ❜

An underground that contained such overground people as the Beatles, and those who were half and half like Allen Ginsberg and William Burroughs.

❛ **It is a completely internal scene: we have our own publishing, our own film-makers, theatres, nightclubs, and so it is a complete society.** ❜

He says now, as he prepares a biography of his friend Ginsberg:

❮ Indica was the place where ideas could be promoted and experimental literature, poetry, ideas from the sixties could be discussed and pushed. It was a sort of editorial statement. It wasn't to make money. It stocked the small literary and mimeo-magazines from America and the underground newspapers, and we had a constituency of people who had an advanced, questioning view of life. The newspaper, *IT*, was designed as a community event where anyone could have input. We finished up catering to the skinheads, just emerging, and to hardcore unreconstructed hippies living in communes in Wales; to vegetarians on one side and bikers who liked nothing better than a McDonald's, on the other. So in the end everyone who felt disaffected from society was catered to. '

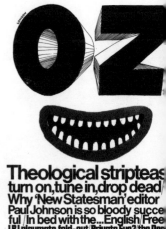

The cover of the first issue of London *OZ*.

IT was fortnightly and cost a shilling (5p) when it hit its stride, which it did quite quickly. A fabulous all-night rave-up was held in the Roundhouse in October 1966 to celebrate the birth. Indica gallery stayed with John Dunbar; Miles went to set up new premises for Indica bookshop and *IT* in Bloomsbury.

'It had the romance of being in a basement', says Tom McGrath, who came from *Peace News* via a respite in rural Wales to edit it.

❮ It was very exciting and exhausting. At the core we had a great spirit and camaraderie with people seriously working, and making things happen. Hoppy would turn up with ideas and streams of news items which we'd get down quickly. Ginsberg's back in town, so and so's fallen down in Ladbroke Grove. Names, unknowns, happy people, victims, jazz people.... We were not in isolation. There was a lot happening. *IT* was read by young people the length and breadth of London, and some older ones, Bohemians and beatniks.'

IT had such romance, hard to imagine now with overground *Time Out* and *City Limits* so available and acceptably alternative. They are respectively the child and grandchild of *IT*, very much of their time and valuable, but the sixties were different times and you'd never have found *IT* in W. H. Smith's. In any case, circulation was well into 10,000 copies without Smith's. Without a glimmer of pretension *IT* did have great contemporary cachet. It was a privilege to be published in it, but just about anybody could be if they were thinking well. It had absolutely rock-solid 'street cred' and yet it was really good fun. There was no cynicism.

Like the Be-In, the basic philosophy of a gathering of the tribes was a vital aspect of *IT*. McGrath was an old radical (though still in his twenties) and keen to bring together the cultural and political left. *IT* also had support from famous avant-garde capitalists. One such fan was the young McCartney, ever keen on self-improvement. He was a friend of Miles and looks back happily on the really basic days of *IT*.

❛ I remember sitting in his flat putting the paper together. That was *the* news-organ of the time, where you could get your little piece of news or views in and do your interview and swear without anyone minding. Because, again, it was a studenty-type thing. You knew it wasn't going to be tut-tutted at by grown-ups. It was good to be involved with Miles on *IT*, and with his friends, like Ginsberg. We were very interested in all of that because we'd come up through the pop world and become known as the cute little headshakers, and that had submerged that slightly offbeat "arty" side of us. *IT* *was* the other side of us.'

Tom McGrath, a Scotsman with a good knowledge of 'straight politics', says today that the excitement of the *IT* offices was in wonderful contrast to the pre-psychedelic politics of radicalism, 'typified by boring meetings and rooms with bare lightbulbs, dusty old books, international this and international that, Marxism, anarchism, various branches of non-violent politics ...'.

❛ When I think about the *IT* office, I remember that great feeling that only came at that time in the sixties, when somebody could come in who was a total stranger and you could tell from the way the person was, and what their attitudes were, that they were OK. You could trust them. There was a mutual support that had nothing to do with money and nothing to do with seeking after fame or anything like that. It only lasted for a very short time, maybe about six months, but it was wonderful throughout that time.

'There would be a striking moment that I'll always remember when everyone would be working away and suddenly the place would become totally silent and you'd know that Bill Burroughs had arrived. I'd have been expecting him with his copy and I would go over to the stairs and Bill would just be standing there ... and it would have silenced everybody.'

The *International Times* had connections with all the other underground publications in France and Holland, but Tom McGrath recalls that the newspapers that counted most came from the United States, the *San Francisco Oracle* – pretty, mystical, lots of acid and go as you please – foremost among them. Berkeley had its *Barb*, radical and serious. The *Los Angeles Free Press* had been around since 1964 – extremely well run and warm to all good causes – and was joined in 1967 by *Open City*. In New York the *East Village Other* had become the cheeky brother/sister of the established *Village Voice*, long treasured by the old radicals. Such newspapers had a readership estimated by mid-1967 at more than a million. In *Oracle* editor Allen Cohen's words, they believed in 'life force'.

One of McGrath's pleasures was associating with the hippest writers and editors without in any way changing his earnest fifties radical style.

❬ They used to say, "Tom, your image isn't right. You're going to have to wear granny specs and a jacket with psychedelic flowers on it," and God knows what else, and I'd say, "This is the way I am". I was able to be myself and, although I might encourage everyone to turn up at some demonstration or big rock concert, I would be at home having a quiet day with the kids – you know, still rooted in basic normality. No matter how freakish and strange the mid-sixties thing was, there was plenty of room for very basic human realities like the love between parent and child. It was a healthy time.

'[*IT*] becoming fashionable was a big surprise and a joy. I mean, when you have spent your time with your head inside books, or playing remote forms of improvised music, you feel you're on a fringe, with rock 'n' roll over there somewhere and us over here, our music supposedly too weird for the public. But in the mid-sixties with mass communication all sorts of thinking and behaving became relevant in the public arena. The gathering of the tribes again, everyone coming together.

'Pop interviews helped *IT* in that we were the first people to run unedited question-and-answer interviews with no interference with what people said. People like McCartney and Lennon and Harrison and Jagger and the rest of them talked about politics and their drug experiences and their mystical explorations in a very open way which no one could read about anywhere else. And this helped them to reach that section of the community they appealed to, and maybe even gave them a broader appeal in that sixties framework.'

The staff of the *International Times*. Some of the brightest and best people in Europe are in this photograph. Doesn't their optimism glow? Or is it the author's fevered rejection of cynicism as a valid concept?

'People came to the *International Times* with all sorts of ideas,' McGrath remembers. 'The ideas might be crazy or they might be sound, but they would come to us, and we were there to be both catalyst and reflector.' Tom McGrath still meets people who read *IT* and remembers it had a big influence on their lives; people who were young then and who still retain the flame of youth.

However, the *International Times*, merely a shilling's worth of views for the young, must have upset someone 'on high' because on the morning of 9 March in big boots came a not so jolly Mr Plod with a search warrant. McGrath remembers:

187

❛ I suddenly heard the police come down the steps. They looked as if they meant business. I picked up my briefcase which held an assortment of things that would have been of great interest to them, and said, "Excuse me," passing this policeman, nice and polite. I wasn't conspicuous; I looked like the janitor. I went out through the bookshop and into the street, along to the Italian restaurant where I used to go for coffee. There was a nice man behind the counter. I said, "Excuse me, will you look after this for me for a while?" and gave him my briefcase and shot back to the office. "Right. I'm the editor. What's going on here?"

'They had come on the pretext of objecting to one front page that had said "Arrest the Home Secretary". In fact they were emptying all of the ashtrays into a bag for analysis, because presumably they thought we were all smoking dope in the office all the time, but we couldn't do that, we were working too hard. Upstairs in the shop they had taken several books which they were categorising as obscene publications. The Chief Inspector instructed his men to look for pictures, not words. They took away *Naked Lunch* and *Memoirs of a Shy Pornographer* and returned them six months later with lots of thumbprints. I hope they enjoyed them. They were obviously out to stop the paper. Now, I still had a Dixon of Dock Green view of the police as a friendly neighbourhood force, avuncular and unthreatening, so I kept fairly calm, but Hoppy was bristling. The police wanted to know what was in the issue about to go to press. There was obviously something they didn't want circulated throughout Britain, which was really a great compliment to what we were doing. They wanted to know where it was being printed, but I wouldn't tell them. So they took all the newspaper's records and the stock that we had for selling mail order. They took everything that they could move, and still we didn't tell them the name of the printers. We were obviously annoying somebody fairly high up the ladder, and they'd decided that we were a threat, that we weren't just fun. And from then on I began to change my attitude to government.'

188

An Arthur Moyse cartoon of the *IT* bust. Despite that serious attempt to infringe civil liberties, the cartoon allows itself many light moments in picture and text.

Funeral symbolism was popular in 1967. Here the friends of *IT* carry a 'coffin' to mark the 'death' of the newspaper after it had been busted.

In fact *IT* lived on and thrived, but the funeral was a good Happening.

Before that, with Aneurin Bevan's widow, Jennie Lee (a fine Scots socialist, fierce in support of the liberty of the individual and the right of free speech), as Arts Minister, there had been a feeling that Wilson's Labour government might be close to *IT*'s ethic. But it wasn't to be. Jennie Lee was not central to a government still locked into rigid, self-protective, unquestioning backing of America in Vietnam, and domestic struggles with the financiers on the one hand and the militant unions on the other. The last thing they wanted was youth's own newspaper spreading some notion of Change Now! across a nation already susceptible to secret messages from the Beatles, the Rolling Stones and UFO.

Miles was at the bust. 'The police had been tipped off that we had run some four-letter words in an interview with Dick Gregory, and they over-reacted to such an extent, seizing things and keeping them for three months, that they were obviously aiming to close the paper down.' In June the *IT* materials were returned without any official apology or explanation. No crimes had been committed. 'No charges were brought. No other business could have survived such behaviour.' But *IT* had bold and powerful friends. Paul McCartney helped out, sometimes paying staff and sometimes the printer. So they were not alone and they survived.

The *International Times* bounced back, unfettered by repression. These were times when the norm was joyful gaiety and the aberration was clampdown – at least, that's how it seemed to me. Tom McGrath wrote a kind of personal manifesto in the aftermath of the raid, published on 13 March in issue 10. It was written fluently and at speed, and the clarion call of unquenchable optimism rang through it to a majestic climax: 'The new movement is slowly, carelessly, constructing an alternative society. It is international, inter-racial, equisexual, with ease. It operates on different conceptions of time and space. The world of the future may have no clocks.'

In five points McGrath summarised the position of all who subscribed to the counter-culture's simple idealism:

(1) It was an inner-directed movement, a common viewpoint rather than a credo or dogma.
(2) It couldn't be suppressed by law. 'You cannot imprison consciousness ... the revolution has taken place in the minds of the young.' The

individual should pursue pleasure without guilt unless he was
impinging on others (shades of J. S. Mill).

(3) The movement was not one of protest but of celebration (as in San
Francisco so in London: street theatre, fun and games. If wet, in the
church hall).

(4) It was not a movement as such; it was just people coming together
and grooving, and should be tempered with British practicality and
common sense. (There was suspicion, said McGrath, of Leary's 'Turn
on, tune in and drop out'. Too easy? Too difficult?)

(5) First and foremost: be happy, be creative, be optimistic in the face of
everything – the H-bomb, poverty, Vietnam.

McGrath saw the rebirth of optimism as miraculous, given the strength
of the opposition. 'The new weapons are love and creativity – wild new
clothes, fashions, strange new music sounds.' Though the new movement
might be weaker than the Campaign for Nuclear Disarmament (previously
the most attractive co-ordinated movement of dissent against the ugly
face of domestic might), McGrath saw that its understanding of McLuhan's
media theories enabled it to send signals across the world with some
force. Mutual admiration was crucial to the underground. Pressed from
without, they found enormous comfort in the joyful attention each section
of the counter-culture paid to the others. There was a real search for unity,
which in June would coalesce comfortably around the great universal
shout of joy from *Sgt Pepper* and the answering cry of 'Message
understood'.

The San Francisco Diggers, however, were strict about whom they
praised. Of all the people in the counter-culture they were the cutting
edge. To be found almost all over the place, full of dash and swagger and
very equitable, they were also the most enigmatic. I liked the idea of them
when word reached me in Los Angeles that they were insisting on
knowing exactly why we wanted to put a festival into Monterey (their
territory, it being near San Francisco), and I liked them more when I met
them, but they were the most challenging people to argue with. They were
actors and satirists, and they had the confidence of the acid generation
sharpened with real intellect, wit and collectivist purity. They lacked
dogma, thank God, and asked only to be left to run their world of Free.
From early on they had the respect and interest of the San Francisco
newspapermen. The liberal churchmen liked them, too, because they were
honest. They showed a pragmatic and compassionate concern for the
influx of so many innocent and unprepared 'seekers' to the Haight. It was
all very well for Uncle Tim to say drop out, said the Diggers: 'But we
have to pick up the pieces.'

Peter Coyote, now a thriving Hollywood actor, was in the sixties a member of the San Francisco mime troupe who formed the core of the Diggers. He first took peyote in the early sixties and saw himself as a creature of the wild. There was in all of the Diggers an honest sense of the nobility of real danger – a formidable yardstick for others to measure themselves by. If you were not *for* them, you were against them, for as they were Free they had always to be right.

Coyote says:

❛ We didn't stand *for* anything but we were about personal authenticity and taking responsibility for your own visions. There was a commitment to total radical overthrow of the culture, an aim that was shared by everyone. Everyone's response to it was different but it was the common denominator that made all personal behaviour meaningful and separated young people from the generation that preceded them, because if they didn't share that premiss, then everything we were doing was nuts!'

He is clear on the essence of Free as the Diggers understood it, and as he still determines it, for he is still young. Few in our story have yet reached fifty and none will accept the limitations of middle-agedness, for what has that to do with Free?

❛ Emotional and intellectual wilderness bear the same relationship to emotional and intellectual suburbia as a coyote does to a miniature poodle. Until people are really thrown on their own resources, until they have their props knocked out from under them, they never know what they are capable of, and in America we had a generation

A street scene in the Haight. Was the picture posed?

191

that was raised in a permissive loony-bin. It was deprived of
adequate tests of personal worth, and so the generation sought out
wild turf by which to measure themselves. It's a necessary part of
growing up.'

Helen Perry, who became managing editor of the journal *Psychiatry*
after being 'acculturated by Haight-Ashbury in mid-life', was extremely
keen on the Diggers, noting that what she termed the 'costume people'
treated them with respect. They took their name from the persecuted
Diggers of Cromwell's England who dug and planted the common land
in towns throughout the country, giving away free the food produced,
both for the good of the people and as a political statement against the
callousness of an administration which seemed not to care that some of
its citizens were starving.

The latter-day Diggers manifested this philosophy by acting it out in
street theatre in an unembarrassed and continuous series of spontaneous
morality plays, in which money was burned before the audience's eyes.
They had been, after all, members of a mime troupe in which audience
participation was central, encouraged and Free. When their altruism and
their satire were combined, they presented a strong challenge to all rigid
forms, be it the high moral seriousness of the anti-war student radicals
or the bureaucracy and autocracy of state and law-enforcement agencies.
They were impossible to tame.

The *San Francisco Chronicle* interviewed them and, true to their
fundamental ethic that they were all one – nameless, amorphous,
interchangeable – no one was quoted by name. The *Chronicle* said: 'Their
burning of ten-dollar bills typifies more than anything else exactly what
the Diggers believe in. They provide goods, not money. They brought
5,000 sandwiches to the Be-In. Arrests and health orders fail to stop
them and arrests have not led to charges.'

Were the Diggers a philanthropic organisation? Peter Berg, one of the toughest of the breed, known in those days as The Hun, thinks it was more subtle than that.

❮ Ralph Gleason coined the phrase "Hippie Robin Hoods" to describe the Diggers, as though they *were* philanthropic, but in fact everybody in the Diggers was very conscious of what they were doing and the entire theme of it was street theatre – *guerilla* street theatre.

'When we undertook an event, the aim was to make something happen and the people who were involved with our events – sometimes two thousand souls – were aware that something was happening. Maybe not at the beginning, but as it took place, they *became* aware.'

Judy Goldhaft, Peter's partner since those happy days, said that life then was a daily theatrical event. 'People thought the Diggers were philanthropic because they were involved with food, housing and clothing, but we just did what we could in the most creative way.'

One Digger event shows what can be achieved if everyone is willing to suspend mundane responses.

❮ People were leaving the Panhandle after a concert and the first item on our Event was to leap through pieces of marbleised paper. I had made a programme of events that said "Carte de Venue and Street Menu", and leaping through paper was the first event. The paper was so wide that you couldn't go down that sidewalk from the Panhandle to Haight without walking through a sheet. Two people held them, one at each end, and we had a stack of them. People jumped through them to gain admission to the street. It was an Artificial Boundary. Once through, they were given penny whistles and rear-view mirrors, which we'd got from a car junkyard, to reflect the sunlight. And when the people were finally gathered in Haight Street they found women in wonderfully outlandish outfits on the roof of a house there, holding posters, spray-painted with the words of a poem by Lenore Kandel. The posters were probably ten feet long and five feet wide, and the women were chanting the poem.'

193

Judy Goldhaft continues:

❮ And then the people on the street started to read the poem, because it was quite big enough to be seen. So when one sheet was finished we'd flip over another, and another, and so the poem was read aloud and there was a chorus – an answering chorus. People began flowing into the street, lights were bouncing everywhere from reflected sunlight. It was twilight and it was wonderful, and then the police arrived, on cue.'

Judy Goldhaft explained that the people the police went after were the women on the rooftop.

‹ They were sure that whatever we were doing shouldn't be happening, so we climbed down from the roof and went up the roof on the other side of the street and did the same thing, reading the poem. And then the police came up there and off we went to another roof and ... well, I don't remember where it all ended but no one was arrested, and by now it was sunset and the event was over. It was pretty wonderful to have a crowd of two thousand watching every detail.'

It was the Diggers' sense of fun the media never could quite express or understand. Peter Coyote says:

‹ Some of my fondest memories (personally as opposed to collectively) have to do with the anarchic quality of communal life. Aside from the folly and idiocy which were equally prevalent, it was extraordinary to live with twenty or thirty people and, by extension, the several hundreds who were involved in a string of fellow-communes: to cook meals, to sit down and eat, play wonderful music for hours and hours, every night. We had a pot into which everybody threw their money, and there was a wonderful book. You just signed for the money you wanted and people were *so* themselves that some would be scrupulously honest and some not. Some would need 15 cents for a pack of gum or 79 cents for two beets and a head of lettuce. Other people would write: "Monday 50 dollars fix my car"; "Tuesday 50 dollars fix my car"; "Wednesday...", and so on. That was the heroin contingent!'

Peter Coyote does not judge. That was how it *was*. Their Reality.

‹ There would be meetings where decisions had to be taken – do I get a starter for the truck or do the kids need shoes? This went on for years. And it was mad but it *worked*. Somehow it worked and it was extraordinary.
'There was a party where about seventy people dug a three-tier pit, fifteen feet across, with a framework over it covered in canvas

and then, stoned out of our gourds, we sang Bach fugues and strange eleven-part harmonies. It was wonderfully collaborative and adventurous. Then we spent a long time on the road with a caravan of nine trucks. Thirty people, eleven kids and nineteen adults camping, just living like free beings. They were very, very carefree, inventive times.'

There *was* something in the air, even if it didn't – despite the fears of the authorities – get into the water.

The Diggers approved of a similar group, the Dutch Provos based in Amsterdam. They were smaller in number but just as influential in their milieu. Robert Jasper Grootveld started the group in 1965 by focusing his attention on a statue in Amsterdam. It had been placed there by the cigarette industry, and depicted a street urchin. Grootveld, himself a heavy smoker, felt that it was wrong to symbolise tobacco addiction with a child, of all things.

The Amsterdam 'White Bicycle', token of the new 'green'/anarchy/anti-car ethic of the Provos, non-violent Dutch dissidents. The idea was that the bicycle, ever popular in Holland, was available to all and could/should be free. So could/should much else. A good Dutch dream.

❝ I thought it was a symbol of corruption that it should be placed there in the newspaper district, and that while the newspapers were busy warning us about cancer their biggest advertiser was what I call "the legalised dope syndicate". I started protesting by writing the word "cancer" on billboards showing a beautiful girl smoking cigarettes. I was put in prison for sixty days and was proud to be there for such a silly thing.

'After that, every Saturday night, week after week, I went to the statue, and youngsters began to hear about this ritual. They shouted with me when I told them: "This statue is the addicted consumer of tomorrow." Before Provo, working-class youth – they were called

Nozem – weren't interested in religion or literature. It was thought they were only interested in hanging around in leather jackets and going to cowboy movies. And then, out of the street youngsters, came this new thing called Provo. It began in 1965 with my ideas about tobacco and the press and a few other ingredients we needed – the police, for example. They were very important, the police. They set me free from going to the statue every Saturday.

'It came about like this: the Lord Mayor of Amsterdam forbade the happenings, so one Saturday evening there was this loudspeaker announcement from the police. They shouted through the neighbourhood streets of the inner city: "The Happening is forbidden. There will be no Happening," etc. And people in the pubs, just standing there, thought: Oh, yes, this is Saturday, let's go to the Happening. So thousands of people went to the Happenings, because of the police.

'And then there was the motorcar. I said: "We need a better enemy than the police. Let's take the holy automobile." Others said: "Yes, you're right." At first they wanted to paint our symbol, a bicycle, in the red and black colours of the anarchists, but we realised white is better, you can see it easier in the dark, and so white became the colour of Provo. White plans were set up – fun, anarchist plans.'

Rob Stolk, a founder member with Grootveld and Roel Van Duijn, remembers those days well but cannot really define Provo. Like Digger it exists in its supporters' behaviour, in the state of collective consciousness that, for instance, 'knew' the automobile was unholy and the bicycle holy. 'White bicycles for all. If you need one, find one, and when you don't need it leave it. Someone else will take it.' He sees much change since then, but many good things remaining.

The great Dutch Provo, Robert Jasper Grootveld at one of his fabled Happenings in Amsterdam watched pleasantly by 'straight' bystanders. One of his protests was against cigarette-smoking, here symbolised by a statue placed by a tobacco company.

196

per Grootveld

'In those days we were seen by the authorities as state enemies, and now they talk about Provo in very nostalgic ways. All our ideas on the pollution of the environment and the way the city was being destroyed were taken over by the established political parties in our country.

'The whole atmosphere in our country – the present liberalism which we love, in which everything is allowed; the way the press today treats any activity or initiative – started in that time. Before the Provos there was only official news, only the official point of view. I think the biggest change in our society today is that now anybody who has a goal has the immediate attention of the mass media.'

Jasper Grootveld was, like the Diggers, an instinctive performer of street theatre.

'I loved myths about Saint Klaus, the saint of Holland. I had many memories of Nicolaus from my childhood. So, in the street, I kept saying: "Klaus will come. Klaus will come. Then there will be light. I am not the light, he is. It's happening, it's happening." Then Klaus *did* come, but it was not Saint Klaus, it was Claus with a "C" who had been in the German Army and who would marry Crown Princess Beatrix. He was not popular in Holland.'

At its height, when the authorities were really concerned about its power, Provo had only about twenty committed members. 'People thought us fantastically powerful,' Jasper recalls. In fact Provo was able to make its presence and philosophy felt by tapping a vast reservoir of support, recruiting ordinary Amsterdam citizens like Irene van der Weetering. 'With Provo, everyone could join in. Everyone felt spoken to. It wasn't an exclusive group. It wasn't just students. That's what pleased me in this eventful time,' she remembers. The symbolic smoke-bombing of the Dutch royal weddings in 1966 and 1967 was a case in point. Irene and many of her friends had been against the marriage of Princess Beatrix to the German Claus, a soldier in the opposing army in the Second World War when people in occupied Holland suffered very badly. 'It was not because we did not want her to marry whomever she wanted but because it was an affront to the people who had been in such a terrible situation, to those who didn't survive the war.'

Had the wedding been in The Hague, the Provos would have been outnumbered, but there were more Provos than public when Princess Beatrix decided to marry in Amsterdam. Irene van der Weetering remembers: 'The supporting public was only a very thin line on both

197

sides of the street. I was in the neighbourhood of the church, and I saw the procession coming and I saw the smoke procession coming up and it was glorious. It was fantastic. It was the most beautiful wedding I've ever seen.'

In 1967 a second Dutch princess, Margriet, married a Dutch commoner, which, it was thought, the *Daily Mail* reported in London, 'might help to heal the rift between the Dutch royal family and the Dutch people, all but one Dutch royal woman having married a German since 1815'. Such pious hopes were lost on the Provos, who were happening-happy, and duly on 10 January the smoke-bombers were out again, this time in The Hague, and three bombs and half a dozen thunderflashes were counted. It was a smaller event than the previous wedding, but it drew attention to dissension in the country and fourteen Provos were hauled in. Pictures of smoke filled the front pages of the newspapers, and as there was no heavy authoritarian crackdown the event was – by the Provos – deemed pleasant and a success. Good publicity and a good joke.

Grootveld is glad there were no real bombs and no violence in Provo. Though they termed their plans 'White' – a Dutch abstraction of the Diggers' concept of Free – they were politically Green. Today Grootveld likes to look back on what he calls 'the magic' of those times.

❻ Magic only means power. We were in need of power or strength to do our thing. My friends Roel and Rob called themselves anarchists. They called me The Magician. I thought: Yes, that's the word for me. A magician is someone who makes things happen.

'Provo lasted two years. It was an idea, a state of mind, a happening. We had Provo printing, Provo cinema, we were provoking. But by the end we had people who were afraid of being called Provos. A Provo was thought to be some club of youngsters: "dirty youngsters" they were called because they had long hair. That had become the image, and it was a sign that we would have to split with Provo. By the summer of 1967 it was over – the first invasion of American hippies came. They had heard something about happenings in Amsterdam and wanted to be there. They had flowers in their hair and these little bells ringing, and they were sitting and sleeping in the Vondelpark.

'It was then I heard this new album, *Sgt Pepper*. Before that I didn't like this cult of pop music, but now I knew this was the poetry of my time, of my days. It was the poetry of the sixties. It was beautiful.'

In the end, as with the Death of Hippie, which would come in October 1967 in San Francisco, the Provos folded themselves. Rob Stolk

remembers the use of rumour to trick Amsterdam University into
believing, in one final prank, that there were valuable Provo archives to
be bought. Their archive was a box of bits and pieces.

◄ In fact it wasn't an archive at all, just some scattered documentation,
if you want to call it that. We spread a rumour via some journalist
that the Provo archive would be sold to an American university, so
Amsterdam University decided to buy the archive itself. They paid
13,000 guilders for it, at that time a huge amount of money, and then
they started a real archive. A lot of people were interested in the
movement but heard about it only when Provo was already dead,
so for us it was really useful. We could say "Go and read about it!"
Now the University has a big department with all kinds of material
and publications of those times, from any country in the world
where something was happening. So now there *is* a big archive.'

After a very busy January starring the Be-In in San Francisco, the
smoke-bombed wedding in The Hague, and the visit of Suzy
Creamcheese and Pot Is Fun to London, the first month of the Great
New Year ended with a concert in London, featuring the Who and Jimi
Hendrix, which was attended by the Beatles and followed by a gathering
of small tribes at a club in the West End. A wonderful year looked
assured for the hippies and hedonists, but in San Francisco the counter-
culture was, for the first time, meeting real opposition. The San Francisco
police were beginning to get tough.

Led by those styled by the *San Francisco Chronicle* 'the Apostles of the
Love Generation', the hippies talked to police chief Thomas Cahill, who
would blow hot and cold by turn but who was rarely *cool* that year. The
hippies complained about various overzealous officers, one of whom was

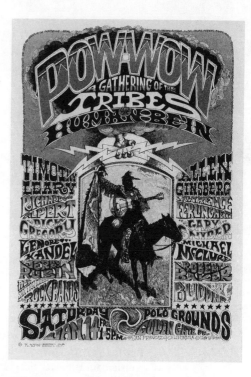

A poster for the Human Be-In in January 1967. The designer was Rick Griffin, one of the design 'stars' of the counter-culture. (What a cast!)

named as Arthur Gerrans. The name would recur in event after event that year, the classic Bad Egg in a Good Novel.

Ron Thelin, who with his brother Jay ran the supremely ethical Psychedelic Shop in the Haight, played down the difficulties the hippies were beginning to face and praised the police: 'We don't think they are bad. Maybe there are three or four bad apples, but they are overall the best in the United States.' High praise from a high priest.

The Psychedelic Shop was a paradigm of the scene in Haight-Ashbury. Its location was just right, its size modest, and its aims free and true. It was almost at the magic meeting-point of Haight Street with Ashbury, selling everything the heart might desire if the head be acid. The brothers themselves had soared angelic, and emerged as freewheeling hospitable young men with a terrific attitude. Always positive, they believed absolutely in the rightness of what they were doing, acting as a conduit for the day-to-day news and views of the counter-culture, selling things at fair and decent prices. Books and records, rare and serious, incense, bells, beads, and dope paraphernalia – previously scattered in specialist places if at all – all these were now concentrated in the Psychedelic Shop, and the Thelins certainly knew how to run it.

Ron Thelin, as cheerful today as he was then, speaks warmly of the times. His father had been a Woolworth's manager right across the street.

❛ I guess I was a merchant's son, likewise my brother. He took care of the business, did the books, while I was out stroking the possibilities of a free and peaceful world. I think capitalism's OK if you think of capital as what you have left after you have your home, your clothing, your food, and you use that to benefit the whole. But we now have corporate capital, which does not benefit the whole: it benefits the pocket-book of individuals.

'The Psychedelic Shop was, in a way, the host point to the street. We put up the first bulletin-boards, and pretty soon it was just a whole wall of messages: "Karen call Rick." It became a meeting-place where people could keep up with whatever was going on. [There had been others – perhaps the Blue Unicorn in Hayer Street was a forerunner.]

'I had a picture in my mind: I could see Haight-Ashbury with cannabis shops and hashish shops where you could go in and buy the finest of all the drugs there were. I believed that drugs should be legal and there should be a choice.

'There was a desire to entertain the possibility of something different, a different way of life away from mundane habit, something that involved free will and trust in God. You can't trick God, but you can sit on a freeway with a coffee-table if you want. It's OK.'

Peter Coyote, a stern observer of the Haight merchants, is none the less approving of the 'coffee-table on the freeway' trick. He says:

❛ The Diggers became synonymous with people who would actualise their fantasies, who would have an idea and do it. So I'll never forget Ron Thelin setting up an impeccable table on the freeway in rush-hour traffic, with linen and crystal and fresh fruit, and three feet away from freeway traffic, bumper to bumper, he ate his breakfast there. The suggestion was that if you wanted to get out of your car and eat – what was stopping you?'

A read-in at the Psychedelic Shop in the Haight 'owned' by the brothers Ron and Jay Thelin

Ron Thelin has never forgotten it, either.

❛ It was the summer solstice, and we were having an event for all of San Francisco. Coyote was involved: he cased twelve different buildings in the city from which twelve of us let off red flares simultaneously. It was a total manifestation of freedom. Then there was this freeway where we set up our table and had our breakfast and watched people going to work – and then, of course, the police came.'

201

Lying down in front of cars came and went as a new and maybe dangerous game, though it was a gesture against traffic rather than a new version of 'Chicken'. The automobile was never the hippies' friend. It was ironic that in the same issue which reported this 'strange new game' the *San Francisco Chronicle* noted in a separate item: 'A total of 47,680 traffic deaths for the nation during the first 11 months of 1966 was reported yesterday by the national safety council.'

The Chalk-In around the time of the Easter happening and the Banana events was a big success. It was real art, of the people, by the people, for the people. The city provided both facilities and chalks. The designs were of the moment.

Interviewed by British Independent Television News in 1967, the very young Ron Thelin was eager to tell the reporter:

❝ I think what's happening in San Francisco is the only meaningful thing that is happening in the country and possibly the world. Right now 60 per cent of the world's resources are controlled by the United States. We have a kind of militant right-wing government which is addicted to symbols and can relate to the world no other way than by symbols. And the only way I can consciously remove myself from it is to consciously drop out of it.'

He explained to the interviewer the value of psychedelics, pleading for understanding and harmony, and for the need to find what we're here for. The Big One. What It's All About. 'LSD psychedelic chemicals are like a microscope to enlarge things,' he explained.

There was no shortage of inspired advice to help save the Haight. The HIP merchants, the poets, the church leaders, all gave the police and city officials a series of suggestions, based on simple broadminded common sense, on how to cope with the city's costumed people and the anticipated influx of new arrivals, variously estimated and projected to number anything from 80,000 to hundreds of thousands. The HIP people advised newcomers: 'Dig it, don't destroy it.' Scott McKenzie was singing that, if we went to San Francisco, we should be sure to wear some flowers in our hair, and furthermore that on arrival we'd meet some gentle people, while the non-hippie natives of the cities were going ape. A quick scamper through the winter in San Francisco shows a relentless resistance to what Chet Helms called 'the rites of passage of the hip young'. On 9 February, Jay Thelin was charged with selling a 'rude' book, to wit Lenore Kandel's *Love Book*. (The Psychedelic Shop had been busted the previous November, too, and Allen Cohen of the counter-cultural newspaper the *Oracle* arrested because he was serving behind the counter at the time.) You could buy a lot of *real* pornography all over San Francisco without hindrance, but it was acidheads' looks at love they wanted to nail. City Lights bookshop was also busted for the *Love Book*. The case went to municipal court but was thrown out. Nevertheless, the scent of harassment lingered in the air.

Out in Berkeley later that month, Charlie Artman, funster and acid politico, attended a meeting in the company of some very straight people

A café window in the Haight. The message, however trite it might seem, *was* love – and inexpensive at that price.

where he sat in a flowing black and purple robe, wearing several crosses and smoking a pipe of dope. He offered it round. No one accepted. 'I will pass out mescaline for home brew,' he promised. One of his opponents in the forthcoming election pledged himself to 'rid the city of malcontents and degenerates' and gave Artman a hard look which was quite wasted on so cheerful a chappie.

On St David's Day, 1 March, Mario Savio, brave young hero of the Free Speech Movement, was gaoled for ninety days and fined $350 for committing a public nuisance. This was the unpleasant climax to thirty months' legal toing and froing following the sit-ins and wrangling over the Free Speech Movement in Berkeley. Savio was and is a great American freedom fighter, who said he was doing it for a free future for his eighteen-month-old son whom he had to leave on entering gaol. Four others were gaoled with Savio, including a pregnant woman. Governor Reagan allowed himself a smile of victory which some considered pyrrhic. He had come to office pledged to 'deal with' student radicals.

There were new raids on hippies in the Haight. Officer Gerrans was now seen as a serious scourge. Signs were carried: 'Turn On, Tune In and Drop Art.'

On 10 March, the day Ralph Gleason praised the January Be-In as
having been a turning-point in American social history, his newspaper
led the front page with a banner: 'Raids on Nude Hippies.' Here was the
long-awaited crackdown on 'Nineteen young Haight-Ashbury types,
including six girls'. (Note the sexism. Alternative version: 'Nineteen
young Haight-Ashbury types including thirteen men'.) In fact the raid
was not in Haight-Ashbury but in Marin County, in a hillside house. 'Pot
had been smelled', two dozen people had been sighted 'cavorting in the
nude'. I always like the imagery of cavorting: a kind of perpetual frolic
in Arcady, long green grass and chiffon scarves waving in a light breeze.
A sign was left at the house: 'We've been busted. Play it cool. Love you
all.'

Also that day there was a report of another bust: three men were
arrested for selling 'erotic posters'. This was the police in what the
Chronicle called 'the new roust of hippies, the first since their knuckles
had been rapped for the unsuccessful bust of Lenore Kandel's *Love Book*'.
There were three counter-culture shops involved: the Blushing Peony,
the House of Richard and the Deadly Excess. Once again, Officer Arthur
Gerrans was present, described in the *Chronicle* as 'the bane of the hippies'.

Four days later the American Council for Civil Liberties demanded and
got the return of hundreds of posters, based on the *Love Book* judgement.
Charges were not pressed, but the feeling of embattlement increased.
Easter came and went in cosmic bliss, however, and after being very
negative on street-chalking pavement art the city itself offered chalks and
facilities. The *Chronicle*, reporting on the chalk-in, had the grace to allow

Bill Graham (*left*) at his
Fillmore ballroom –
admission three dollars

their writer, Michael Mahoney, to note rather beautifully: 'A slender brown-skinned girl in T-shirt and blue jeans was working, completely absorbed, her straight glossy black hair brushing the floral pattern she was building up.'

Meanwhile the city's churchmen were speaking of the Diggers as 'the executive branch of the hippie movement'. Concerned churchmen were looking to them for advice, and on the first day of spring they got it. The Diggers told the monthly meeting of the Episcopalian diocese that the city could be invaded by hundreds of thousands of young, indigent and hungry people in the summer. The clergymen took note and voted unanimously to condemn the Commission for Parks and Recreation for a resolution passed the previous week preventing the use of the parks for resting, sleeping or like purposes.

The City's response to the counter-culture and its supporters was blunt and unimaginative. Police Chief Cahill said: 'Law, order and health must prevail. These hippies do not have the courage to face the reality of life they are trying to escape.' The *Chronicle* reports Cahill turning his fire on the Diggers, questioning their forecast of an invasion, and stating: 'The Diggers are definitely more against the police than in favour of cooperating with us.' He announced that police patrols would be stepped up. Mayor Shelley said that the hippie vagrants' presence could cause 'chaotic conditions detrimental to themselves and others'. The banner across the front of the *Chronicle* read: 'The War on Hippies: Mayor Acts.'

The health chief, interestingly named Ellis D. Sox, was now working closely with Cahill and the Mayor, and on 25 March it was announced there would be a blitz on houses in the Haight by a twelve-man team of health inspectors. 'Young people of good background are creating a slum,' it was stated.

On 29 March it was reported that the hippies had been given a clean bill of health. The *Chronicle* reported: ' "The situation is not as bad as we thought," said Mr Sox.' Improvement notices were issued against only sixty-five of the 1,400 buildings, and only sixteen of those had been issued to 'occupants whose bizarre dress and communal living habits could class them as hippies'. Mr Sox denied that there was an attempt to squeeze or force out unconventional inhabitants but said the watch would go on. The Haight-Ashbury Neighborhood Council issued a statement, 'resenting the gratuitous criticism of our community. It ill accords with the best of San Francisco tradition to seek to outlaw one lifestyle in favour of that lifestyle apparently more congenial to public officials whose only duty after all is to serve the public and not dominate it.'

There was more than a hint of Founding Fathers in the tone of that and subsequent statements from HANC, the Diggers and other, after all, very *American* movements.

However, the nagging and nudging went on. Bus routes were closed to 'protect school children from having to travel through this No Man's Land akin to Sodom of Biblical Days', a spokesman was reported as saying. Ralph Gleason had to point out that not only were the Haight people an asset to the community, but they were also productive people with rights. The Avalon and Fillmore ballrooms employed dozens of people, there were 200,000 copies of posters going out in series, there was work and creative energy stimulated by the Haight stores, the Job Co-op, the *Oracle*, the PRINT Mint, and the Communications Company.

(One of the great features of the counter-culture was the speed with which people could get their views printed up and on the streets. Called 'broadsides', some of these emanated from the Diggers, suggesting responses to a given situation, confrontation or whatever; others came from Beat veteran Chester Anderson's Com-Co. They were mimeographed cheaply and quickly, and supplemented the underground press, itself a marvel of fast and colourful communication. Today's teenagers can thank those writers with heart for the best of today's young journalism. Broadside journalism was unjaded and quite undegraded by advertising. Of course, its co-opting by the year's end into the free capitalist society was inevitable, but it set standards of truth, sincerity and immediacy which, rarely attained today, still stand as a benchmark.)

Gleason spoke out against the rerouting of buses, saying that no one had to like the hippies or their lifestyle, but they were equal in the eyes of the law and we ought to keep it that way. The costumed people agreed, and on 4 April they took to the streets and had a 'walk-in'. Two thousand of them proclaimed 'Streets are for people'. The police sent in 150 men, pulled in twenty-six young men and six young women. A hippie spokesman said that, no matter, there would be a happening every week and the city officials had better understand it. Priests backed the street people, but the chief lay officer of the Episcopalians resigned and stated the case for the opposition with some colour: '[These] people reject the moral code of our society. They curse and swear, are admitted fornicators, are physically unclean, and reject if not despise the law. I believe they are un-Christian and immoral.' His bishop did not agree. Some San Francisco churchmen were blessedly liberal.

The founder of the Limeliters folk-group, Lou Gottlieb, had fallen foul of the law with his remedy for homelessness, the Morning Star ranch way out of town which he saw as a 'pilot study in an alternative way of life. It should be a place where people who can't make it in a straight society can demonstrate a style of life that emphasises *being* not doing.' He said that his guests would be people who 'cannot live in the Great Society'.

The place was busted for being an illegal, 'organised' camp. Gottlieb

defied anyone to prove that it was organised. There were reports of
'people of both sexes showing their private parts', and some quite
offputting stories of people using makeshift lavatories with 'toilet paper
around the place'. Even in the counter-culture there was a limit to what
middle-class Americans would tolerate, and having used toilet paper
hanging around longer than a few minutes was definitely outside that
limit.

It was a big bust, involving the FBI, the sheriff's department, the
county supervisors, a probation officer and a judge. By the autumn, the
ranch had been declared an organised camp, but Lou Gottlieb was not
allowed to pursue his generous dream. His motives had been pure and
very let-it-all-hang-out, but he was right – there *was* no organisation, and
that, it was clear, was one of the things that made the world go round.
Civilisation, after all, had as much to do with drains as with successful
adventure in inner space.

Commerce was ambivalent. Five days after bus routes had been closed
so as to protect the innocent young from seeing the guilty young, another
company, Gray Line Buses, organised a tourist bus through the Haight.
'Hippies at My Window,' ran the slogan for the tours. The blurb on the
promotional literature read: 'The only foreign tour within the continental
limits of the USA.' The *Chronicle*, reporting on the tour, said: 'When
word spread through the bus about "the journey through psychedelphia",
as driver-guide Dee Briggs put it, interest in the other wonders of San
Francisco seemed desultory.' The reporter, J. Campbell Bruce,
commented: 'Most had never seen a live hippie.'

Britain's Independent Television News also reported on the Haight in
this period. The narration of their film featured the coach-driver's spiel:

❝ This is the new avant-garde left-bank area of San Francisco which

207

has evolved and developed over the past years.... It is the belief of these people that we have done a very poor job of running our government and way of life.'

The soundtrack featured two old ladies sitting on the bus, reading the Gray Line *Guide to Hippie Language*, beginning with the word 'speed' and passing through 'teeny bopper', 'turn on', 'weed'. The women were astonished by what they read and saw. It was, after all, very new to America.

The *Chronicle* reported faithfully:

◄ "Nobody seems to know what hippies are yet," said Dr Robert Allen, a Memphis surgeon. Chicago dentist Dr Elsenbaum said: "They're beginning to infiltrate Chicago now, kids with long hair." A Mrs Costanza said that the hippies indulged in free love. "Their parents send them money for LSD." But hippie on the bus, Stan Miklose, with his western boots, shoulder-length hair, jeans, turtle neck sweater and car coat, said he was a busy poster painter. "I *must* work to support my wife and child."

'A tourist commented: "He speaks so well, as if he had a college education." The tourists were genuinely interested.

'Miklose commented: "It was bound to happen. When someone creates a thing of beauty, an Eiffel Tower, a great painting, the public comes to it. We hippies have created something beautiful – it's natural the public should come to see."'

An awareness of the arrogance of hindsight prevents my claiming to have seen the beginning of the end in those April days when the nights began to shorten and the brown hills behind the Haight began to green. In her book *The Human Be-In* Helen Perry has a chapter title 'The Haight-Ashbury before the Tour Buses Came Through'. It was her wisdom and good fortune to get in there and fall in love with innocence before the Summer of Love. It was my misfortune and mistake to get there when it was just too late. But I treasure beyond measure the sharing in Los Angeles of some of the aspirations expressed in the San Francisco council's announcement of their plans for that Summer of Love.

On Thursday, 6 April, the *San Francisco Chronicle* ran a two-column panel, written once again sympathetically by Mike Mahoney. The title was 'Nice Happenings'; the headline 'Good Hippies Summer Plans'. As with the dark-haired girl at the Chalk-In, so at the press conference for the Summer of Love, Mahoney showed an eye for a pretty girl. 'As television and radio newsmen hovered over their equipment, a winsome young thing in tights and a skirt clear up to h-e-r-e circulated among them, passing out cups of coffee and pieces of toast with butter and apricot marmalade. They had not been as well treated in many a conference.'

It was a beginning full of promise, but little over a week later an event held in the Haight's Kezar Stadium was to test the consciousness and conscience of the costumed people. By the time the Summer of Love was fully upon us the cry was not so much for 'peace and love' as a part of the long-haired switched-on lifestyle, but for peace in Vietnam, an end to a war that should never have begun.

'Now' day march past the Panhandle, Golden Gate Park

Blows for Freedom: boot
and club on the steps of the
Pentagon

SIX

OUT,
DEMONS,
OUT

By 1967 I didn't know anybody who actually supported the war, but perhaps that tells you more about the people I associated with than about public opinion because it wasn't until the end of 1967 that more were against it than were for it.

By the end of 1966 the United States had nearly half a million troops in Vietnam; massacres and tortures were commonplace; there were said to be half a million Vietnamese civilians dead already, and Johnson 'was not going to negotiate with terrorists'.

In fact it was becoming more and more clear to an appalled audience in Europe and America that the war in Vietnam was a horrifying and disgraceful manifestation of state-sponsored terrorism. It emerged in 1967 that defoliation of the jungle was commonplace, and that Laos had been bombed for three years without Congress being made aware of it. (The same thing was to happen to Cambodia during Nixon's administration.) No amount of saluting and bands and flag-waving today can wipe out the stain on the reputation of those who ran the United States in the sixties and early seventies, and who put young men into the field to enforce their own position.

Recruits to the front ranks of opponents to the war were always welcomed by us, the 'angels', for that is how we saw ourselves, and reviled by them, the 'devils', which is how we saw LBJ and his gang, led in battle by General Westmoreland, who prosecuted the war with such cruelty and ruthlessness, and on the home front by politicians like Dean Rusk, Secretary of State, who believed America must win at any price.

Two disparate recruits who were emotionally and physically impressive were Dr Benjamin Spock, whose *Baby and Child Care* had dominated the upbringing of many of the young now finding the courage to explore their psyche in gentler ways than their predecessors, and Muhammad Ali, the most famous heavyweight champion of the world, whose skill had enchanted millions and raised the status of the sport far in advance of its standing during the reigns of Sonny Liston and Floyd Patterson. As a result of their stand against the war, both dissidents found themselves in trouble.

Dr Spock was arrested, and Ali was stripped of his title. Each well over six feet tall, and therefore towering over their interviewers physically as well as morally, they both appeared on the newsreels talking up a spiritual storm.

'The American people are terribly concerned about the danger to our country and the devastation of the war,' said the Doctor, grave-eyed behind his famous spectacles, talking at the induction centre for recruits in Lower Manhattan. 'People here think that the war is disastrous from every point of view; an immoral war, an illegal war, a war that's hurting the United States more than it's hurting our opponents. It hasn't accomplished anything.'

At the induction centre in Houston, Texas, an officer in charge announced: 'Mr Muhammad Ali has just refused to be inducted into the United States armed forces. Notification of his refusal has been made to the United States Attorney, the State Director of the selective service system and the local selective service board for whatever action is deemed to be appropriate.'

Before his stand, Ali had been promised a safe home-based spell in the service (similar to Ronald Reagan's in the Second World War), staging morale-boosting fights, and receiving status and 'real honour' for accepting the draft. But if he refused it, he was told, white America would rise against him, and blacks whose many sons *were* in Vietnam would see him as a traitor.

He chose to refuse the draft. He told a special hearing: 'I know my image with the American public is completely ruined because of the stand I take. If I could do otherwise I wouldn't jeopardise my life by walking the streets of America, especially in the South with no bodyguard. I do it because I mean it. I will not participate in this war.'

So Ali, heavyweight champion of the world, had his boxing licence rescinded, was sentenced to five years in gaol (though this was reversed on appeal after three years' legal wrangling), was picked up and gaoled for ten days on an old motoring rap, was exiled from boxing for three years, and received an avalanche of hate mail. Time, however, was on his side and, coupled with his own particular courage, it gave him the heavyweight championship all over again in 1974. But in his own words he had 'lost the seven best years of a boxer's life'.

The most clean-cut of American groups, the Beach Boys – today Reagan's vaunted favourites – offered up Carl Wilson to Uncle Sam's darker nature: he was charged with draft evasion in Los Angeles Superior Court in May and released on $40,000 bail so that he could fly to England where the group were, in one *New Musical Express* readers' poll, considered the World's Top Group. He said on arrival in Manchester: 'I am an objector on the grounds of conscience. I have to make them believe me or the alternative is gaol for three years. But I have feelings about these things and I feel absolutely certain that the worst will not happen. I only hope I'm right.'

He was. He was not gaoled, and unlike Ali his licence to 'practise his trade', art, couldn't be revoked. His stand was none the less bold and decent. The Beach Boys could have had a lot to lose, but by now the

Muhammad Ali in Texas, speaking to an arts-festival audience in Denton

'pop world' was substantially liberal/radical so that his stand was admired. After completing some voluntary service, Carl was back in action doing what he did best, making good vibrations.

The only pop singer in my circle of friends to do any service at all was Drake Levin of Paul Revere and the Raiders, a dissenter with an equable nature who settled for six months' activity in the National Guard. He gave up his place in the Raiders, but he never gave a damn about anything anyway and by 1967 was a cheerful hippie. Revere himself, like Carl a client of mine, had peeled potatoes in a mental home rather than kill.

Meanwhile less famous 'hell, no, we won't go' draft-resisters were leaving the country in their tens of thousands, welcomed by Canada and Sweden. Draft-card burning in public became a favourite Happening. The hardcore counter-culturalists were so solidly for the anti-war movement that it is truly shocking to see how far to the right things have swung as I write now. To the sixties young, costumed people or straight, the idea of shooting strangers in far-off jungles was ludicrous beyond all imaginings. As Jim Dickson says: 'People didn't want to go to Vietnam not so much because we had a reason why we shouldn't go but because nobody had a good reason why we should. If you're going to be expected to go kill somebody, or take a chance on getting killed, you want a reason.'

There were all sorts of exemptions to the draft: being married was an early form; later, being married *with children*. Students were exempt, though students with bad grades were removed from exemption in 1966, and by May 1967 several members of the House Armed Services Committee were ready to disregard the first Amendment (the one referring to freedom of speech!) when it came to draft-resisters. There had been for a couple of months a House view that students should not be allowed exemptions if anti-war demonstrations took place on campus. There was also, I thought, a fair argument from hippies that students should not be a special case when so many uneducated, uninformed and unprotected young people – especially blacks – were being drafted, sent to Vietnam and killed, with few questions asked and none answered.

Blacks in that year were no better off than in 1966 or the previous year, which had seen the riots in the Watts ghetto in Los Angeles, a horrible tragedy mirrored in Barry McGuire's protest hit 'Eve of Destruction', which was written by P. F. Sloan, a protégé of Monterey's Lou Adler. The race riots continued in the cities into 1967, but although there was common cause between hippies and blacks against the Man (authority) there was little communal action. Blacks were not the chosen 'Outsiders' of the white counter-culturalists. Blacks were becoming too militant for 'long-hair' tastes, with a burgeoning self-awareness, a feeling of belonging

214

A speech from the 'Peace Lord' at Kezar Stadium in San Francisco. Contemporary captions put the total crowd at 60,000 – the largest peace demonstration to date (then) in West Coast history. May it not be necessary again....

to a separate nation with its own tough leaders: H. Rap Brown, Eldridge Cleaver, Huey Newton, Bobby Seale, Stokely Carmichael, who were quite removed from bells and beads and incense-holding street theatricals. That indeed is why this book is so 'white'. That is how it was in 1967 in San Francisco, London and Amsterdam. Hungry for change we may have been, but our consciousness was white and romantic, if not knowingly racist.

Kezar Stadium stands in Golden Gate Park. On 15 April 1967 it was the venue for a test of the anti-Vietnam consciousness of the neighbourhood, and of the city and country beyond. The nationwide event was called the Spring Mobilisation and took the form of a march, speeches, and a very little music. Numerically it was a very big success: 60,000 people turned out, representing every shade of anti-war opinion. Again the tribes gathered peacefully, but there was a feeling that the politicos who spoke and the organisers who organised were grumpy theorists while the 'costumed people', of Helen Perry's felicitous description, were the actual embodiment of peacefulness. The Mobilisation was felt to have been too serious by the young (and all accounts have the vast majority of the audience aged twenty-five or under) and too subversive by the Establishment.

The city's Mayor Shelley, anxious to declare for the authorities, proclaimed a counter-measure, a 'US Servicemen Appreciation Week'. Reagan sent goodwill messages to that from the Governor's Mansion. Dean Rusk said that anti-war demonstrations (they took place all over America that day) would have 'the net effect of prolonging the war rather than shortening it' (Nixon said the war would last another five years anyway), and averred that 'LBJ and the Congress spoke for the United States. Demonstrators didn't.'

The Diggers wouldn't have agreed. They took their street theatre to Kezar and broke the lock on the gates to the field there to let in Country Joe and the Fish. The latter were not really welcome, not being 'serious' enough, but Charles Artman, the LSD 'priest' who had been busted for carrying LSD in his crucifix, declared: 'When the hippies turn on the peace movement, you've got a combination that will inherit the earth.' Eighty assorted servicemen tried to crash the event. There were 350 policemen to keep order, and no injuries.

The actor Robert Vaughn and the black representatives Julian Bond and Coretta King were among the speakers. A warm wave of assent greeted the warning from a platform speaker, 'Moral values will wither away in the hypocritical name of nationalism', but the young were not primarily interested in speeches and went looking for music. The stadium was emptying as it became Mrs King's turn to speak. Her husband was speaking in New York. He had a year to live.

The parachutist from the Be-In turned up or, rather, floated down again. There were demonstrators in warpaint, Indian costumes, feathers and flowers. Much more fun than speeches. Los Angeles peaceniks were noted by the *San Francisco Chronicle*, as were Physicians for Peace and other 'respectable' interest groups.

Lyn Ludlow, a reporter covering the event for the *San Francisco Chronicle*, submitted a balanced appraisal. She described the march as orderly, and didn't labour the matter of litter – there was plenty left after the event for there was no kitchen mantra at Kezar; this was not a love-in. The biggest cheer, she reported, was for Robert Sheer: 'the bearded anti-war activist, politician and editor from Berkeley'. She also quoted the administration view: 'The world-wide communist apparatus is working very hard in the demonstrations.'

Lyndon Baines Johnson in the Texas White House was said to be collating reports on the countrywide anti-war protests. J. Edgar Hoover of the FBI was known to be 'watching anti-war people'. A government spokesman would admit only that 'reports were coming in to LBJ on a regular basis'. The spokesman, George Christian, repeated: 'The President regularly got reports.' The press agency, United Press International, reported Christian as claiming he 'had announced such reports in the past'. But he 'couldn't remember when'. Neither could newsmen. Well, well. The times were *indeed* a-changin'. Was the Great Society now spying on its members as they openly exercised the very right they were defending in Vietnam at such a cost? Yes.

It was not, by now, getting better all the time and it was going to get much worse. The Summer of Love was going to be complicated.

By the early summer of 1967 I was writing to any underground paper within reach about the madness of fighting the Vietcong – real 'freedom fighters'. Then in June came the news of a calculated and brutal crackdown on peace marchers at Century City in Los Angeles. *Open City*, the new friendly rival to the *Los Angeles Free Press*, ran a story by its editor, John Bryan, a good friend of mine, raving about the inequity of the police treatment of differing groups. Where the Los Angeles police chief, Thomas Reddin, was happy to turn a blind eye to rave-ups by the American Legion and Shriners at drunken conventions, he had declared what seemed very much like war on the demonstrators who gathered outside the Century Plaza Hotel to protest at the visit of the hated President Johnson, now seen as the arch-betrayer of Camelot.

Open City quoted Reddin as saying: 'Love-ins, be-ins, sit-ins have gradually degenerated into riots, or at least exhibitions of rampant anarchy masquerading as peaceful protest. Where thousands can engage in what is their right to dissent and demonstrate, tens of thousands are inconvenienced by the demonstrations.' Reddin proposed a change in city

More battering, this time at Oakland Induction Center, California. Two hundred officers used clubs and gas. There were two thousand anti-draft demonstrators including Joan Baez. She and 106 others were gaoled for ten days. This was 17 October, in mid-week – a few days before the worldwide marches and protests.

ordinances, prohibiting 'parades, the use of sound equipment, and the use of parks, at the discretion of the police'. The response from the American Council for Civil Liberties was swift and all-American. Spokesman Ed Cray said:

> ❝ The law is not for the convenience of the police. The police may find it convenient to have gatherings like these banned but I imagine that the British Crown once found the Sons of Liberty inconvenient also.
>
> 'The real front line is the Constitution itself and the Bill of Rights ... many opinions should be aired in times of crisis. Where there is hesitation to criticize official policy there is much danger to a free society. It is essential that as much wisdom be obtained about that policy as possible.'

The ordinances were not changed, but in July and August there was continuing police reaction against gatherings of the costumed people in Griffith Park, Los Angeles. The result could have been anticipated: the kids became more politicised.

And of course much the same was happening in San Francisco, though there, as Ron Thelin had said, the police were 'the best in America' – something that could never be said for either the Los Angeles Police Department or the Los Angeles County Sheriff's Department, that of the Sunset Strip riots. Chief Cahill of the San Francisco Police had warned that the law must be obeyed, and when, on 16 June, ten street dancers – nine men and one woman – were gaoled for the maximum forty-five days the court stated: 'Those who commit violence and incite it must accept the consequences. Unlawful disorder during these times of turmoil simply leads to more serious lawlessness.' Anti-war undertones rumbled on.

217

The sentences arose from a wild night when 2,000 hippies and tourists had danced and 'cavorted' at the intersection of Haight with Ashbury, and a phalanx of policemen six abreast had swept the street clear. A paddy-wagon was immobilised.

There were other round-ups. It seemed always to be raining. Where now was the Summer of Love? On 21 June, the *Chronicle* reported: 'It arrived at dawn in a fog bank atop twin peaks.'

'There were strong vibrations of love,' Randall de Leon, a hippie, was quoted as telling the *San Francisco Chronicle*, having stood 'in an almost frozen pose on the windy crest of the easternmost ridge of twin peaks, one arm pointing above his head at the faint unremitting appearances of the sun'. In the Haight later he joined a gathering stream of thousands heading to Golden Gate Park. The *Chronicle*'s Jack Viels reported:

War

❝ They celebrated making it through the spring and communed with the Gods, spirits, forces, influences and people present during the solstice. They lay down in a green meadow for a giant psychedelic picnic; they lay in the daisies and tied colourful paper flowers to ordinary trees and bushes, laboriously created elaborate and exotic shrines along the meadow borders and listened to a turned-on symphony of bongos, bells, whistles, flutes, guitars, an occasional trumpet and sax, drums and cymbals. A hippie stroked the nose of a police horse while the cop wrote out a parking ticket. There was a barbecue. At set of sun they marched to the sea to see the rising of the moon. Now the summer of love had begun.'

At the start of the summer, with the Diggers providing accommodation wherever they could stay ahead of unsympathetic visits from the inspectors of Ellis D. Sox, with the San Francisco Free Clinic picking up some mostly drug-related casualties, and with the church urging tolerance, it is a pity the authorities didn't respond as generously as they could have done. Then there just might have been real hope for the Summer of Love.

Helen Perry says that those furthest removed remained the most intolerant – the immediate neighbourhood became increasingly sympathetic towards the responsible leadership of the Diggers, the honest traders, the sheltering churches, but the city fathers and institutions became more and more punitive, more and more frightened. The police, in Helen Perry's words, 'finally, frankly harassed the young people'.

Meanwhile, growing anti-war feeling made strange bedfellows of hippies and politicians. On 23 September, Governor Romney, competing against Richard M. Nixon for nomination as Republican leader, decided to go electioneering among the hippies. He was running for President but was 'getting his ass whupped' for telling the press that when he went to Vietnam he got the impression he was 'being brainwashed' by the military–political duopoly running the war. Of course, it is a matter of public record that leaders who actually went to Vietnam, as well as those who merely received reports, were the victims of clever snow-jobs, but then it was no way to run for President to admit it! He was welcomed in the Panhandle as nowhere else. Governor Romney, a Mormon, couldn't actually endorse the dopers of the Haight but he munched corn, accepted a present of some cigarette-papers, talked to church leaders, met some runaways, visited the Black People's Free Store, and left with a flower and a smile. He did not become President of the United States.

Former Californian governor Edmund 'Pat' Brown, father of subsequent governor, Jerry, publicly announced that there was a growing feeling against the war. While he didn't believe a peace delegation could actually beat a Johnson delegation, there was 'impatience from sincere people who didn't *understand* the situation'. Hardly *brave* words, but bolder than some. We clung to any straws tossed to us by the Establishment. *We* knew the war was wrong, and outside America there were moves afoot to discredit the American government's stance.

Bertrand Russell and Jean-Paul Sartre, two key figures in modern philosophy, were named respectively honorary and executive presidents of a 'war crimes tribunal' set up in Sweden in Russell's name to 'try' the United States and 'compile a dossier of atrocities and criminal deeds committed against the citizens of Vietnam'. The committee around these two distinguished thinkers and secular saints was international and impressive: Simone de Beauvoir, Stokely Carmichael, James Baldwin and David Dellinger among them. These last three were American activists. The chairman of the tribunal was Vladimir Dedijer. There had been an earlier plan to hold the sessions in Paris, but the French government had at the last minute withdrawn hospitality, and the Swedes, who maintained a solidly anti-war stance, welcomed the tribunal to Stockholm.

It was held in two sessions. The first was in May 1967, and the second in November. Among the charges it was alleged that:

> **◖ The air force of the United States has dropped in Vietnam four million pounds of bombs daily. If this continues at this rate to the end of the year, the total will constitute a greater mass of explosives than it unloaded on the entire Pacific theatre during the whole of the Second World War. In the South, the US forces and their docile Saigon allies have herded eight million people, peasants and their families into barbed wire encampments under the surveillance of the political police. Chemical poisons have been and are being used to defoliate and render barren tens of thousands of acres of farmland**

'... more than five hundred thousand Vietnamese men, women and children have perished under this onslaught.'

When Bertrand Russell's secretary, American Ralph Schoenman, appeared before the tribunal he brought with him the great man's speech. 'The tribunal is revolutionary,' he said on behalf of Bertrand Russell. 'We have no armies and no gallows. We lack power, even the power of mass communication. It is overdue that those without power sit in judgement over those who have it. This is a test we must meet alone if need be. We are responsible before history.'

This was pure Counter-Cultural Speak, as good as anyone had heard from the poets or the Beats. That it came from an Englishman of whom many hippies had never even heard is not important: out there, in Scandinavia, sober and wise men were talking their language and saying brave things about the 'terrible' leaders of the Free World!

It was said to be a 'rigged tribunal'. The British activist Tariq Ali wouldn't disagree. 'One could say exactly that about the Nuremberg War Crimes Tribunal, that you had people there who believed that what had been done was immoral. Its main impact was to draw attention to what was going on in Vietnam, on the level of genocide, which it succeeded in doing.'

Tariq Ali, no hippie, was, however, a well-loved figure in counter-cultural politics. He occupied a high place in the hate list compiled by the Right, and that was good enough for most of us. His own view of the 'costumed people' is generous.

In 1967 lots of people were still in process of formation; their ideas, their music, even their lifestyles had still not gelled out. And overlying all this was the feeling that things had to change. Those of us who were politically on the left knew the sort of change we wanted; the hippies, the lifestylers, the libertarians were not so sure of their aims but they felt that there was something very wrong with the world. And this common feeling brought us all together on demonstrations, at meetings.... Though I never went to a love-in, there were many of those, and rock concerts. They all brought together politics and culture in a way that had not been seen before and hasn't since.'

Tariq Ali went to Hanoi on behalf of Bertrand Russell in December 1966 and January 1967.

I remember travelling at night because that was when the bombing was the lightest. I remember we were about to be taken into a hospital in North Vietnam but the radar spotted bombers and they

delayed our visit. When we went, an hour later, the entire hospital had been destroyed. That war left its mark on a whole generation for good and bad. It meant a lot to us. I was there as an investigator/observer for the tribunal, taking notes, which became very difficult as I saw people dying or being killed. You had to remove yourself and take the notes on their behalf. *For their sake.*'

Harold Wilson, the British premier who backed America throughout the war despite a substantial body of opinion on the British left against the American action, had earlier refused the request of Lord Russell that the tribunal be held in London. 'He was scared of the Americans,' says Tariq Ali. But because of the tribunal's passion and sheer intellectual weight there was a substantial communication gain. People *heard* about it. Jane Fonda, then married to Roger Vadim and living in Paris, followed the news of the tribunal's findings with mounting horror. Previously influenced by her famous middle-of-the-road liberal father, Henry, she became seriously politicised by the war, shifted leftwards and earned considerable notoriety because of it. Likewise her brother Peter, who boldly refused induction into the forces and spoke endlessly and publicly against the violence in Vietnam. Such people had influence and access. In London, Tariq Ali was busy drumming up more anti-war feeling. He says now:

❛ The Vietnamese had told us, "We can win the war here on the ground but in order to expedite its conclusion, we need support from our friends in Europe and North America. What you can do is influence your government," and so there was a very clear call for international solidarity in the mood of the year. We felt the world was all one, all struggles were linked to each other.'

Tariq Ali: 'Things had to change.'

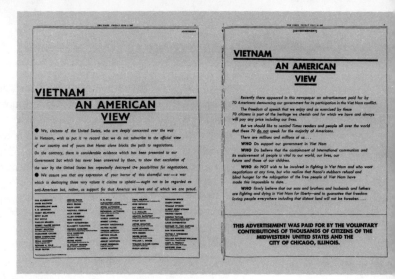

Tariq Ali and his friends set up the Vietnam Solidarity Campaign, 'very clearly not as an organisation which was neutral in the war, or an organisation which just wanted peace, but as an organisation which wanted peace from victory. It wanted the Vietnamese to win. This was, if you like, a substitute for what in Spanish Civil War days would have been the International Brigade, but we were called on to fight the war in our own homeland in order to bring peace closer, and we did that.'

In London *The Times* that summer had become quite a popular advertising medium for dissenting views. In those days when it was a great Great Newspaper, the supplication of support for minority causes somehow carried more weight, elicited more trust, if it appeared in *The Times*. There had been a full-page advertisement entitled 'Vietnam – An American View' which read, in part: 'We, citizens of the United States … do not subscribe to the official view of our country and of yours that Hanoi alone blocks the path to negotiations. On the contrary there is considerable evidence … to show that escalation of the war by the United States has repeatedly destroyed the possibility for negotiations.' It concluded: 'We assure you that any expression of your horror at this shameful war – a war which is destroying those very values it claims to uphold – ought not to be regarded as anti-American but, rather, as support for that America we love and of which we are proud.'

The 'view' was signed by some extraordinarily distinguished, famous and disparate Americans including James Baldwin, Marlon Brando, Noam Chomsky, Jules Feiffer, Allen Ginsberg, Arthur Miller, Mike Nichols, Philip Roth, Pete Seeger, Susan Sontag, Robert Lowell, Sam Wanamaker, and about two dozen very senior professors among the seventy signatories.

An answering full-page advertisement appeared six weeks later. It conceded the right of free speech but asserted: 'These 70 *do not* speak for the majority of Americans.... There are millions and millions of

222

us ... who do believe that the containment of international communism and its enslavement of people is vital to our world, our lives, our future and those of our children.'

It was stated, in conclusion, that the advertisement was paid for by 'the voluntary contributions of thousands of citizens of the Midwestern United States, and the City of Chicago, Illinois'. And thus, with an inexorable shift towards the liberal view, was battle fully joined in 1967. But, incredibly, Johnson would resign and there would be two Nixon election victories, fought on the fashionable 'peace' platform, before the war ended.

Abbie Hoffman, who had long been a civil rights activist and peace campaigner, saw the direction the anti-war tide was taking in New York.

❝ After the early be-ins, which were just an expression of philosophy without any political thrust, it was possible by Easter to have 40,000 gathering in the Peace Parade in the Sheep-Meadow, three times the number on Fifth Avenue in the *regular* Easter Parade, which had Cardinal Spellman, that blesser of those who went to Vietnam, posing for pictures behind a machine-gun. We had the freaks in the park for peace.'

Hoffman saw 'The Street' as crucial symbolism of the movement for change. Just as the Diggers and our costumed heroes and heroines took to the streets in San Francisco whenever they wanted to make a point, so Hoffman on the East Coast saw its potential as an arena for anti-war consciousness.

❝ For middle-class Americans the street is an extremely important symbol because your whole inculturation experience is geared around keeping you out of the street – there's violence in the street, there's dirty women in the street, if you lose your job you'll be in the street ... so, don't stay in the street! The idea is to keep everybody indoors. So, when you come to challenge the powers that be, inevitably you find yourself on the kerbstone of indifference, wondering: "Should I play it safe and stay on the sidewalks, or should I go into the street?" And it's the ones that hit the street first that are the leaders. It's the ones that are taking the most risks that will ultimately effect the change in society. I'm not just speaking of the street as a physical, actual street ... it's also the street of what we used to call "Prime Time" because of the impact of TV. It's the "Prime Time" street that's in your head that you have to destroy.

'When we began resisting the war in Vietnam, resistance was not popular at all – there was a very small percentage of people and

223

they were getting the shit kicked out of them – but slowly the numbers grew. I'm not going to say it was ever a majority – I don't believe majorities make these kind of changes – but it became enough people to stop the war in Vietnam because of pressure here, because of civil war in our own country. At no time in Western civilisation had a foreign war been stopped in this way. It had become a generational war.'

There began, all over America in the Summer of Love, to be talk of a Great Demonstration against the war. It was a natural evolution.

Allen Cohen, editor of the *Oracle*, traces the origins of the demonstration back to the time of the Be-In, when he and the hippies started to talk to the Berkeley activists. He had been reading a book by Lewis Mumford called *The City in History* in which the author describes the Pentagon as being a structure from a previous period in history, and warns that not until it is destroyed will there be a just and peaceful world.

Cohen says: 'I read this excerpt to Michael Bowen and Jerry Rubin, and I suggested that we direct our energies toward the Pentagon, to exorcising it in a magic ceremony. Michael liked that idea because he was into the theatre of politics, we were into the magic of living, and so the two ideas merged.'

The Human Be-In – with its blending of spirituality, political inactivism, all-welcome-with-bells, just *being* – set the metaphysical stage for the harnessing of the counter-culture to the planned march on the Pentagon in October 1967. There had been demonstrations before, God knows, all over the world for better or for worse. Some good ones had turned out badly, and some badly motivated ones had turned out well for evil men – Nuremberg, for instance. It was immediately apparent that if the October demonstration were to *succeed*, be audible, simple and understandable, it would have to be visible, very well organised and, above all, peaceful. The idea of an 'exorcism' was deeply attractive to the counter-culture and oddballs everywhere. Could the Pentagon really be purged of evil, bloodlessly?

Ed Sanders of the Fugs, Abbie Hoffman, Ponderosa Pine (then still Keith Lampe, ex-soldier, ex-newsman), Allen Ginsberg and Allen Cohen were all enthusiastic about the idea of visiting exorcism, levitation and other indignities on the terrifying building/institution.

Ponderosa Pine remembers their meetings in New York:

◄ All of us had been living on the East Coast, but we had a surprise visitor, Michael Bowen, who had been to Mexico to consult with shamans on the matter of levitation. We were just trying to put together an imaginative project with media appeal, we didn't expect

Ponderosa Pine

the building actually to leave terra firma, but this fellow arrived with ideas on how to make it happen and I began to see there was an interesting difference between East Coast and West Coast: East Coast being more into media projects, and West Coast more into lifestyle.

'A friend of mine realised that the new left at that time had controlled all of the language to the press about the action. They – the new left – had the bullhorns and they kept everything their way until the marshals arrived to club people, when the hippies took the skull-bashing and the gaol time. And my friend said: "This is unjust, and if this is what's happening why shouldn't there be some kind of loose media representation of the hippies? Not with tight

Black uprisings. Burn, baby, burn. July 1967. Such was the white attitude to these events, the caption at the time failed to name the city. It could be anywhere in urban America.

leadership, not hierarchical, very informal." And we began to add other characteristics. Since a lot of people were becoming paranoid under swiftly increasing police pressure, we thought the new group should have a sense of humour.'

Yippies were born.
Ed Sanders remembers:

❛ Someone [Cohen and Bowen] came up with their idea for exorcism and levitation modelled on the Catholic or Episcopalian exorcism, so we said, "Let's do it," had meetings at my bookstore where I consulted a Hittite book. I studied linguistics at college, so I dug up some phrases, and some Graeco-Roman magic formulae I knew, and cobbled together all this stuff. We made other plans, too. An

'The Death of Hippie'

American Indian was to circle the Pentagon with a trail of cornmeal; we were going to get a cow, which is the symbol of Hathar, the Egyptian sky-deity, the benevolent patroness of arts and schools, and bring that into the proceedings.'

So the plotting progressed between the East and West Coast anti-war pranksters. To the costumed ones it seemed like a lot more fun than Kezar, where even Country Joe Macdonald had not been allowed more than a few minutes' playing-time. The march on Washington would now be 'Haight Meets East Village and Has a Ball'. So successfully had the Diggers brought playfulness to the street that many activists, tired of speeches or serious confrontation, now saw the hippies as being firmly on their side. A splendid time was guaranteed for all at the expense of the government and what Abbie Hoffman called 'their fucking war'. Meanwhile, the Haight had become a peepshow visited by pressmen from all around the world, by tourists and runaways and celebrities, whether George Harrison and Paul McCartney, or Rudolf Nureyev and Margot Fonteyn. These latter two improbable exquisites were found hiding on a roof and arrested on suspicion of being part of the counter-culture – to the delight of the hippies, who would have been very happy to recruit at that level. No charges were brought. The dancers had merely been curious sightseers.

Ron Thelin of the Psychedelic Store, once among the most optimistic of the Haight people, had seen too much of the dream dissipated that summer under the media spotlight. Where at the announcement of a 'Summer of Love' he had seen the chance of purchasing a hall where they could teach crafts, carpentry, cooking, the making of clothes, and hold concerts and lectures, he now saw the whole hippie ethos shrivelling and dying in the fierce glare of media attention.

He says now:

‹ The effect of the media on the Haight was powerful. We use this media-tool all the time to convey our ideas, and it's one of the miracles of this age that an idea can be communicated to, say, Zaïre, Africa, instantly. But "The Death of Hippie" was about that, too – the way the media entrapped people into imitating what it was to have been. That's what happens with the media: people imitate. It's not from their own souls, from their own conviction, it's just imitation. That's why we held the "Death of Hippie" event. It was to beat the media at their own game. Say: "Don't do it because someone else is doing it. Do it because that's how *you* feel about it." '

All in all, Ron Thelin decided, it was time to turn off, tune out and drop away from the Haight. The *San Francisco Chronicle* announced on 4 October: 'The hippie movement, according to its own spokesmen, is dead. [Now] it's, well, to give it a name, instead of the hippies, the freebies. Beards are out; beads are out; even pot may be out. Now the touchstone is to be free – free especially of the hippie designation.'

The *Chronicle* quoted Ron Thelin: 'I have had it. [In the spirit of Thoreau] we're getting rid of all these possessions. We want to concentrate on how it feels to be free, every minute of the day.' Describing Ron as 'the first of the freebies', the *Chronicle* quoted him: 'the hippies, with their own hungry consent, were the creation of TV, radio and the newspapers. The media cast nets, created bags for the identity-hungry to climb into ... your face on TV, your style immortalised without soul in the captions of the *Chronicle*. NBC says you exist, ergo I am.' Thelin also said, 'It must all go – a victim of narcissism and plebeian vanity,' and he promised that now the boundaries of the San Francisco hippie world were down and would be replaced by a will to be free that went beyond Haight-Ashbury, 'which had been portioned to us by the media police and the tourists who came to the zoo to see the captive animals. We growled fiercely behind the bars we accepted but now we are no longer hippies....'

Today Ron Thelin casts a loving look at events around those three days in October that culminated in the Funeral of Hippie on 6 October.

‹ On the day of the death, we gave everything away. We stayed open all night. A guy from Vietnam gave me a medal of St Michael. We played records in the shop for whoever came. We played *Sgt Pepper's Lonely Hearts Club Band* a lot that night. We gave away books, we gave away other people's stuff [a lot of things were left there on consignment], the records, the whole shebang. We wrote a little funeral notice mourning this "hippie", this beaded creature of habit

'The Death of Hippie.' The people who *lived* their beliefs tired of media-induced 'narcissism and plebeian vanity' and buried their hippie past to reaffirm their desire to be Free of all attachments to possessions and image. In the power-play, symbols had to be met with symbols. The game worked.

227

it was becoming, and we carried a coffin down Haight Street and people threw beads and trinkets and other belongings into the coffin. Then it was taken down to the Panhandle and burned. I think [the gesture] succeeded.

'It was that feeling of giving and sharing which marked the Death of Hippie, and the end of the Psychedelic Shop. Then I cashed in the life insurance policy that my father bought me, got a white panel truck which we called the Free News Truck, and headed on out. Two weeks later I was in Washington, DC, for the exorcism of the Pentagon.'

Abbie Hoffman and all the rest were busy making preparations there.

‹ A friend and I went to the Pentagon, measured it, got arrested, got a lot of publicity. We said we were finding out how many witches we would need and so on. We went on TV talk-shows, doing things, saying things – it was all satire, all tongue-in-cheek, but good satire. You know twenty-five per cent of the people are going to believe you anyway.'

Certainly there was a lot of speculation developing during the run-up to the demonstration at the Pentagon. It ranged over possibilities as diverse as chaos on the streets, terrible injuries, maybe the awful spectacle of the devil's own building actually rising into the air and hurling itself and contents down on top of a defenceless city. What if there were nuclear devices in the Pentagon? And, if the thing didn't get levitated but was actually exorcised, whither would the demons scatter and what would they do among the ignorant populace? Would the Furies at last be loosed over a sinful nation, careless of God, bent on genocide? Did America not now deserve such retribution?

The march began by the Lincoln Memorial on the morning of 21 October, in the heart of governmental, ceremonial, sentimental, Home-of-the-Brave Washington. Norman Mailer, who later wrote the Pulitzer Prize-winning *Armies of the Night* based around the events of the year of the march, a brilliant demonstration of history fanning a novelist's creative fires, admits in the book that on arrival in the empty expanse of the North Area parking-lot of the Pentagon he had the bizarre and secret desire to be back in New York for a party. He realised instantly how clever the government had been to route the marchers directly to an empty lot as big as five football pitches. In such an unromantic venue, without the drama of facing troops at the Pentagon's gates, there was time to think such disloyal thoughts. That was how totalitarianism bred apathy, he thought. Clever!

Like so many events noble in conception, brave in execution and aggrandised in memory, the Pentagon happening was all sorts of muddle and untidiness. There should be no suggestion that it did not work, but reality always leaves a lot to be desired, and marches, however well organised, are not the dramatic torch-bearing crowd scenes of the movies. There are always all manner of irregularities. Which pace do we march at and in what order? Mailer and his two respected cosmopolitan companions, the poet Robert Lowell and the critic Dwight Macdonald, were meant to be in the front row of notables leading off from Lincoln Memorial at the head of a crowd which Mailer estimated at 50,000 but others guessed to be anything between 25,000 and 250,000. (Allen Cohen puts it at 100,000.)

In his description of the march – alas, too lengthy to be quoted in full here – Mailer asks us to imagine a mass of people

‹ bored for hours by speeches, now elated at the beginning of the March, now made irritable by delay, now compressed, all old latent pips of claustrophobia popping out of the crush, and picture them as they stepped out toward the bridge [over the Potomac], monitors in the lead … next the line of notables, with tens then hundreds of lines squeezing up behind, helicopters overhead, police gunning motor cycles, cameras spinning their gears like the winging of horse flies, TV cars bursting at the seams with hysterically overworked technicians, sun beating down overhead – this huge avalanche of people rumbled forward thirty feet and came to a stop in disorder, the lines behind breaking and warping and melding into themselves to make a crowd not a parade. Some jam-up at the front, just what no one knew, now they were moving again.'

Flowers down the barrels. A famous picture. It is still travelling the world – as you can see – and says so much. 'The Pentagon is not the absolute authority of the universe,' says Allen Ginsberg. 'The human spirit is the absolute authority.'

229

And so it went till they reached the parking-lot, hardly the heroic confrontation which was the reason why Mailer, maverick, pugilist and every good person's hero-writer, was there. He *had* to get arrested, get noticed. It was a duty. Fearing the possibility of a long wait, and the subsequent dissipation of his impulse for self-sacrifice, he made his way to a barrier, climbed over, crossed into police lines, insisted on arrest and got it – manfully so.

On his way he met the Fugs. They were there as a performing band, and as fierce glamorous figures in the anti-war movement they were crucial to the script of the Great Mobilisation. As costumed people, they were in goodly extended company.

The counter-culture, hippie no longer, was there in great number. This was their march and it would be the last in which ex-hippies would outnumber new yippies. Mailer reports that many were dressed like the legion of Sgt Pepper's band. There was a long, happy, zestful procession of free people in every sort of outfit from Batman to old Hollywood, both armies of the Civil War, the French Foreign Legion, every sort of ethnic dress, regional garb, armour, tropical gear. For some, their fancy dress was their daily apparel, white men and women dressed as local Indians and many wearing the loose apparel of the East. There were some real Indians but few blacks by now, they having left to stage their own march. Professors marched with their students.

All of divided America was represented in or against the march, the America which saw itself in initials: SCLC, Southern Christian Leadership

Conference; SDS, Students for Democratic Society, and the rest of the day-to-day, fair-play-for-decency radical movements; but there were by now brave new dissident factions exemplified by Veterans Against the War in Vietnam. The Reverend William Sloane Coffin, Jun., Chaplain of Yale, was a prominent figure in the front rank of protesters while remaining unequivocal in his respect for those actually fighting the war. When nearly a thousand young men had turned in their draft cards at the Justice Department on the day prior to the march – a criminal offence – he had stated: 'Many of us are veterans, and all of us have the highest sympathy for our boys in Vietnam. They know what a dirty bloody war it is.' But he warned that there would be no 'cleansing water' if military victory spelled moral defeat. He had sympathy, too, for the families who were losing their loved ones in an unjust war. It was to show solidarity with the young and equal detestation of elderly politicians and the military–industrial complex that good American people like Coffin were there. He was a brave bulky man who would later use his muscle to wrestle to the floor a member of the American Nazi Party who had attacked and felled Britain's Clive Jenkins, there as a guest and speaker.

Ed Sanders today remembers the Fugs' part in the adventure:

◄ We were playing a psychedelic peacock-feather venue in Washington – you know, two thousand people waving peacock feathers or whatever – and we used the money to rent a flatbed truck. The Liberation News Service got us a speaker system and we pulled this in as close to the Pentagon as we could and set up a huge Day-Glo dollar bill on canvas as a backdrop, and we played. Shirley Clarke was filming, Kenneth Anger the film-maker was underneath the flatbed, burning tarot cards and hissing and sing-songing some sibillant lines of arcane wisdom.'

The Fugs – the East Coast poets, musicians, performers and anarchists who were *right out there* for an end to the war. 'Out, demons, out,' they chanted at the Pentagon as it 'rose in the air' in many imaginings.

Ed Sanders remembers Mailer and Macdonald and Lowell coming by. He saw their respectably dressed presence as weird but interesting. The Fugs, in multicoloured capes, chanted 'Out, Demons, out,' their wailing – in Norman Mailer's words – 'mournful as the wind in a cave'. This was a mighty incantation and not to be lightly dismissed in Sanders's modest aside of today: 'We jibberished this thing out.'

In *Armies of the Night* Mailer gives this episode a whole chapter with the wonderful title 'The Witches and the Fugs'. Sanders's own contemporary document is a leaflet entitled *Exorcism and Levitation Demonstration Held at the Pentagon, October 1967*. It is surmounted by ancient Greek characters above a drawing of the Pentagon with the statement: 'A magic rite to exorcize the Spirits of murder, violence & creephood from the Pentagon.' A list of ten items follows:

Ed Sanders, recalls Mailer, chanted:

232 ‘ "In the name of the generative power of Priapus, in the name of totality, we call upon the demons of the Pentagon to rid themselves of the cancerous tumours of the war generals, all the secretaries and soldiers who don't know what they're doing, all the intrigue, bureaucracy and hatred, all the spewing coupled with prostate cancer in the deathbed. Every Pentagon general lying alone at night with a tortured psyche and an image of death in his brain, every general lying alone, every general lying alone." And then again: "Out, Demons, out. Out, Demons, out" while bells, cymbals, drums and brass made their own plea.'

To the question 'Was the levitation successful?' Ed Sanders replies: 'Well, the war went on to '75, so does that answer it? ... I don't know ... basically it was a self-fulfilling prophecy, a bunch of people trying to be creative when there was nothing we could actually do to stop the war.'

The Pentagon did not lift off the ground, nor did the building turn orange; but, then, there was, and always will be, that image of the flower down the barrel of a rifle. Ed Sanders smiles to remember: 'All those soldiers were out there with their trembling rifles, and for the first time I got to insert roses into the barrels of rifles. Those poor twenty-year-old kids were thinking: "Here's some guy in striped pants shoving roses down my M16." That was fun. I liked doing that.'

Allen Cohen was at the fun end of the event, too. He remembers that there was an application for a permit for a human chain to circle the Pentagon. It was not granted.

◄ It was the one thing not allowed. They allowed marching to the Pentagon from the Lincoln Memorial across the river to the parking-lot, and they allowed having a demonstration on its steps and on the grass in front of it, but they disallowed people joining hands around it and so we decided to rent a plane, fill it with flowers, circumnavigate the Pentagon from above and drop flowers into the middle of the building, which is an empty space. The FBI somehow got to hear about it ... and the guys who were going to do it were turned back at the airport with a carload of flowers. They came back to the demonstration with the flowers. We brought them up to the line of sheriffs and marshals and gave them out to people. That was the origin of the pictures of the rifles with the flowers in them, and flowers dropping from the helmets of soldiers.'

There was comparatively little violence from the demonstrators – not so much as in Main Street, Big Town, on a Saturday night. There was, however, real cruelty from the marshals and soldiers towards the marchers. Norman Mailer was arrested with kid gloves in comparison to the treatment meted out to demonstrators later that day and night. There were 1,000 other arrests, and charges were brought against 600 of those detained. Only twelve demonstrators, however, were charged with assault and only two brought to trial, both subsequently acquitted. But what of the assaults on demonstrators by marshals and soldiers? Throughout the day there had been repeated random arrests. As darkness fell, the few thousand remaining marchers assembled on the steps to the Pentagon. In *Armies of the Night*, Mailer quotes several horrifying eyewitness accounts of the level of violence used against the demonstrators on the Pentagon steps by Vietnam veteran paratroopers. Margie Stamberg, for instance, reported in the *Washington Free Press* on the especially harsh treatment of female demonstrators.

233

Allen Cohen

‹ With bayonets and rifle butts they moved first on the girls in the front line, kicking them, jabbing at them again and again with guns, busting their heads and arms to break the [demonstrators'] chain of arms.... One hundred people were methodically beaten and carried away to the paddy wagons.'

In the same newspaper a second observer, Thorne Dreyer, reported:

‹ The cops began to get really brutal, moving into the group in a wedge and smashing heads with billy clubs. These beautiful little hippy chicks had tears streaming down their faces, but they weren't about to move.'

Lyndon Johnson later congratulated his enforcers on their outstanding performance against 'the irresponsible acts of violence and lawlessness by many of the demonstrators'. It was his ghost-written response to Sanders's chant; 'Out, demonstrators, out,' cried LBJ. But in the next six months Johnson would be on television saying he would not seek re-election, and the mantle would pass to the shoulders of that next great President, Richard M. Nixon.

The Pentagon march marked the drawing up of lines between the activist and the pacifist, the costumed young against the uniformed young and their officer masters. In Allen Ginsberg's words:

‹ This was a massive popular demonstration against the war, striking directly into the Pentagon, in which the final image was of flower power with a kid sticking his flower into the barrel of a frightened

Where are they now?

soldier's gun, both the same age, both the same image of youth.

'I think it demystified the authority of the Pentagon, and in that sense we *did* levitate it. Before that the Pentagon was grounded ... in the authority of public approval, and the feeling that it was so rich and so big that it couldn't make a big mistake. Afterwards the public decided that the Pentagon was wrong. It was as simple as that. So the levitation of the Pentagon *was* a success. It must be understood for what it was – a poetic metaphor; basically a triumph of the human imagination over heavy metal materialism.

'The Pentagon was not the absolute authority of the universe. *The human spirit is the absolute authority*. The problem was named, the consciousness of the public was raised. By February 1968, Gallup reported that fifty-two per cent of the American people thought the war a big mistake.'

Allen Cohen sees the day as one of mixed blessings.

❮ Like all demonstrations this one produced a feeling of solidarity, of outrage, and it brought the two parts of the movement a little closer together. But as with all things there's a pendulum, and those who didn't like the violence that erupted from the most radical parts of the movement on the march separated out even further. So there were both effects.'

The hippies who became the yippies moved into 1968 with plans for further disruption. The 'play' element was part of the 1967 mentality, and 1968 would be more serious.

Theodore Roszak, in his book *The Making of a Counter Culture*, is generous to the concept of demonstration as theatre, carnival or magic.

● Before we decide that the policy of "no politics" cannot work, with its recourse to indirection, involvement by seduction, and subliminal persuasion, let us be honest about one thing. If violence and injustice could be eliminated from our society by heavy intellectual research and ideological analysis, by impassioned oratory and sober street rallies, by the organisation of bigger unions or lobbies or third parties or intricate coalitions, by the "flat ephemeral pamphlet and boring meeting", by barricades, bullets or bombs, then we should long since have been living in the New Jerusalem.

'Instead we are living in the thermonuclear technocracy. Given the perfectly dismal (if undeniably heroic) record of traditional radicalism in America, why should the dissenting young assume

If you go to Grosvenor Square, be sure to wear some flour in your hair

236

that the previous generations have much to tell them about practical politics?'

Amen.

James Reston, the much respected, very senior columnist of the *New York Times*, in his syndicated verdict on the demonstration said that Washington was: 'A sad, brooding city because everyone seemed to have lost in the anti-war siege of the Pentagon.' He saw the event as having been 'taken over by the militant minority'. Reston was never knowingly simplistic, but he was not inside the skins of the costumed ones, those whom Ed Sanders called 'the peacock feather people', who had actually done what they set out to do: bring music, love and flowers to a mad, bad place. Reston noted 'peace symbols' in the parade, and a sign on a wall: 'LSD NOT LBJ.'

Nevertheless, the demonstrators had drawn enormous numbers of defenders on to the streets, including 2,500 soldiers with fixed bayonets, plus marshals, police, and all the rest of the metal and leather paraphernalia of power. Across in Japan, much nearer the hideous war they were protesting against, reports spoke of a demonstration of 200,000 people. All over Europe the counter-culture orchestrated simultaneous anti-war protests, conspicuously in London and Amsterdam. Twenty years later, Tariq Ali remembers the London march.

❝ The police and our campaign were surprised by the size of the crowd that turned up outside the American embassy. It was small in comparison to what happened later, in 1968, but large for us then. Ten to twelve thousand people, I think. We charged the embassy and actually got to the glass doors. ... And then there was a moment of panic: "What do we do now?" And in that moment of panic the police regrouped and drove us off down the steps again. The next day someone pointed out that this moment of delay must have been an instinct for survival among the demonstrators. Inside the embassy there were armed Marines, and as we would technically have been on American soil they could have done what they liked.

'The demonstration itself was a very interesting mixture of political hippies wearing badges – "Make Love Not War" – and flower people handing blooms to the police. It was a weird affair but very effective, and the next day it was reported in shocked tones by the press.'

237

Though a serious-minded man, Tariq Ali has sympathy for those who experienced their dissent on the level of clothes and sexual liberation: 'Even the most frivolous forms of protest had a sort of element of humanity about them and they at least made you laugh. The American yippies took this to extremes, and we even considered using their methods.'

One plan involved the delivery of ten truckloads of cow dung to Harold Wilson in 10 Downing Street. The other involved swallowing pieces of bacon with strings attached, to be pulled out in front of Wilson, thus 'throwing-up' over the Prime Minister. Both were discarded as impractical, but it says something of the mood of the times that they were considered at all.

In similar iconoclastic anti-war vein, Norman Mailer, over on 'The Merv Griffin Show' in New York, accused of having used 'four-lettered words' at the demonstration, told Griffin: 'I think this war's more obscene than all dirty four-letter words and all the dirty words American authors put into all the dirty books you ban in your libraries. I think one minute in the mind of General Westmoreland is more obscene than all those words put together.'

And that was the beginning of the end of intellectual support for the Vietnam War. Now 'we' were *all* the counter-culture: Dr Spock, Norman Mailer, Tariq Ali, the Beatles, Allen Ginsberg. Now the youth of America was on fire with righteous democratic passion. Hell, no, they *wouldn't go*. From then until the end of the year, the activists and the pacifists and the (now officially ex-) hippies either drifted towards rural life, retrenched in the cities or geared for further anti-war provocation.

Country Joe Macdonald is eloquent upon the nature of our hopes then. He recalls his feelings at the Human Be-In at the beginning of the year.

❛ I was convinced that at this gathering of the tribes that the stage would come where the princes and princesses of the tribes and a noble, kind, courageous race of people would change the destiny of the planet for ever and we would all live happily ever after.'

And?

❛ And the outcome was quite different to what I thought. Much confusion and reality set in. It was the beginning and the end of some childish and Utopian dream but I think it was very important that it happened because there was now a brand-new consciousness and it was so appealing that it circled the entire planet. People now had to deal with it – with what became known eventually as the Woodstock consciousness.'

Life goes on.

239

For some 1967 is overlaid
with a melancholy cast
symbolised by the violence
and all too visible finality of
the death of Che Guevara.
He became an instant hero
in legend and on poster for
the young. His courage
was something to aspire to
and he had what Jeff Nuttall
called 'rapacious good
looks'.

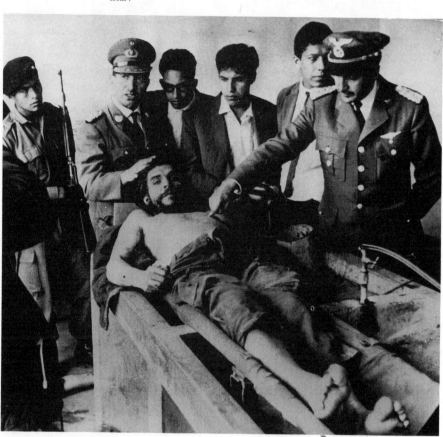

EPILOGUE

Write us as ones who tried to love our fellow-men. It wasn't always easy. Though we said it and sang it over and over again, that all we needed was love, it turned out to be more complicated than that. Still and all, it was a *sort* of Arcady, and we're still alive and well to prove it.

In this passing phase of the late twentieth century there is much more evident selfishness and ill-temper, but as Jack Kerouac said to Allen Ginsberg: 'Walking on water wasn't built in a day.' We have found that by applying that optimism with generosity to our immediate environment much can be improved, or sustained in better shape, than is possible in the scramble to acquire personal wealth. David Simpson of the Diggers calls it 'bioregionalism' – a long word for looking at one's surroundings, what is required to sustain it, how it relates to the rest of the planet, how to fit into it so that when you take what you need you are not leaving a wasteland. That applies everywhere – to the countryside, to the city, to the suburbs. Simpson believes, as I do, that a powerful legacy of the sixties is a sense of the fragility and the complexity of the relationship between ourselves and where we live. The growth of such organisations as Greenpeace, Friends of the Earth, the greater awareness of older bodies like the Council for the Protection of Rural England, the attention each political party (certainly in most of Europe) has to pay to 'Green' notions are part of the legacy of the sixties.

I agree, too, with Peter Coyote, who sees most of the people he knew pursuing their lives with the same attention to individual responsibility for one's fellows. As he says, people's style has changed; it doesn't matter whether their hair is long or short, but their 'religious' communion with nature and man's better self remains undiminished. Coyote believes that the Reagan years are a temporary reaction: 'They are a reaction by the forces that were maybe threatened a little too assiduously during the sixties, so that they have regrouped to remind themselves that the world paradigm they understood has not completely shattered.'

But it *is* shattered, and the times they are a-changing. Coyote hopes –

and I hope – that today's young will leave the door open for more people to see this change, not as something born of a failed drug-induced euphoria, but as a *good change* that will gradually develop so that each time around the spiral we can get a little wisdom and the group consciousness will click just a notch higher. We ask that today's young judge us without cynicism. We have learned that the battle is between love and fear. We need not necessarily fear what Leary has termed the OT, the Overwhelming Threat. If we do not fuel that Pentagonic myth, it may die. What, after all, could Daniel Ortega do to the Kansas farmer that market forces have not already done?

The Dutch Provos, disbanded now but alive and thriving spiritually, see in Holland much room for hope. Roel van Duijn says Amsterdam is still a city of action groups; older people have changed their behaviour and acknowledge the three principles of green politics that embody the old white (bicycle) dream: quality of living conditions, direct democracy and open spirituality.

Caroline Coon, young and terrifically active in London on behalf of the busted ones of that and subsequent years, saw more than many others the double standards of the defenders of the *status quo*. Today, she believes that much was saved from the period: 'Twenty years ago hippies had no power, only an ideal. Today we are beginning to see the ideology wield power.'

Ron Thelin, now living in the country outside San Francisco, describes 1967 as a time when

❝ There was this door that was blown open by God, and light shone in on the world, huge amounts of light, at first blinding; and then a vision of the beautiful world started to be realised, and for about a year and a half the world felt it was really true. *Sgt Pepper*. **Hey, it's really going to happen. And then fear and habit and inertia and doubt started to push the door closed. They're still pushing. Reagan is pushing hard now. "No, no, let's keep to what we know about. No drugs! Oh God! No smoke. Close the door." But there's still a light under the door. And a friend of mine told me: "You know, a door can always be opened again." ❞**

After the Summer of Love, after the march on the Pentagon, after the triumph of *Sgt Pepper*, still in the record charts as autumn deepened into winter, hippies were becoming yippies (members of the Youth International Party), and the Beatles were editing something called *Magical Mystery Tour* and preparing to open the Apple boutique, the first commercial manifestation of Apple. Apple was to incorporate film, publishing, records, electronics and retail. I would be press officer, and

Cass Elliott and Jimi Hendrix when all the world was young and everything was possible. They were two of a kind in attitude but each was a self-invention defying imitation. Cass was unafraid, fat and free; Jimi was wild and truly Far-Out. Both died a long time ago but their auras and reputations are intact.

we would all live together in a heavenly land somewhere near Norwich. Some of these dreams came true. There was a grand ball and party at the Royal Lancaster Hotel in London to celebrate the completion of *Magical Mystery Tour*, the first Apple film, made for television. The guests were asked to wear fancy dress. In that year of music, love and flowers, I went as Hitler.

The year hadn't been all that wonderful for millions of people outside the world of inner spacemen. The narrative has slipped by many events, some large, world-famous and quite shattering, or small and remembered and appreciated by a handful who respect what Hannah More has termed the peace that springs from the large aggregate of little things.

There was a furious and costly armed struggle in the Middle East between the state of Israel and Egypt with combined Arab support. It became known as the Six-Day War, and the region remains in turmoil twenty years later, though Israel and Egypt made a kind of peace in the seventies. There were in 1967 continued uprisings by repressed blacks in the United States. That nation is still split, though fresh subdivisions have emerged and turned attention from the black struggle – Hispanics, the poor whites, the homeless of all groups, the outcasts of Reagan's America.

In 1967, Che Guevara died. So did Vivien Leigh. The first at the hands of Bolivian heavies with help from the CIA, the other after several battles against depression and terrible debilitation. Francis Chichester, fit and fierce, sailed round the world, alone, in a yacht. He was sixty-six. On his return he was knighted. Elvis Presley at last married Priscilla Beaulieu in Las Vegas. A brilliant, if quirky, lyric tenor named Tiny Tim became a star. Sandie Shaw won the Eurovision Song Contest with 'Puppet on a String'. The British government outlawed pirate radio. Radios Caroline and London, operating from ships off the east coast of England, had attracted millions of listeners. Now the BBC responded with its own pop radio station, Radio 1, employing several former pirate stars, notably Kenny Everett, a brilliant and very psychedelic broadcaster – quite the best of the new British disc jockeys who had learned some American tricks and anglicised them. Some – nameless ones – were dreadful. In San Francisco two disc jockeys – first Larry Miller, then Tom Donahue – had pioneered progressive free-form radio, daring to play long album-tracks back to back without funny voices or inane chatter. In Britain a Liverpudlian broadcaster who called himself John Peel did the same on his own show, 'The Perfumed Garden'. The best new game in radioland was to choose your own favourites and play 'em. Unheard of before 1967 on legal airwaves.

There would be, for the rest of the sixties and the seventies, ample new music fostered by the evolution of free-form lyrics and musical adventure.

Jimmy Webb and Harry Nilsson were two to spring to national attention in 1967, both working out of Los Angeles, both young and buccaneering and intelligent. Webb wrote mainly for others, though he was an engaging performer and made good records. Nilsson, one of my dearest friends in the years that followed, had a unique voice and towering personality that caused the post-1967 Beatles to name him their 'favourite American group'. Webb and Nilsson had musical roots deeper than 1967, but the strong new growth came in that year, as it did for so many of those other young musicians for whom the psychedelic summer had been such a liberation. No more suits or tight collars; with one bound everybody – the dream ran – could be free.

Was love all we needed? The question is asked today. George Harrison reaches for Sir Walter Scott's poem, 'The Lay of the Last Minstrel', to reply: 'Love rules the court, the camp, the grove, / And men below, and saints above; / For love is heaven, and heaven is love.'

Abbie Hoffman: 'It's nice to have, as is peace, but it is not [all you need], and this is basically the flaw, I think, in Beatles politics. *Justice* is all you need.'

Tariq Ali says that love is very nice, but that he had taken it up with John Lennon: 'It was a naïve anthem, and could not be an anthem for the movement, certainly not for the Vietnamese fighting in Vietnam, or the black South Africans or Nicaraguans today.'

Peter Blake believes that one can get a long way on love: 'But it isn't all you need. The Beatles were also extremely rich at that point and they were extremely talented and they were brilliant musicians.'

Allen Cohen raises doubts about the simplistic approach of the message:

❮ Unless we change who controls the institutions of society and the heart of the institutions, and bring love and compassion into them, the institutions will stay the same and all the love in the world won't change them; they're very ingrained in everything that we do. '

David Simpson believes that love of the planet and of human life as part of that planet is all we need. Peter Coyote would say, yes, love is all we need if that love be the expression of devotion and appreciation of the universe. One of the authors of the song is less certain: 'Is love all you need? I don't know really. I don't know what you need, you know. I'm just some feller, and I haven't got any answers. We're all just individuals. I don't think there's anyone who's got the answers.' So says Paul McCartney.

Yet the 'answers' keep on coming.

Allen Ginsberg:

❝ I would say awareness is all you need, and then love proceeds from awareness. I think the saying "Love is all you need" is a sentimentalisation because "love", after all, is a word and anybody can interpret it differently, but I think "awareness" is a little more ample.'

Timothy Leary:

❝ Love is not all you need. Love is just a beginning. Love without intelligence, love without precision, love without discrimination, love without an evolutionary sense, love that doesn't grow and change, [that sort of] love is the biggest addiction of all, like drugs and television or anything else – it's a great ally but a terrible master to be enslaved to.'

Leary is roguish about 1967:

❝ I give us this credit. We were willing to be holy fools. We were willing to make asses of ourselves. But let's not hang these portraits of our foolish selves on the walls of the Smithsonian Institute.'

Ron Thelin says that you need truth, not just love: 'You have to have a heart. You have to speak from the heart. But you have to speak the truth.' Paul Kantner says: 'The idea is noble, and it was the idea that, I think, imbued the whole age. It is one of the main things you need, and if you don't have that all the rest of the stuff doesn't really matter.' I would say that we need more than love. Love is very important, but we need sobriety and a lot of positive energy, and we need to know where our next meal is coming from.

In Arcadian dreams in times to come there will be a belief that somehow things will turn out all right. More danced than dramatised, these times will astonish the people no less than those through which we have lived in this book. And in T. S. Eliot's words, '... the end of all our exploring will be to arrive where we started, and know the place for the first time.'

Elvis and Priscilla married in Las Vegas in a time capsule of their own choosing. His fame was undimmed throughout psychedelia and other manias but many fans turned away in this period and never dreamed of the great revival that began at the end of the following year.

245

CHRONICLE OF EVENTS

1966

Oct 6	LSD outlawed in United States
10	Party at Roundhouse, London, to launch *International Times*
15	Bobby Seale and Huey Newton launch Black Panther Party in Oakland, Calif.
Nov	CAFF demonstrations on Sunset Strip, Los Angeles (young and showbiz people demonstrating against teenage curfew; some arrests)
Dec 23	Opening of UFO; Pink Floyd début there
26	*Time* awards 'Man of the Year' to 'The Younger Generation'

1967

Jan 1	Giant Freakout at the Roundhouse, London
	Giant Freakout at Winterland, San Francisco, including Jefferson Airplane, Grateful Dead, Quicksilver Messenger Service
4	Donald Campbell killed on Coniston Water
10	Provos 'bomb' royal wedding, Amsterdam
14	'The Gathering of the Tribes': the Human Be-In, Golden Gate Park, San Francisco
27	America, Russia and Britain sign treaty banning nuclear weapons in space

28	Three Apollo astronauts killed in fire at Cape Kennedy
Feb 12	Keith Richards's house-party raided, West Wittering, Sussex
17	'Penny Lane'/'Strawberry Fields Forever' released in Britain London School of Economics 'Daffodil Protest' march
March	Spring freakouts in Los Angeles and New York
9	*International Times* offices raided Berkeley Be-In, Berkeley, Calif.
18	*Torrey Canyon* oil-tanker disaster
30	*Sgt Pepper* cover photo session at Michael Cooper's studio
April 8	Sandie Shaw wins Eurovision Song Contest with 'Puppet on a String'
3–12	Paul McCartney visits San Francisco, Denver and Los Angeles
12	Ken Kesey on drugs charges
15	400,000 march on United Nations building to demonstrate against Vietnam War
27	Expo 67 opens in Montreal, Canada Beach Boy Carl Wilson indicted for failing to report for draft induction
28	Muhammad Ali at Houston Induction Center (licence rescinded)
29	'Fourteen-Hour Technicolor Dream' at Alexandra Palace, London
30	'Love-In' in Detroit ends in police riot
May	Greece kicks out long-hairs 'Smoke-In' at Speaker's Corner, London 'End of Provo' event in Vondelpark, Amsterdam

247

3–10	Russell Tribunal in Stockholm finds America guilty in Vietnam
10	Mick Jagger and Keith Richards in court in Chichester Brian Jones arrested at home
14	'Provo' declares itself dead
19	BBC bans 'A Day in the Life' Party at Brian Epstein's flat to launch *Sgt Pepper*
21	'Youth for Peace in Vietnam' rally in Trafalgar Square
25	John Lennon's newly painted Rolls-Royce collected in Weybridge
26	Pink Floyd at Queen Elizabeth Hall, London
28	Sir Francis Chichester home to Plymouth
30	Eastern province breaks away from Nigeria; civil war
June 1	*SGT PEPPER* RELEASED IN BRITAIN
	SOMA founded (Society of Mental Awareness) John Hopkins to prison for nine months A Day of Violence in Aden Advertisement in *The Times* against American involvement in Vietnam, signed by American intelligentsia
2	*SGT PEPPER* RELEASED IN AMERICA
	Berlin demonstration against Shah of Iran; Benno Ohnesborg shot dead Mick Jagger and Keith Richards in court; Brian Jones attends
3	Boston race riots
5–10	Six-Day War
16	Beatles on cover of *Life*; Paul McCartney admits taking LSD
16–18	Monterey Pop Festival
18	Paul McCartney's twenty-fifth birthday

19	Billy Graham (in London) and Spiro Agnew condemn Paul McCartney
23	Peace March, Century City, Los Angeles (Lyndon Johnson visiting)
25	'All You Need Is Love' satellite broadcast
	Muhammad Ali receives five-year sentence for refusal to join the Army
27	Mick Jagger and Keith Richards found guilty at West Sussex Assizes
28	Death of Jayne Mansfield in car crash
29	Rolling Stones sentenced to prison
July	Foundation of 'Release' organisation to help people raided, or 'busted', for drugs Foundation of Arts Lab, London 'Dialectics of Liberation' Congress, London London demonstration against *News of the World* for informing on Rolling Stones
1	Leader in *The Times*: 'Who Breaks a Butterfly on a Wheel?' *Time* cover-story: 'The Hippies: Anatomy of a Sub-Culture'
7	'All You Need Is Love'/'Baby You're a Rich Man' released in Britain
10	British Medical Association meeting on 'Drugs'
14	Advertisement in *The Times* supporting American involvement in Vietnam (counter to advertisement of 1 June)
11–15	Race riots, Newark, NJ
16	'Legalise Pot' rally, Hyde Park, London
23	Turkish earthquake 'Love-In', Griffith Park, Los Angeles

23–7	Race riots, Detroit, Mich.
24	Advertisement in *The Times* concerning cannabis
27	Royal Assent to Sexual Offences Act (legalising homosexual acts between consenting adults)
31	Mick Jagger appeals, wins, flown in 'World in Action' helicopter
Aug	Marine Broadcasting Act scuttles pirate radios
	'Breathalyser' introduced in Britain
8	George and Pattie Harrison tour Haight-Ashbury, Los Angeles
14	Closing of pirate radio stations
19	Anti-drug march in Sunderland
24	Ringo and Maureen's son Jason born
	John, Paul and George first meet Maharishi at Hilton Hotel, London
25	Beatles and partners go to Bangor to attend Transcendental Meditation seminar
25–7	'Festival of the Flower Children', Woburn Abbey, including Bee Gees, Alan Price, Marmalade
26	Brian Epstein dies
29	Brian Epstein buried in Liverpool
Sept 3	Hippies' LSD demonstration, Speaker's Corner, London
30	John Lennon, George Harrison and Maharishi on 'David Frost Show'
Oct 2	Grateful Dead busted, San Francisco

6	'Death of Hippie' procession, San Francisco (first anniversary of LSD being made illegal)
8	Death of Che Guevara
9	First edition of *Rolling Stone*
11	The Move sued by Harold Wilson
18	Première of *How I Won the War*
19	Joan Baez (and 122 others) arrested at Oakland Induction Center; Governor Reagan commends police
21	'Exorcism of the Pentagon', Washington, DC, march, including Norman Mailer and the Fugs Also marches in London, Paris, Bonn, etc.
27	Royal Assent to Abortion Act (becomes law on 27 April 1968) Royal Assent to Dangerous Drugs Act
30	Brian Jones on drugs charge
31	Brian Jones on bail; demonstrations at court
Nov	Pound devalued by 14.3 per cent
13	Martin Luther King receives award in Newcastle
14	'Hello Goodbye' / 'I Am the Walrus' released in Britain
Dec	Owsley busted in possession of 868,000 trips ($4.3 million) Youth International Party founded by Abbie Hoffman, Jerry Rubin and Paul Krassner
4–6	Whitehall Street, New York, anti-draft demonstration
7	Opening of Apple shop, 94 Baker Street
26	*Magical Mystery Tour* shown on BBC television

British Number One Singles in 1967

1966 1 December 'Green Green Grass of Home': **Tom Jones**

19 January 'I'm a Believer': **Monkees**

16 February 'This Is My Song': **Petula Clark**

2 March 'Release Me': **Engelbert Humperdinck**

13 April 'Somethin' Stupid': **Frank and Nancy Sinatra**

27 April 'Puppet on a String': **Sandie Shaw**

18 May 'Silence Is Golden': **Tremeloes**

8 June 'A Whiter Shade of Pale': **Procol Harum**

19 July 'All You Need Is Love': **Beatles**

9 August 'San Francisco (Be Sure to Wear Flowers in Your Hair)': **Scott McKenzie**

6 September 'The Last Waltz': **Engelbert Humperdinck**

11 October 'Massachusetts': **Bee Gees**

8 November 'Baby Now That I've Found You': **Foundations**

22 November 'Let the Heartaches Begin': **Long John Baldry**

6 December 'Hello Goodbye': **Beatles**

American Number One Singles in 1967

1966	**31 December**	'I'm a Believer': **Monkees**
	18 February	'Kind of a Drag': **Buckinghams**
	4 March	'Ruby Tuesday': **Rolling Stones**
	11 March	'Love Is Here': **Supremes**
	18 March	'Penny Lane': **Beatles**
	25 March	'Happy Together': **Turtles**
	15 April	'Somethin' Stupid': **Frank and Nancy Sinatra**
	13 May	'The Happening': **Supremes**
	20 May	'Groovin'': **Young Rascals**
	3 June	'Respect': **Aretha Franklin**
	1 July	'Windy': **Association**
	29 July	'Light My Fire': **Doors**
	19 August	'All You Need Is Love': **Beatles**
	26 August	'Ode to Billy Joe': **Bobbie Gentry**
	23 September	'The Letter': **Box Tops**
	21 October	'To Sir with Love': **Lulu**
	25 November	'Incense & Peppermints': **Strawberry Alarm Clock**
	2 December	'Daydream Believer': **Monkees**
	30 December	'Hello Goodbye': **Beatles**

BIBLIOGRAPHY

Bronson, Fred, *The Billboard Book of Number One Hits* (London: Guinness, 1985).

Capps, Benjamin, *The Great Chiefs* (New York: Time-Life, 1975).

Coleman, Ray, *John Lennon* (London: Sidgwick & Jackson, 1984).

Davies, Hunter, *The Beatles* (London: Heinemann, 1968).

Edelstein, Andrew J., *The Pop Sixties* (New York: World Almanac, 1969).

Eisen, Jonathan (ed.), *The Age of Rock: Sounds of the American Cultural Revolution* (New York: Random House, 1985).

Gans, David, and Simon, Peter, *Playing in the Band: An Oral and Visual Portrait of the Grateful Dead* (New York: St Martin's Press, 1985).

Gleason, Ralph J., *The Jefferson Airplane and the San Francisco Sound* (New York: Ballantine Books, 1969).

Haynes, Jim, *Thanks for Coming* (London: Faber, 1984).

Hewat, Tim (ed.), *Rolling Stone File* (London: Panther, 1967).

Hewison, Robert, *Too Much: Art and Society in the Sixties* (London: Methuen, 1986).

Huxley, Aldous, *The Doors of Perception* (Harmondsworth: Penguin, 1968).

Kooper, Al, *Backstage Passes: Rock 'n' Roll Life in the Sixties* (New York: Stein & Day, 1977).

Laing, R. D., *The Politics of Experience and the Bird of Paradise* (Harmondsworth: Penguin, 1967).

Lee, Martin A., and Shlain, Bruce, *Acid Dreams* (New York: Grove Press, 1985).

McDonough, Jack, *San Francisco Rock: The Illustrated History of San Francisco Rock Music* (San Francisco, Calif.: Chronicle Books, 1985).

Mailer, Norman, *Armies of the Night* (Harmondsworth: Penguin, 1968).

Martin, George, *All You Need Is Ears* (London: Macmillan, 1979).

Mellers, Wilfred, *Twilight of the Gods: The Beatles in Retrospect* (London: Faber, 1973).

Melly, George, *Revolt into Style* (London: Allen Lane, 1970).

Miller, Jim, *The Rolling Stone History of Rock and Roll* (London: Picador, 1981).

Muhammad Ali, *The Greatest: My Own Story* (London: Hart-Davis, MacGibbon, 1975).

Nuttall, Jeff, *Bomb Culture* (London: MacGibbon & Kee, 1968).

Perry, Charles, *The Haight-Ashbury: A History* (New York: Rolling Stone Press, 1984).

Perry, Helen, *The Human Be-In* (London: Allen Lane, 1968).

Phillips, Michelle, *California Dreamin'* (New York: Warner Books, 1986).

Rice, Jo and Tim, Gambaccini, Paul, and Read, Mike, *The Guinness Book of Hit Singles*, 5th edn (London: Guinness Superlatives, 1985).

Roszak, Theodore, *The Making of a Counter-Culture* (Garden City, NY: Doubleday, 1969).

Sculatti, Gene, and Seay, David, *San Francisco Nights: The Psychedelic Music Trip* (New York: St Martin's Press, 1985).

Steinberg, Cobbett, *Reel Facts: The Movie Book of Records* (New York: Random House, 1978).

Taylor, Norman, *Narcotics: Nature's Dangerous Gifts* (New York: Dell, 1949).

Wells, Brian, *Psychedelic Drugs: Psychological, Medical and Social Issues* (Harmondsworth: Penguin, 1973).

Photographic
Acknowledgements

The Publishers have made every attempt to contact the owners of the photographs appearing in this book. In the few instances where they have been unsuccessful they invite the copyright holders to contact them direct.

For colour photograph acknowledgements *see* list of colour plates, black and white acknowledgements as follows:

A & M records: 151
Amsterdam University/Ab Pruis: 196
Amsterdam University/Koen Wessing: 195, 199
Gene Anthony: 50, 56, 69, 81, 92, 95, 96, 101, 102, 131, 133, 137, 140, 162, 165, 166, 167, 169, 170, 173, 174, 191, 192, 200–1, 203, 204, 207, 209
Backnumbers: 184 bottom
Backnumbers/Arthur Moyse: 188
Beat Publications: 18–19, 38
British Library/Mail Newspapers: 28
British Library/Mirror Group Newspapers: 116
British Library/News International: 113, 115, 222 left and right
Colorific/Paul S Conklin: 229
Michael Cooper: 37 top
Dogz Dinna Produx: 37 bottom
Granada Television: 25, 32, 98, 108, 119, 164, 197, 224, 233
Graham Keen: 33, 70, 91, 154, 178, 183, 184 top
Kobal Collection: 158, 161
London Features International: 44
Monterey International Pop Festival: 80
Pictorial Press: 22, 30, 49, 53, 59, 65, 73, 243
Popperfoto: 23, 71, 84, 105, 118, 125, 127, 144, 147, 157, 177, 210, 213, 214, 225, 226, 227, 235, 236, 239, 240, 245
Rex Features: 46, 60, 62, 66–7, 68, 74, 77, 78, 83, 87, 110, 122, 129, 132, 152, 153, 234
Adam Ritchie: 187, 230
Charles Royal: 139
Ed Sanders: 232
Syndication International: 27, 34, 55, 134, 143, 181,182, 189, 221
Derek Taylor: 12
Topham Picture Library: 16, 21, 43, 88, 106, 148, 217, 218